Hands-On Machine Learning for Cybersecurity

Safeguard your system by making your machines intelligent using the Python ecosystem

Soma Halder
Sinan Ozdemir

BIRMINGHAM - MUMBAI

Hands-On Machine Learning for Cybersecurity

Commissioning Editor: Sunith Shetty
Acquisition Editor: Nelson Morris
Content Development Editor: Ronnel Mathew
Technical Editor: Sagar Sawant
Copy Editor: Safis Editing
Project Coordinator: Namrata Swetta
Proofreader: Safis Editing
Indexer: Rekha Nair
Graphics: Jisha Chirayil
Production Coordinator: Aparna Bhagat

First published: December 2018

Production reference: 1281218

Published by Packt Publishing Ltd.
Livery Place
35 Livery Street
Birmingham
B3 2PB, UK.

ISBN 978-1-78899-228-2

www.packtpub.com

mapt.io

Mapt is an online digital library that gives you full access to over 5,000 books and videos, as well as industry leading tools to help you plan your personal development and advance your career. For more information, please visit our website.

Why subscribe?

- Spend less time learning and more time coding with practical eBooks and Videos from over 4,000 industry professionals

- Improve your learning with Skill Plans built especially for you

- Get a free eBook or video every month

- Mapt is fully searchable

- Copy and paste, print, and bookmark content

Packt.com

Did you know that Packt offers eBook versions of every book published, with PDF and ePub files available? You can upgrade to the eBook version at www.packt.com and as a print book customer, you are entitled to a discount on the eBook copy. Get in touch with us at customercare@packtpub.com for more details.

At www.packt.com, you can also read a collection of free technical articles, sign up for a range of free newsletters, and receive exclusive discounts and offers on Packt books and eBooks.

Contributors

About the authors

Soma Halder is the data science lead of the big data analytics group at Reliance Jio Infocomm Ltd, one of India's largest telecom companies. She specializes in analytics, big data, cybersecurity, and machine learning. She has approximately 10 years of machine learning experience, especially in the field of cybersecurity. She studied at the University of Alabama, Birmingham where she did her master's with an emphasis on Knowledge discovery and Data Mining and computer forensics. She has worked for Visa, Salesforce, and AT&T. She has also worked for start-ups, both in India and the US (E8 Security, Headway ai, and Norah ai). She has several conference publications to her name in the field of cybersecurity, machine learning, and deep learning.

Sinan Ozdemir is a data scientist, start-up founder, and educator living in the San Francisco Bay Area. He studied pure mathematics at the Johns Hopkins University. He then spent several years conducting lectures on data science there, before founding his own start-up, Kylie ai, which uses artificial intelligence to clone brand personalities and automate customer service communications. He is also the author of *Principles of Data Science*, available through Packt.

About the reviewers

Chiheb Chebbi is a Tunisian InfoSec enthusiast, author, and technical reviewer with experience in various aspects of information security, focusing on the investigation of advanced cyber attacks and researching cyber espionage. His core interest lies in penetration testing, machine learning, and threat hunting. He has been included in many halls of fame. His talk proposals have been accepted by many world-class information security conferences.

I dedicate this book to every person who makes the security community awesome and fun!

Dr. Aditya Mukherjee is a cybersecurity veteran with more than 11 years experience in security consulting for various Fortune 500's and government entities, managing large teams focusing on customer relationships, and building service lines. He started his career as an entrepreneur, specializing in the implementation of cybersecurity solutions/cybertransformation projects, and solving challenges associated with security architecture, framework, and policies.

During his career, he has been bestowed with various industry awards and recognition, of which the most recent are most innovative/dynamic CISO of the year-2018, Cyber Sentinel of the year, and an honorary doctorate–for excellence in the field of management.

I would like to Thank the people who supported me through the process for this book. My mother, without who's support anything I do wouldn't be possible. The writers of this book - Soma & Sinan for their hard work & dedication in bringing out a quality literature. A Big thanks to the Packt team for creating a wonderful, enabling & fostering learning environment & Nidhi for her co-ordination in bringing out the final product that is in your hands.

Packt is searching for authors like you

If you're interested in becoming an author for Packt, please visit `authors.packtpub.com` and apply today. We have worked with thousands of developers and tech professionals, just like you, to help them share their insight with the global tech community. You can make a general application, apply for a specific hot topic that we are recruiting an author for, or submit your own idea.

Table of Contents

Preface

The damage that cyber threats can wreak upon an organization can be incredibly costly. In this book, we use the most efficient and effective tools to solve the big problems that exist in the cybersecurity domain and provide cybersecurity professionals with the knowledge they need to use machine learning algorithms. This book aims to bridge the gap between cybersecurity and machine learning, focusing on building new and more effective solutions to replace traditional cybersecurity mechanisms and provide a collection of algorithms that empower systems with automation capabilities.

This book walks you through the major phases of the threat life cycle, detailing how you can implement smart solutions for your existing cybersecurity products and effectively build intelligent and future-proof solutions. We'll look at the theory in depth, but we'll also study practical applications of that theory, framed in the contexts of real-world security scenarios. Each chapter is focused on self-contained examples for solving real-world concerns using machine learning algorithms such as clustering, k-means, linear regression, and Naive Bayes.

We begin by looking at the basics of machine learning in cybersecurity using Python and its extensive library support. You will explore various machine learning domains, including time series analysis and ensemble modeling, to get your foundations right. You will build a system to identify malicious URLs, and build a program for detecting fraudulent emails and spam. After that, you will learn how to make effective use of the k-means algorithm to develop a solution to detect and alert you about any malicious activity in the network. Also, you'll learn how to implement digital biometrics and fingerprint authentication to validate whether the user is a legitimate user or not.

This book takes a solution-oriented approach to helping you solve existing cybersecurity issues.

Who this book is for

This book is for data scientists, machine learning developers, security researchers, and anyone who is curious about applying machine learning to enhance computer security. Having a working knowledge of Python, the basics of machine learning, and cybersecurity fundamentals will be useful.

What this book covers

Chapter 1, *Basics of Machine Learning in Cybersecurity*, introduces machine learning and its use cases in the cybersecurity domain. We introduce you to the overall architecture for running machine learning modules and go, in great detail, through the different subtopics in the machine learning landscape.

Chapter 2, *Time Series Analysis and Ensemble Modeling*, covers two important concepts of machine learning: time series analysis and ensemble learning. We will also analyze historic data and compare it with current data to detect deviations from normal activity.

Chapter 3, *Segregating Legitimate and Lousy URLs*, examines how URLs are used. We will also study malicious URLs and how to detect them, both manually and using machine learning.

Chapter 4, *Knocking Down CAPTCHAs*, teaches you about the different types of CAPTCHA and their characteristics. We will also see how we can solve CAPTCHAs using artificial intelligence and neural networks.

Chapter 5, *Using Data Science to Catch Email Fraud and Spam*, familiarizes you with the different types of spam email and how they work. We will also look at a few machine learning algorithms for detecting spam and learn about the different types of fraudulent email.

Chapter 6, *Efficient Network Anomaly Detection Using k-means*, gets into the various stages of network attacks and how to deal with them. We will also write a simple model that will detect anomalies in the Windows and activity logs.

Chapter 7, *Decision Tree- and Context-Based Malicious Event Detection*, discusses malware in detail and looks at how malicious data is injected in databases and wireless networks. We will use decision trees for intrusion and malicious URL detection.

Chapter 8, *Catching Impersonators and Hackers Red Handed*, delves into impersonation and its different types, and also teaches you about Levenshtein distance. We will also learn how to find malicious domain similarity and authorship attribution.

Chapter 9, *Changing the Game with TensorFlow*, covers all things TensorFlow, from installation and the basics to using it to create a model for intrusion detection.

Chapter 10, *Financial Fraud and How Deep Learning Can Mitigate It*, explains how we can use machine learning to mitigate fraudulent transactions. We will also see how to handle data imbalance and detect credit card fraud using logistic regression.

Chapter 11, *Case Studies*, explores using SplashData to perform password analysis on over one million passwords. We will create a model to extract passwords using scikit-learn and machine learning.

To get the most out of this book

Readers should have basic knowledge of cybersecurity products and machine learning.

Download the example code files

You can download the example code files for this book from your account at www.packt.com. If you purchased this book elsewhere, you can visit www.packt.com/support and register to have the files emailed directly to you.

You can download the code files by following these steps:

1. Log in or register at www.packt.com.
2. Select the **SUPPORT** tab.
3. Click on **Code Downloads & Errata**.
4. Enter the name of the book in the **Search** box and follow the onscreen instructions.

Once the file is downloaded, please make sure that you unzip or extract the folder using the latest version of:

- WinRAR/7-Zip for Windows
- Zipeg/iZip/UnRarX for Mac
- 7-Zip/PeaZip for Linux

The code bundle for the book is also hosted on GitHub at `https://github.com/PacktPublishing/Hands-on-Machine-Learning-for-Cyber-Security`. In case there's an update to the code, it will be updated on the existing GitHub repository.

We also have other code bundles from our rich catalog of books and videos available at `https://github.com/PacktPublishing/`. Check them out!

Download the color images

We also provide a PDF file that has color images of the screenshots/diagrams used in this book. You can download it here: `http://www.packtpub.com/sites/default/files/downloads/9781788992282_ColorImages.pdf`.

Conventions used

There are a number of text conventions used throughout this book.

`CodeInText`: Indicates code words in text, database table names, folder names, filenames, file extensions, pathnames, dummy URLs, user input, and Twitter handles. Here is an example: "The SVM package available in the `sklearn` package."

A block of code is set as follows:

```
def url_has_exe(url):
  if url.find('.exe')!=-1:
      return 1
  else :
      return 0
```

When we wish to draw your attention to a particular part of a code block, the relevant lines or items are set in bold:

```
dataframe = pd.read_csv('SMSSpamCollectionDataSet',
delimiter='\t',header=None)
```

Any command-line input or output is written as follows:

```
$ mkdir css
$ cd css
```

Bold: Indicates a new term, an important word, or words that you see onscreen. For example, words in menus or dialog boxes appear in the text like this. Here is an example: "Select **System info** from the **Administration** panel."

 Warnings or important notes appear like this.

 Tips and tricks appear like this.

Get in touch

Feedback from our readers is always welcome.

General feedback: If you have questions about any aspect of this book, mention the book title in the subject of your message and email us at customercare@packtpub.com.

Errata: Although we have taken every care to ensure the accuracy of our content, mistakes do happen. If you have found a mistake in this book, we would be grateful if you would report this to us. Please visit www.packt.com/submit-errata, selecting your book, clicking on the Errata Submission Form link, and entering the details.

Piracy: If you come across any illegal copies of our works in any form on the Internet, we would be grateful if you would provide us with the location address or website name. Please contact us at copyright@packt.com with a link to the material.

If you are interested in becoming an author: If there is a topic that you have expertise in and you are interested in either writing or contributing to a book, please visit authors.packtpub.com.

Reviews

Please leave a review. Once you have read and used this book, why not leave a review on the site that you purchased it from? Potential readers can then see and use your unbiased opinion to make purchase decisions, we at Packt can understand what you think about our products, and our authors can see your feedback on their book. Thank you!

For more information about Packt, please visit packt.com.

Basics of Machine Learning in Cybersecurity

1

The goal of this chapter is to introduce cybersecurity professionals to the basics of machine learning. We introduce the overall architecture for running machine learning modules and go through in great detail the different subtopics in the machine learning landscape.

There are many books on machine learning that deal with practical use cases, but very few address the cybersecurity and the different stages of the threat life cycle. This book is aimed at cybersecurity professionals who are looking to detect threats by applying machine learning and predictive analytics.

In this chapter, we go through the basics of machine learning. The primary areas that we cover are as follows:

- Definitions of machine learning and use cases
- Delving into machine learning in the cybersecurity world
- Different types of machine learning systems
- Different data preparation techniques
- Machine learning architecture
- A more detailed look at statistical models and machine learning models
- Model tuning to ensure model performance and accuracy
- Machine learning tools

What is machine learning?

A computer program is said to learn from experience E with respect to some class of tasks T and performance measure P, if its performance at tasks in T, as measured by P, improves with experience E.

- Tom M. Mitchell

Machine learning is the branch of science that enables computers to learn, to adapt, to extrapolate patterns, and communicate with each other without explicitly being programmed to do so. The term dates back 1959 when it was first coined by Arthur Samuel at the IBM Artificial Intelligence Labs. machine learning had its foundation in statistics and now overlaps significantly with data mining and knowledge discovery. In the following chapters we will go through a lot of these concepts using cybersecurity as the back drop.

In the 1980s, machine learning gained much more prominence with the success of **artificial neural networks** (**ANNs**). Machine learning became glorified in the 1990s, when researchers started using it to day-to-day life problems. In the early 2000s, the internet and digitization poured fuel on this fire, and over the years companies like Google, Amazon, Facebook, and Netflix started leveraging machine learning to improve human-computer interactions even further. Voice recognition and face recognition systems have become our go-to technologies. More recently, artificially intelligent home automation products, self-driving cars, and robot butlers have sealed the deal.

The field of cybersecurity during this same period, however, saw several massive cyber attacks and data breaches. These are regular attacks as well as state-sponsored attacks. Cyber attacks have become so big that criminals these days are not content with regular impersonations and account take-overs, they target massive industrial security vulnerabilities and try to achieve maximum **return of investment** (**ROI**) from a single attack. Several Fortune 500 companies have fallen prey to sophisticated cyber attacks, spear fishing attacks, zero day vulnerabilities, and so on. Attacks on **internet of things** (**IoT**) devices and the cloud have gained momentum. These cyber breaches seemed to outsmart human **security operations center** (**SOC**) analysts and machine learning methods are needed to complement human effort. More and more threat detection systems are now dependent on these advanced intelligent techniques, and are slowly moving away from the signature-based detectors typically used in **security information and event management** (**SIEM**).

Problems that machine learning solves

The following table presents some of the problems that machine learning solves:

Use case Domain	Description
Face recognition	Face recognition systems can identify people from digital images by recognizing facial features. These are similar to biometrics and extensively use security systems like the use of face recognition technology to unlock phones. Such systems use three-dimensional recognition and skin texture analysis to verify faces.
Fake news detection	Fake news is rampant specially after the 2016 United States presidential election. To stop such yellow journalism and the turmoil created by fake news, detectors were introduced to separate fake news from legitimate news. The detectors use semantic and stylistic patterns of the text in the article, the source of article, and so on, to segregate fake from legit.
Sentiment analysis	Understanding the overall positivity or negativity of a document is important as opinion is an influential parameter while making a decision. Sentiment analysis systems perform opinion mining to understand the mood and attitude of the customer.
Recommender systems	These are systems that are able to assess the choice of a customer based on the personal history of previous choices made by the customer. This is another determining factor that influences such systems choices made by other similar customers. Such recommender systems are extremely popular and heavily used by industries to sell movies, products, insurances, and so on. Recommender systems in a way decide the go-to-market strategies for the company based on cumulative like or dislike.
Fraud detection systems	Fraud detection systems are created for risk mitigation and safe fraud according to customer interest. Such systems detect outliers in transactions and raise flags by measuring anomaly coefficients.
Language translators	Language translators are intelligent systems that are able to translate not just word to word but whole paragraphs at a time. Natural language translators use contextual information from multilingual documents and are able to make these translations.
Chatbots	Intelligent chatbots are systems that enhance customer experience by providing auto responses when human customer service agents cannot respond. However, their activity is not just limited to being a virtual assistant. They have sentiment analysis capabilities and are also able to make recommendations.

Why use machine learning in cybersecurity?

Legacy-based threat detection systems used heuristics and static signatures on a large amount of data logs to detect threat and anomalies. However, this meant that analysts needed to be aware of how normal data logs should look. The process included data being ingested and processed through the traditional **extraction, transformation, and load (ETL)** phase. The transformed data is read by machines and analyzed by analysts who create signatures. The signatures are then evaluated by passing more data. An error in evaluation meant rewriting the rules. Signature-based threat detection techniques, though well understood, are not robust, since signatures need to be created on-the-go for larger volumes of data.

Current cybersecurity solutions

Today signature-based systems are being gradually replaced by intelligent cybersecurity agents. Machine learning products are aggressive in identifying new malware, zero day attacks, and advanced persistent threats. Insight from the immense amount of log data is being aggregated by log correlation methods. Endpoint solutions have been super active in identifying peripheral attacks. New machine learning driven cybersecurity products have been proactive in strengthening container systems like virtual machines. The following diagram gives a brief overview of some machine learning solutions in cybersecurity:

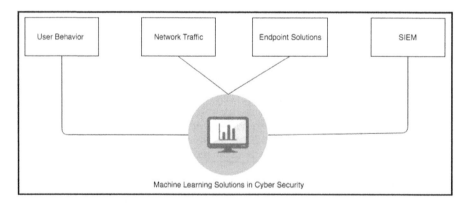

In general, machine learning products are created to predict attacks before they occur, but given the sophisticated nature of these attacks, preventive measures often fail. In such cases, machine learning often helps to remediate in other ways, like recognizing the attack at its initial stages and preventing it from spreading across the entire organization.

Many cybersecurity companies are relying on advanced analytics, such as user behavior analytics and predictive analytics, to identify advanced persistent threats early on in the threat life cycle. These methods have been successful in preventing data leakage of **personally identifiable information** (**PII**) and insider threats. But prescriptive analytics is another advanced machine learning solution worth mentioning in the cybersecurity perspective. Unlike predictive analytics, which predicts threat by comparing current threat logs with historic threat logs, prescriptive analytics is a more reactive process. Prescriptive analytics deals with situations where a cyber attack is already in play. It analyzes data at this stage to suggest what reactive measure could best fit the situation to keep the loss of information to a minimum.

Machine learning, however, has a down side in cybersecurity. Since alerts generated need to be tested by human SOC analysts, generating too many false alerts could cause alert fatigue. To prevent this issue of false positives, cybersecurity solutions also get insights from SIEM signals. The signals from SIEM systems are compared with the advanced analytics signals so that the system does not produce duplicate signals. Thus machine learning solutions in the field of cybersecurity products learn from the environment to keep false signals to a minimum.

Data in machine learning

Data is the fuel that drives the machine learning engine. Data, when fed to machine learning systems, helps in detecting patterns and mining data. This data can be in any form and comes in frequency from any source.

Structured versus unstructured data

Depending on the source of data and the use case in hand, data can either be structured data, that is, it can be easily mapped to identifiable column headers, or it can be unstructured, that is, it cannot be mapped to any identifiable data model. A mix of unstructured and structured data is called **semi-structured data**. We will discuss later in the chapter the differing learning approaches to handling these two type of data:

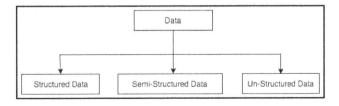

Labelled versus unlabelled data

Data can also be categorized into labelled and unlabelled data. Data that has been manually tagged with headers and meaning is called **labelled**. Data that has not been tagged is called **unlabelled data**. Both labelled and unlabelled data are fed to the preceding machine learning phases. In the training phase, the ratio of labelled to unlabelled is 60-40 and 40-60 in the testing phase. Unlabelled data is transformed to labelled data in the testing phase, as shown in the following diagram:

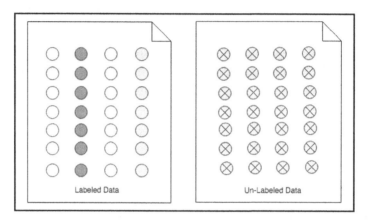

Machine learning phases

The general approach to solving machine learning consists of a series of phases. These phases are consistent no matter he source of data. That is, be it structured or unstructured, the stages required to tackle any kind of data are as shown in the following diagram:

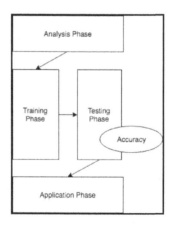

We will discuss each of the phases in detail as follows:

- **The analysis phase**: In this phase, the ingested data is analyzed to detect patterns in the data that help create explicit features or parameters that can be used to train the model.
- **The training phase**: Data parameters generated in the previous phases are used to create machine learning models in this phase. The training phase is an iterative process, where the data incrementally helps to improve the quality of prediction.
- **The testing phase**: Machine learning models created in the training phase are tested with more data and the model's performance is assessed. In this stage we test with data that has not been used in previous phase. Model evaluation at this phase may or may not require parameter training.
- **The application phase**: The tuned models are finally fed with real-world data at this phase. At this stage, the model is deployed in the production environment.

Inconsistencies in data

In the training phase, a machine learning model may or may not generalize perfectly. This is due to the inconsistencies that we need to be aware of.

Overfitting

The production of an analysis that corresponds too closely or exactly to a particular set of data, and may therefore fail to fit additional data or predict future observations reliably.

- Oxford Dictionary

Overfitting is the phenomenon in which the system is too fitted to the training data. The system produces a negative bias when treated with new data. In other words, the models perform badly. Often this is because we feed only labelled data to our model. Hence we need both labelled and unlabelled data to train a machine learning system.

The following graph shows that to prevent any model errors we need to select data in the optimal order:

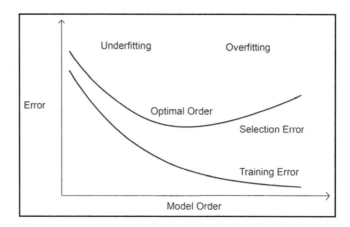

Underfitting

Underfitting is another scenario where model performs badly. This is a phenomenon where the performance of the model is affected because the model is not well trained. Such systems have trouble in generalizing new data.

For ideal model performance, both overfitting and underfitting can be prevented by performing some common machine learning procedures, like cross validation of the data, data pruning, and regularization of the data. We will go through these in much more detail in the following chapters after we get more acquainted with machine learning models.

Different types of machine learning algorithm

In this section, we will be discussing the different types of machine learning system and the most commonly used algorithms, with special emphasis on the ones that are more popular in the field of cybersecurity. The following diagram shows the different types of learning involved in machine learning:

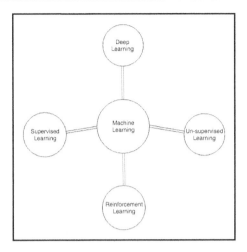

Machine learning systems can be broadly categorized into two types: supervised approaches and unsupervised approaches, based on the types of learning they provide.

Supervised learning algorithms

Supervised learning is where a known dataset is used to classify or predict with data in hand. Supervised learning methods learn from labelled data and then use the insight to make decisions on the testing data.

Supervised learning has several subcategories of learning, for example:

- **Semi-supervised learning**: This is the type of learning where the initial training data is incomplete. In other words, in this type of learning, both labelled and unlabelled are used in the training phase.
- **Active learning**: In this type of learning algorithm, the machine learning system gets active queries made to the user and learns on-the-go. This is a specialized case of supervised learning.

Some popular examples of supervised learning are:

- **Face recognition**: Face recognizers use supervised approaches to identify new faces. Face recognizers extract information from a bunch of facial images that are provided to it during the training phase. It uses insights gained after training to detect new faces.
- **Spam detect**: Supervised learning helps distinguish spam emails in the inbox by separating them from legitimate emails also known as **ham** emails. During this process, the training data enables learning, which helps such systems to send **ham** emails to the inbox and spam emails to the Spam folder:

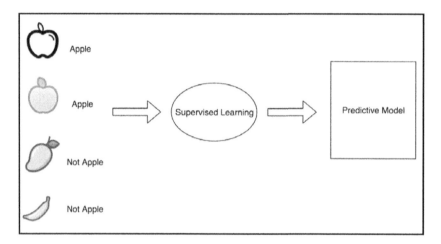

Unsupervised learning algorithms

The unsupervised learning technique is where the initial data is not labelled. Insights are drawn by processing data whose structure is not known before hand. These are more complex processes since the system learns by itself without any intervention.

Some practical examples of unsupervised learning techniques are:

- **User behavior analysis**: Behavior analytics uses unlabelled data about different human traits and human interactions. This data is then used to put each individual into different groups based on their behavior patterns.

- **Market basket analysis**: This is another example where unsupervised learning helps identify the likelihood that certain items will always appear together. An example of such an analysis is the shopping cart analysis, where chips, dips, and beer are likely to be found together in the basket, as shown in the following diagram:

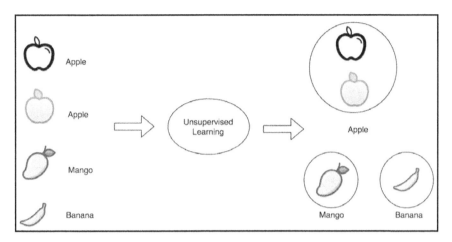

Reinforcement learning

Reinforcement learning is a type of dynamic programming where the software learns from its environment to produce an output that will maximize the reward. Here the software requires no external agent but learns from the surrounding processes in the environment.

Some practical examples of reinforcement learning techniques are:

- **Self driving cars**: Self driving cars exhibit autonomous motion by learning from the environment. The robust vision technologies in such a system are able to adapt from surrounding traffic conditions. Thus, when these technologies are amalgamated with complex software and hardware movements, they make it possible to navigate through the traffic.

- **Intelligent gaming programs**: DeepMind's artificially intelligent G program has been successful in learning a number of games in a matter of hours. Such systems use reinforcement learning in the background to quickly adapt game moves. The G program was able to beat world known AI chess agent Stockfish with just four hours of training:

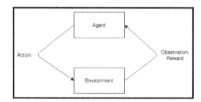

Another categorization of machine learning

Machine learning techniques can also be categorized by the type of problem they solve, like the classification, clustering, regression, dimensionality reduction, and density estimation techniques. The following diagram briefly discusses definitions and examples of these systems:

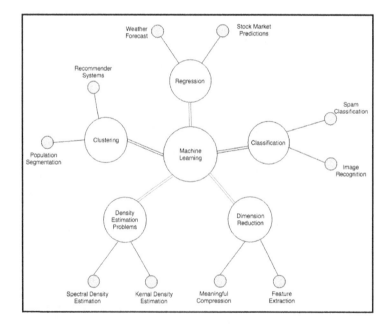

In the next chapter, we will be delving with details and its implementation with respect to cybersecurity problems.

Classification problems

Classification is the process of dividing data into multiple classes. Unknown data is ingested and divided into categories based on characteristics or features. Classification problems are an instance of supervised learning since the training data is labelled.

Web data classification is a classic example of this type of learning, where web contents get categorized with models to their respective type based on their textual content like news, social media, advertisements, and so on. The following diagram shows data classified into two classes:

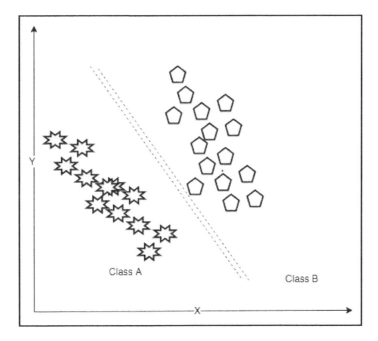

Clustering problems

Clustering is the process of grouping data and putting similar data into the same group. Clustering techniques use a series of data parameters and go through several iterations before they can group the data. These techniques are most popular in the fields of information retrieval and pattern recognition. Clustering techniques are also popularly used in the demographic analysis of the population. The following diagram shows how similar data is grouped in clusters:

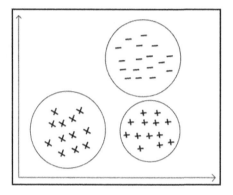

Regression problems

Regressions are statistical processes for analyzing data that helps with both data classification and prediction. In regression, the relationship between two variables present in the data population is estimated by analyzing multiple independent and dependent variables. Regression can be of many types like, linear regression, logistic regression, polynomial regression, lasso regression, and so on. An interesting use case with regression analysis is the fraud detection system. Regressions are also used in stock market analysis and prediction:

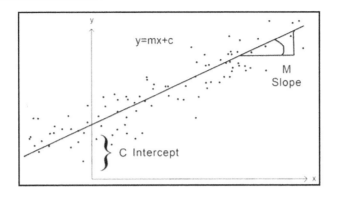

Dimensionality reduction problems

Dimensionality reduction problems are machine learning techniques where high dimensional data with multiple variables is represented with principle variables, without loosing any vital data. Dimensionality reduction techniques are often applied on network packet data to make the volume of data sizeable. These are also used in the process of feature extraction where it is impossible to model with high dimensional data. The following screenshot shows high-dimensional data with multiple variables:

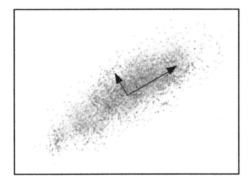

Density estimation problems

Density estimation problems are statistical learning methods used in machine learning estimations from dense data that is otherwise unobservable. Technically, density estimation is the technique of computing the probability of the density function. Density estimation can be applied on path-parametric and non-parametric data. Medical analysis often uses these techniques for identifying symptoms related to diseases from a very large population. The following diagram shows the density estimation graph:

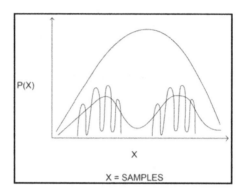

Deep learning

Deep learning is the form of machine learning where systems learn by examples. This is a more advanced form of machine learning. Deep learning is the study of deep neural networks and requires much larger datasets. Today deep learning is the most sought after technique. Some popular examples of deep learning applications include self driving cars, smart speakers, home-pods, and so on.

Algorithms in machine learning

So far we have dealt with different machine learning systems. In this section we will discuss the algorithms that drive them. The algorithms discussed here fall under one or many groups of machine learning that we have already covered.

Support vector machines

Support vector machines (**SVMs**) are supervised learning algorithms used in both linear and non linear classification. SVMs operate by creating an optimal hyperplane in high dimensional space. The separation created by this hyperplane is called **class**. SVMs need very little tuning once trained. They are used in high performing systems because of the reliability they have to offer.

SVMs are also used in regression analysis and in ranking and categorization.

Bayesian networks

Bayesian network (**BN**) are probabilistic models that are primarily used for prediction and decision making. These are belief networks that use the principles of probability theory along with statistics. BN uses **directed acyclic graph** (**DAG**) to represent the relationship of variables and any other corresponding dependencies.

Decision trees

Decision tree learning is a predictive machine learning technique that uses decision trees. Decision trees make use of decision analysis and predict the value of the target. Decision trees are simple implementations of classification problems and popular in operations research. Decisions are made by the output value predicted by the conditional variable.

Random forests

Random forests are extensions of decision tree learning. Here, several decisions trees are collectively used to make predictions. Since this is an ensemble, they are stable and reliable. Random forests can go in-depth to make irregular decisions. A popular use case for random forest is the quality assessment of text documents.

Hierarchical algorithms

Hierarchical algorithms are a form of clustering algorithm. They are sometimes referred as the **hierarchical clustering algorithm** (**HCA**). HCA can either be bottom up or agglomerative, or they may be top down or divisive. In the agglomerative approach, the first iteration forms its own cluster and gradually smaller clusters are merged to move up the hierarchy. The top down divisive approach starts with a single cluster that is recursively broken down into multiple clusters.

Genetic algorithms

Genetic algorithms are meta-heuristic algorithms used in constrained and unconstrained optimization problems. They mimic the physiological evolution process of humans and use these insights to solve problems. Genetic algorithms are known to outperform some traditional machine learning and search algorithms because they can withstand noise or changes in input pattern.

Similarity algorithms

Similarity algorithm are predominantly used in the field of text mining. Cosine similarity is a popular algorithm primarily used to compare the similarity between documents. The inner product space of two vectors identifies the amount of similarity between two documents. Similarity algorithms are used in authorship and plagiarism detection techniques.

ANNs

ANNs are intelligent computing systems that mimic the human nervous system. ANN comprises multiple nodes, both input and output. These input and output nodes are connected by a layer of hidden nodes. The complex relationship between input layers helps genetic algorithms are known like the human body does.

The machine learning architecture

A typical machine learning system comprises a pipeline of processes that happens in a sequence for any type of machine learning system, irrespective of the industry. The following diagram shows a typical machine learning system and the sub-processes involved:

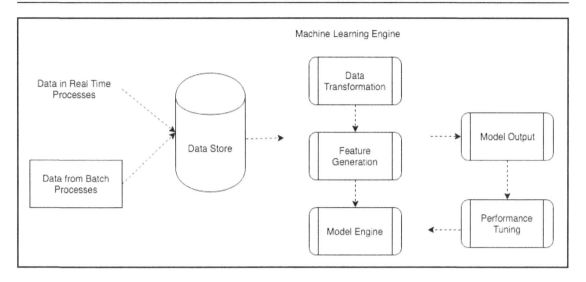

Data ingestion

Data is ingested from different sources from real-time systems like IOTS (CCTV cameras), streaming media data, and transaction logs. Data that is ingested can also be data from batch processes or non-interactive processes like Linux cron jobs, Windows scheduler jobs, and so on. Single feed data like raw text data, log files, and process data dumps are also taken in by data stores. Data from **enterprise resource planning (ERP)**, **customer relationship management (CRM)**, and **operational systems (OS)** is also ingested. Here we analyze some data ingestors that are used in continuous, real-time, or batched data ingestion:

- **Amazon Kinesis**: This is a cost-effective data ingestor from Amazon. Kinesis enables terabytes of real-time data to be stored per hour from different data sources. The **Kinesis Client Library (KCL)** helps to build applications on streaming data and further feeds to other Amazon services, like the Amazon S3, Redshift, and so on.

- **Apache Flume**: Apache Flume is a dependable data collector used for streaming data. Apart from data collection, they are fault-tolerant and have a reliable architecture. They can also be used in aggregation and moving data.

- **Apache Kafka**: Apache Kafka is another open source message broker used in data collection. This high throughput stream processors works extremely well for creating data pipelines. The cluster-centric design helps in creating wicked fast systems.

Some other data collectors that are widely used in the industry are Apache Sqoop, Apache Storm, Gobblin, Data Torrent, Syncsort, and Cloudera Morphlines.

Data store

The raw or aggregated data from data collectors is stored in data stores, like SQL databases, NoSQL databases, data warehouses, and distributed systems, like HDFS. This data may require some cleaning and preparation if it is unstructured. The file format in which the data is received varies from database dumps, JSON files, parquet files, avro files, and even flat files. For distributed data storage systems, the data upon ingestion gets distributed to different file formats.

Some of the popular data stores available for use as per industry standards are:

- **RDBMS (relational database management system)**: RDBMS are legacy storage options and are extremely popular in the data warehouse world. They store data retaining the **Atomicity, Consistency, Isolation, and Durability (ACID)** properties. However, they suffer from downsides are storage in volume and velocity.
- **MongoDB**: MongoDB is a popular NoSQL, document-oriented database. It has a wide adoption in the cloud computing world. It can handle data in any format, like structured, semi- structured, and unstructured. With a high code push frequency, it is extremely agile and flexible. MongoDB is inexpensive compared with other monolithic data storage options.
- **Bigtable**: This is a scalable NoSQL data base from Google. Bigtable is a part of the reliable **Google Cloud Platform (GCP)**. It is seamlessly scalable, with a very high throughput. Being a part of GCP enables it to be easily plugged in behind visualization apps like Firebase. This is extremely popular among app makers, who use it to gather data insights. It is also used for business analytics.
- **AWS Cloud Storage Services**: Amazon AWS is a range of cloud storage services for IOT devices, distributed data storage platforms, and databases. AWS data storage services are extremely secure for any cloud computing components.

The model engine

A machine learning model engine is responsible for managing the end-to-end flows involved in making the machine learning framework operational. The process includes data preparation, feature generation, training, and testing a model. In the next section we will discuss each of this processes in detail.

Data preparation

Data preparation is the stage where data cleansing is performed to check for the consistency and integrity of the data. Once the data is cleansed, the data is often formatted and sampled. The data is normalized so that all the data can be measured in the same scale. Data preparation also includes data transformation where the data is either decomposed or aggregated.

Feature generation

Feature generation is the process where data in analyzed and we look for patterns and attributes that may influence model results. Features are usually mutually independent, and are generated from either raw data or aggregated data. The primary goal of feature generation is performing dimensionality reduction and improved performance.

Training

Model training is the phase in which a machine learning algorithm learns from the data in hand. The learning algorithm detects data patterns and relationships, and categorizes data into classes. The data attributes need to be properly sampled to attain the best performance from the models. Usually 70-80 percent of the data is used in the training phase.

Testing

In the testing phase we validate the model we built in the testing phase. Testing is usually done with 20 percent of the data. Cross validations methods help determine the model performance. The performance of the model can be tested and tuned.

Performance tuning

Performance tuning and error detection are the most important iterations for a machine learning system as it helps improve the performance of the system. Machine learning systems are considered to have optimal performance if the generalized function of the algorithm gives a low generalization error with a high probability. This is conventionally known as the **probably approximately correct (PAC)** theory.

To compute the generalization error, which is the accuracy of classification or the error in forecast of regression model, we use the metrics described in the following sections.

Mean squared error

Imagine for a regression problem we have the line of best fit and we want to measure the distance of each point from the regression line. **Mean squared error (MSE)** is the statistical measure that would compute these deviations. MSE computes errors by finding the mean of the squares for each such deviations. The following shows the diagram for MSE:

$$MSE = \sum n(Pi - Ai)2/n$$

Where $i = 1, 2, 3...n$

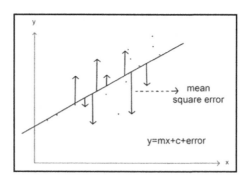

Mean absolute error

Mean absolute error (MAE) is another statistical method that helps to measure the distance (error) between two continuous variables. A continuous variable can be defined as a variable that could have an infinite number of changing values. Though MAEs are difficult to compute, they are considered as better performing than MSE because they are independent of the square function that has a larger influence on the errors. The following shows the MAE in action:

$$MAE = \sum ni|Pi - Ai|/n$$

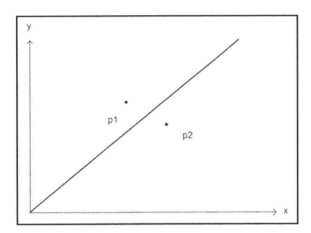

Precision, recall, and accuracy

Another measure for computing the performance for classification problems is estimating the precision, recall, and accuracy of the model.

Precision is defined as the number of true positives present in the mixture all retrieved instances:

$$Precision(P) = TruePositive/(TruePositive + FalsePositive)$$

Recall is the number of true positives identified from the total number of true positives present in all relevant documents:

$$Recall = TruePositive/(TruePositive + FalseNegative)$$

Accuracy measures the percentage of closeness of the measured value from the standard value:

$$Accuracy = (TruePositive + TrueNegative)/(TruePositive + TrueNegative + FalsePositive + FalseNegative)$$

Fake document detection is a real-world use case that could explain this. For fake news detector systems, precision is the number of relevant fake news articles detected from the total number of documents that are detected. Recall, on the other hand, measures the number of fake news articles that get retrieved from the total number of fake news present. Accuracy measures the correctness with which such a system detects fake news. The following diagram shows the fake detector system:

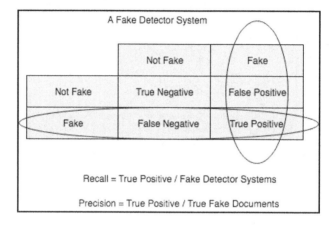

How can model performance be improved?

Models with a low degree of accuracy and high generalization errors need improvement to achieve better results. Performance can be improved either by improving the quality of data, switching to a different algorithm, or tuning the current algorithm performance with ensembles.

Fetching the data to improve performance

Fetching more data to train a model can lead to an improvement in performance. Lowered performance can also be due to a lack of clean data, hence the data needs to be cleansed, resampled, and properly normalized. Revisiting the feature generation can also lead to improved performance. Very often, a lack of independent features within a model are causes for its skewed performance.

Switching machine learning algorithms

A model performance is often not up to the mark because we have not made the right choice of algorithm. In such scenarios, performing a baseline testing with different algorithms helps us make a proper selection. Baseline testing methods include, but are not limited to, k-fold cross validations.

Ensemble learning to improve performance

The performance of a model can be improved by ensembling the performance of multiple algorithms. Blending forecasts and datasets can help in making correct predictions. Some of the most complex artificially intelligent systems today are a byproduct of such ensembles.

Hands-on machine learning

We have so far established that machine learning is used heavily in industries and in the field of data driven research. Thus let's go through some machine learning tools that help to create such machine learning applications with both small or larger-scale data. The following flow diagram shows the various machine learning tools and languages that are currently at our disposal:

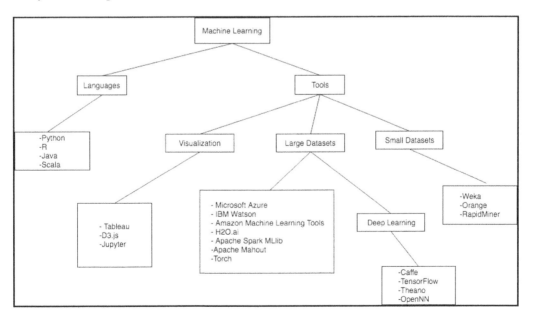

Python for machine learning

Python is the preferred language for developing machine learning applications. Though not the fastest, Python is extensively adapted by data scientists because of its versatility.

Python supports a wide range of tools and packages that enable machine learning experts to implement changes with much agility. Python, being a scripting language, is easy to adapt and code in. Python is extensively used for the **graphical user interfaces (GUI)** development.

Comparing Python 2.x with 3.x

Python 2.x is an older version compared to Python 3.x. Python 3.x was first developed in 2008 while the last Python 2.x update came out in 2010. Though it is perfectly fine to use table application with the 2.x, it is worthwhile to mention that 2.x has not been developed any further from 2.7.

Almost every machine learning package in use has support for both the 2.x and the 3.x versions. However, for the purposes of staying up-to-date, we will be using version 3.x in the uses cases we discuss in this book.

Python installation

Once you have made a decision to install Python 2 or Python 3, you can download the latest version from the Python website at the following URL:

```
https://www.python.org/download/releases/
```

On running the downloaded file, Python is installed in the following directory unless explicitly mentioned:

- For Windows:

```
C:\Python2.x
C:\Python3.x
```

- For macOS:

```
/usr/bin/python
```

- For Linux:

```
/usr/bin/python
```

A Windows installation will require you to set the environment variables with the correct path.

To check the version of Python installed, you can run the following code:

```
import sys
print ("Python version:{}",format(sys.version))
```

Python interactive development environment

The top Python **interactive development environments** (**IDEs**) commonly used for developing Python code are as follows:

- Spyder
- Rodeo
- Pycharm
- Jupyter

For developmental purposes, we will be using IPython Jupyter Notebook due to its user-friendly interactive environment. Jupyter allows code transportation and easy mark-downs. Jupyter is browser-based, thus supporting different types of imports, exports, and parallel computation.

Jupyter Notebook installation

To download Jupyter Notebook, it is recommended that you:

- First download Python, either Python 2.x or Python 3.x, as a prerequisite for Jupyter Notebook installation.
- Once the Python installation is complete, download Anaconda from the following link, depending on the operating system where the installation is being done. Anaconda is a package/environment manager for Python. By default, Anaconda comes with 150 packages and another 250 open source package can be installed along with it:

  ```
  https://www.anaconda.com/download/
  ```

- Jupyter Notebook can also be installed by running the following commands:

```
pip install --upgrade pip
pip3 install jupyter
```

If the user is on Python 2, `pip3` needs be replaced by `pip`.

After installation, you can just type `jupyter notebook` to run it. This opens Jupyter Notebook in the primary browser. Alternatively, you can open Jupyter from Anaconda Navigator. The following screenshot shows the Jupyter page:

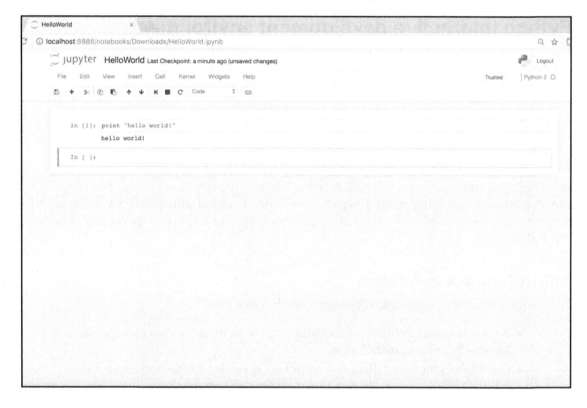

Python packages

In this section, we discuss packages that form the backbone for Python's machine learning architecture.

NumPy

NumPy is a free Python package that is used to perform any computation task. NumPy is absolutely important when doing statistical analysis or machine learning. NumPy contains sophisticated functions for solving linear algebra, Fourier transform, and other numerical analysis. NumPy can be installed by running the following:

```
pip install numpy
```

To install this through Jupyter, use the following:

```
import sys
!{sys.executable} -m pip install numpy
```

SciPy

SciPy is a Python package that is created on top of the NumPy array object. SciPy contains an array of functions, such as integration, linear algebra, and e-processing functionalities. Like NumPy, it can also be installed likewise. NumPy and SciPy are generally used together.

To check the version of SciPy installed on your system, you can run the following code:

```
import scipy as sp
print ("SciPy version:{}",format(sp.version))
```

Scikit-learn

Scikit-learn is a free Python package that is also written in Python. Scikit-learn provides a machine learning library that supports several popular machine learning algorithms for classification, clustering, regression, and so on. Scikit-learn is very helpful for machine learning novices. Scikit-learn can be easily installed by running the following command:

```
pip install sklearn
```

To check whether the package is installed successfully, conduct a test using the following piece of code in Jupyter Notebook or the Python command line:

```
import sklearn
```

If the preceding argument throws no errors, then the package has been successfully installed.

Scikit-learn requires two dependent packages, NumPy and SciPy, to be installed. We will discuss their functionalities in the following sections. Scikit-learn comes with a few inbuilt datasets like:

- Iris data set
- Breast cancer dataset
- Diabetes dataset
- The Boston house prices dataset and others

Other public datasets from `libsvm` and `svmlight` can also be loaded, as follows:

```
http://www.csie.ntu.edu.tw/~cjlin/libsvmtools/datasets/
```

A sample script that uses scikit-learn to load data is as follows:

```
from sklearn.datasets import load_boston
boston=datasets.load_boston()
```

pandas

The pandas open source package that provides easy to data structure and data frame. These are powerful for data analysis and are used in statistical learning. The pandas data frame allows different data types to be stored alongside each other, much unlike the NumPy array, where same data type need to be stored together.

Matplotlib

Matplotlib is a package used for plotting and graphing purposes. This helps create visualizations in 2D space. Matplotlib can be used from the Jupyter Notebook, from web application server, or from the other user interfaces.

Let's plot a small sample of the iris data that is available in the `sklearn` library. The data has 150 data samples and the dimensionality is 4.

We import the `sklearn` and `matplotlib` libraries in our Python environment and check the data and the features, as shown in the following code:

```
import matplotlib.pyplot as plt
from sklearn import datasets
iris = datasets.load_iris()
```

```
print(iris.data.shape) # gives the data size and dimensions
print(iris.feature_names)
```

The output can be seen as follows:

```
Output:
(150, 4)
['sepal length (cm)', 'sepal width (cm)', 'petal length (cm)', 'petal width
(cm)']
```

We extract the first two dimensions and plot it on an X by Y plot as follows:

```
X = iris.data[:, :2] # plotting the first two dimensions
y = iris.target
x_min, x_max = X[:, 0].min() - .5, X[:, 0].max() + .5
y_min, y_max = X[:, 1].min() - .5, X[:, 1].max() + .5
plt.figure(2, figsize=(8, 6))
plt.clf()plt.scatter(X[:, 0], X[:, 1], c=y, cmap=plt.cm.Set1,
  edgecolor='k')
plt.xlabel('Sepal length')
plt.ylabel('Sepal width')
```

We get the following plot:

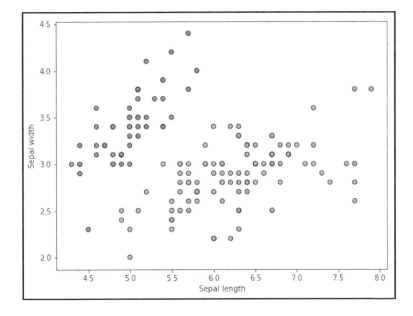

Mongodb with Python

MongoDB can store unstructured data that is fast and capable of retrieving large amounts of data over a small time. MongoDB uses a JSON format to store data in rows. Thus, any data without a common schema can be stored. We will be using MongoDB in the next few chapters because of its distributed nature. MongoDB has a fault tolerant distribution by shredding the data into multiple servers. MongoDB generates a primary key as you store data.

Installing MongoDB

To install MongoDB on your Windows, macOS, or Linux systems, run the following steps:

1. Download MongoDB from the download center from the following link for a windows or Mac system:

   ```
   https://www.mongodb.com/download-center
   ```

2. On a Linux system you can download it from:

   ```
   sudo apt-get install -y mongodb-org
   ```

3. MongoDB requires a separate repository of its own where you can extract and store the contents upon installation
4. Finally you can start the MongoDB service

PyMongo

To use MongoDB from within Python we will be using the PyMongo Library. PyMongo contains tools that helps you to work with MongoDB. There are libraries that act as an object data mapper for MongoDB, however PyMongo is the recommended one.

To install PyMongo, you can run the following:

```
python -m pip install pymongo
```

Alternatively, you can use the following:

```
import sys
!{sys.executable} -m pip install pymongo
```

Finally, you can get started with using MongoDB by importing the PyMongo library and then setting up a connection with MongoDB, as shown in the following code:

```
import pymongo
connection = pymongo.MongoClient()
```

On creating a successful connection with MongoDB, you can continue with different operations, like listing the databases present and so on, as seen in the following argument:

```
connection.database_names() #list databases in MongoDB
```

Each database in MongoDB contains data in containers called **collections**. You can retrieve data from these collections to pursue your desired operation, as follows:

```
selected_DB = connection["database_name"]
selected_DB.collection_names() # list all collections within the selected
database
```

Setting up the development and testing environment

In this section we will discuss how to set up a machine learning environment. This starts with a use case that we are trying to solve, and once we have shortlisted the problem, we select the IDE where we will do the the end-to-end coding.

We need to procure a dataset and divide the data into testing and training data. Finally, we finish the setup of the environment by importing the ideal packages that are required for computation and visualization.

Since we deal with machine learning use cases for the rest of this book, we choose our use case in a different sector. We will go with the most generic example, that is, prediction of stock prices. We use a standard dataset with *xx* points and *yy* dimensions.

Use case

We come up with a use case that predicts the onset of a given few features by creating a stock predictor that ingests in a bunch of parameters and uses these to make a prediction.

Data

We can use multiple data sources, like audio, video, or textual data, to make such a prediction. However, we stick to a single text data type. We use scikit-learn's default diabetes dataset to to come up with a single machine learning model that is regression for doing the predictions and error analysis.

Code

We will use open source code available from the scikit-learn site for this case study. The link to the code is available as shown in the following code:

```
http://scikit-learn.org/stable/auto_examples/linear_model/plot_ols.html#sph
x-glr-auto-examples-linear-model-plot-ols-py
```

We will import the following packages:

- `matplotlib`
- `numPy`
- `sklearn`

Since we will be using regression for our analysis, we import the `linear_model`, `mean_square_error`, and `r2_score` libraries, as seen in the following code:

```
print(__doc__)
# Code source: Jaques Grobler
# License: BSD 3 clause
import matplotlib.pyplot as plt
import numpy as np
from sklearn import datasets, linear_model
from sklearn.metrics import mean_squared_error, r2_score
```

We import the diabetes data and perform the following actions:

- List the dimension and size
- List the features

The associated code for the preceding code is:

```
# Load the diabetes dataset
diabetes = datasets.load_diabetes()
print(diabetes.data.shape) # gives the data size and dimensions
print(diabetes.feature_names
print(diabetes.DESCR)
```

The data has 442 rows of data and 10 features. The features are:

```
['age', 'sex', 'bmi', 'bp', 's1', 's2', 's3', 's4', 's5', 's6']
```

To train the model we use a single feature, that is, the `bmi` of the individual, as shown:

```
# Use only one feature
diabetes_X = diabetes.data[:, np.newaxis, 3]
```

Earlier in the chapter, we discussed the fact that selecting a proper training and testing set is integral. The last 20 items are kept for testing in our case, as shown in the following code:

```
# Split the data into training/testing sets
diabetes_X_train = diabetes_X[:-20]#everything except the last twenty
itemsdiabetes_X_test = diabetes_X[-20:]#last twenty items in the array
```

Further we also split the targets into training and testing sets as shown:

```
# Split the targets into training/testing sets
diabetes_y_train = diabetes.target[:-20]
everything except the last two items
diabetes_y_test = diabetes.target[-20:]
```

Next we perform regression on this data to generate results. We use the testing data to fit the model and then use the testing dataset to make predictions on the test dataset that we have extracted, as seen in the following code:

```
# Create linear regression object
regr = linear_model.LinearRegression()
#Train the model using the training sets
regr.fit(diabetes_X_train, diabetes_y_train)
# Make predictions using the testing set
diabetes_y_pred = regr.predict(diabetes_X_test)
```

We compute the goodness of fit by computing how large or small the errors are by computing the MSE and variance, as follows:

```
# The mean squared error
print("Mean squared error: %.2f"
 % mean_squared_error(diabetes_y_test, diabetes_y_pred))
# Explained variance score: 1 is perfect prediction
print('Variance score: %.2f' % r2_score(diabetes_y_test, diabetes_y_pred))
```

Finally, we plot the prediction using the Matplotlib graph, as follows:

```
# Plot outputs
plt.scatter(diabetes_X_test, diabetes_y_test, color='black')
plt.plot(diabetes_X_test, diabetes_y_pred, color='blue', linewidth=3)
plt.xticks(())
plt.yticks(())
plt.show()
```

The output graph looks as follows:

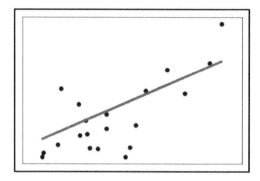

Summary

In this chapter, we have gone through the basics of machine learning. We briefly discussed how machine learning fits into daily use cases and its relationship with the cybersecurity world. We also learned the different aspects of data that we need to know to deal with machine learning. We discussed the different segregation of machine learning and the different machine learning algorithms. We also dealt with real-world platforms that are available on this sector.

Finally, we learned the hands-on aspects of machine learning, IDE installation, installation of packages, and setting up the environment for work. Finally, we took an example and worked on it from end to end.

In the next chapter, we will learn about time series analysis and ensemble modelling.

2
Time Series Analysis and Ensemble Modeling

In this chapter, we will study two important concepts of machine learning: time series analysis and ensemble learning. These are important concepts in the field of machine learning.

We use these concepts to detect anomalies within a system. We analyze historic data and compare it with the current data to detect deviations from normal activities.

The topics that will be covered in this chapter are the following:

- Time series and its different classes
- Time series decomposition
- Analysis of time series in cybersecurity
- Prediction of DDoS attack
- Ensemble learning methods and voting ensemble methods to detect cyber attacks

What is a time series?

A time series is defined as an array of data points that is arranged with respect to time. The data points are indicative of an activity that takes place at a time interval. One popular example is the total number of stocks that were traded at a certain time interval with other details like stock prices and their respective trading information at each second. Unlike a continuous time variable, these time series data points have a discrete value at different points of time. Hence, these are often referred to as discrete data variables. Time series data can be gathered over any minimum or maximum amount of time. There is no upper or lower bound to the period over which data is collected.

Time series data has the following:

- Specific instances of time forming the timestamp
- A start timestamp and an end timestamp
- The total elapsed time for the instance

The following diagram shows the graphs for **Housing Sales** (top-left), **Treasury Bill Contracts** (top-right), **Electricity Production** (bottom-left), and **Dow Jones** (bottom-right):

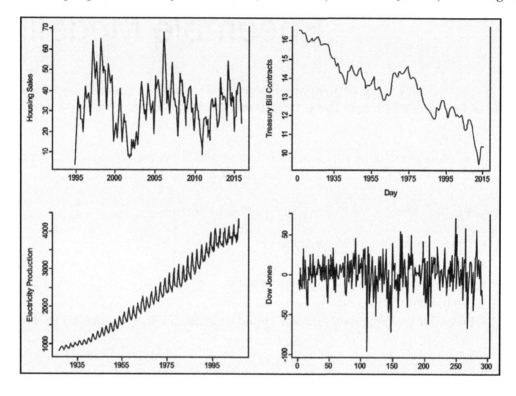

Time series analysis

Time series analysis is the study of where time series data points are mined and investigated. It is a method of interpreting quantitative data and computing the changes that it has undergone with respect to time. Time series analysis involves both univariate and multivariate time analysis. These sorts of time-based analysis are used in many areas like signal processing, stock market predictions, weather forecasting, demographic related-predictions, and cyber-attack detection.

Stationarity of a time series models

A time series needs to be stationary or else building a time series model on top is not technically possible. This can be called a prerequisite for model building. For a stationary time series, the mean, variance, and autocorrelation are consistently distributed over time.

The following graphs show the wave forms for **Stationary Time Series** (top) and **Non-Stationary Time series** (bottom):

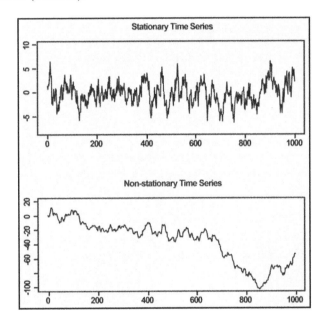

Strictly stationary process

A strictly stationary process is a process with a random probability distribution, such that its joint probability distribution is independent of time.

Strong sense stationarity: A time series T is called strongly or strictly stationary if two or more random vectors have equal joint distribution for all indices and integers, for example:

$$Random\ vector\ 1 = \{\ Xt1,\ Xt2,\ Xt3,\ ...,\ Xtn\}$$

$$Random\ vector\ 2 = \{\ Xt1 +s,\ Xt2 + s,\ Xt3+s,\ ...,\ Xtn +s\}$$

- *s* is all integers
- *t1..tn* is all indices

Weak or wide sense stationarity: A time series T is called weakly stationary if it has a shift invariance for the first and second moments of the process.

Correlation in time series

In this section, we will be learning about autocorrelation and partial autocorrelation function.

Autocorrelation

In order to choose two variables as a candidate for time series modeling, we are required to perform a statistical correlation analysis between the said variables. Here each variable, the Gaussian curve, and Pearson's coefficient are used to identify the correlation that exists between two variables.

In time series analysis, the autocorrelation measures historic data called lags. An **autocorrelation function (ACF)** is used to plot such correlations with respect to lag. In Python the autocorrelation function is computed as follows:

```
import matplotlib.pyplot as plt
import numpy as np
import pandas as p
from statsmodels.graphics.tsaplots import plot_acf
data = p.Series(0.7 * np.random.rand(1000) + 0.3 * np.sin(np.linspace(-9 *
np.pi, 9 * np.pi, num=1000)))
plot_acf(data)
pyplot.show()
```

The output for the preceding code is as follows:

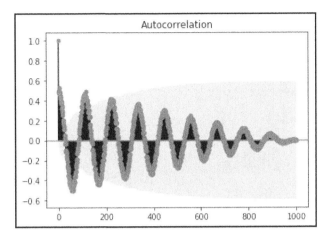

Partial autocorrelation function

Partial autocorrelation function (PACF) can be defined as a time series where there is a restricted or incomplete correlation between the values for shorter time lags.

PACF is not at all like ACF; with PACE the autocorrelation of a data point at the current point and the autocorrelation at a period lag have a direct or indirect correlation. PACF concepts are heavily used in autoregressive models.

In Python, the PACF function can be computed as follows:

```
import matplotlib.pyplot as plt
import numpy as np
import pandas as p
from statsmodels.graphics.tsaplots import plot_pacf
data = p.Series(0.7 * np.random.rand(1000) + 0.3 * np.sin(np.linspace(-9 *
np.pi, 9 * np.pi, num=1000)))
plot_pacf(data, lag = 50)
pyplot.show()
```

The output for PACF can be seen as shown:

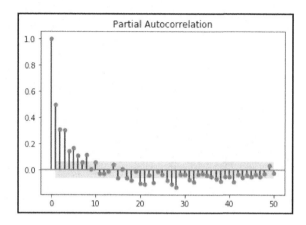

Classes of time series models

Based on the use-case type that we have in hand, the relationship between the number of temporal sequences and time can be distributed among multiple classes. Problems bucketed into each of these classes have different machine learning algorithms to handle them.

Stochastic time series model

Stochastic processes are random mathematical objects that can be defined using random variables. These data points are known to randomly change over time. Stochastic processes can again be divided into three main classes that are dependent on historic data points. They are **autoregressive (AR)** models, the **moving average (MA)** model, and **integrated (I)** models. These models combine to form the **autoregressive moving average (ARMA)**, the **autoregressive integrated moving average (ARIMA)**, and the **autoregressive fractional integrated moving average (ARFIMA)**. We will use these in later sections of the chapter.

Artificial neural network time series model

Artificial neural network (ANN) is an alternative to stochastic processes in time series models. ANN helps in forecasting, by using regular detection and pattern recognition. It uses this intelligence to detect seasonalities and helps generalize the data. In contrast with stochastic models like multilayer perceptrons, **feedforward neural network (FNN)**, and **time lagged neural network (TLNN)** are mainly used in nonlinear time series models.

Support vector time series models

A **support vector machine (SVM)** is another accurate non-linear technique that can be used to derive meaningful insight from time series data. They work best when the data is non-linear and non-stationary. Unlike other time series models, SVMs can predict without requiring historic data.

Time series components

Time series help detect interesting patterns in data, and thus identify the regularities and irregularities. Their parameters refer to the level of abstraction within the data. A time series model can thus be divided into components, based on the level of abstraction. These components are the systematic components and non-systematic components.

Systematic models

These are time series models that have recurring properties, and the data points show consistency. Hence they can be easily modeled. These systematic patterns are trends, seasonality, and levels observed in the data.

Non-systematic models

These are time series models that lack the presence of seasonal properties and thus cannot be easily modeled. They are haphazard data points marked against time and lack any trend, level, or seasonality. Such models are abundant in noise. Often inaccurate data collection schemes are responsible for such data patterns. Heuristic models can be used such non-systematic models.

Time series decomposition

Time series decomposition is a better way of understanding the data in hand. Decomposing the model creates an abstract model that can be used for generalization of the data. Decomposition involves identifying trends and seasonal, cyclical, and irregular components of the data. Making sense of data with these components is the systematic type of modeling.

In the following section, we will look at these recurring properties and how they help analyze time series data.

Level

We have discussed moving averages with respect to time series before. The level can be defined as the average or mean of a bunch of time series data points.

Trend

Values of data points in a time series keep either decreasing or increasing with time. They may also follow a cyclic pattern. Such an increase or decrease in data point values are known as the **trend** of the data.

Seasonality

The values of data point increases or decreases are more periodic, and such patterns are called **seasonality**. An example of this behavior could be a toy store, where there is an increase and decrease in the amount of toys sold, but in the Thanksgiving season in November, every year there is a spike in sales that is unlike the increase or decrease seen rest of the year.

Noise

These are random increases or decreases of values in the series. We will be generally dealing with the preceding systematic components in the form of additive models, where additive models can be defined as the sum of level, trend, seasonality, and noise. The other type is called the multiplicative model, where the components are products of each other.

The following graphs help to distinguish between additive and multiplicative models. This graph shows the additive model:

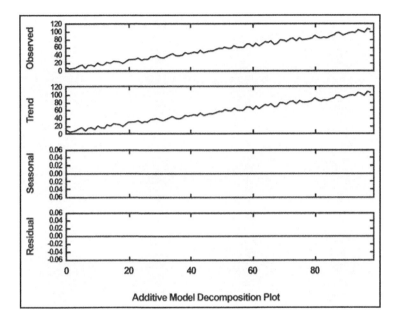

Additive Model Decomposition Plot

Since data decomposition has a major role in data analyzing, we understand these different components by using `pandas` inbuilt dataset that is the "International airline passengers: monthly totals in thousands, Jan 49 – Dec 60" dataset. The dataset contains a total of 144 observations of sales from the period of 1949 to 1960 for Box and Jenkins.

Let's import and plot the data:

```
from pandas import Series
from matplotlib import pyplot
airline = Series.from_csv('/path/to/file/airline_data.csv', header=0)
airline.plot()
pyplot.show()
```

The following graph shows how there is a seasonality in data and a subsequent increase in the height(amplitude) of the graph as the years have progressed:

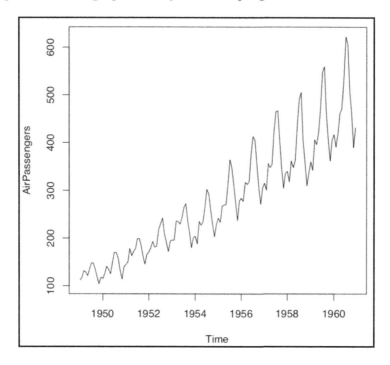

We can mathematically compute the trend and the seasonality for the preceding graph with an additive model as shown:

```
from pandas import Series
from matplotlib import pyplot
from statsmodels.tsa.seasonal import seasonal_decompose
airline = Series.from_csv('/path/to/file/airline_data.csv', header=0)
result = seasonal_decompose(airline, model='additive')
result.plot()
pyplot.show()
```

The output for the preceding code is as shown follows:

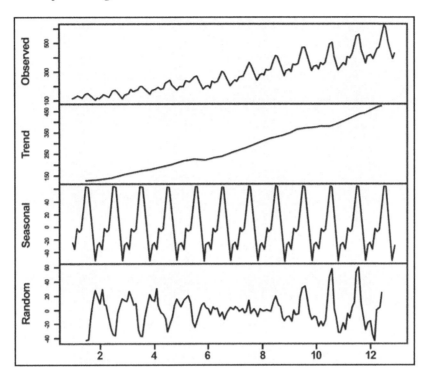

The preceding graph can be interpreted as follows:

- **Observed**: The regular airline data graph
- **Trend**: The observed increase in trend
- **Seasonality**: The observed seasonality in the data
- **Random**: This is first observed graph after removing the initial seasonal patterns

Use cases for time series

In the *Signal processing* section, we will discuss the different fields where time series are utilized to extract meaningful information from very large datasets. Be it social media analysis, click stream trends, or system log generations, time series can be used to mine any data that has a similar time-sensitive approach to data collection and storage.

Signal processing

Digital signal processing uses time series analysis to identify a signal from a mixture of noise and signals. Signal processing uses various methods to perform this identification, like smoothing, correlation, convolution, and so on. Time series helps measure deviations from the stationary behaviors of signals. These drifts or deviations are the noise, as follows:

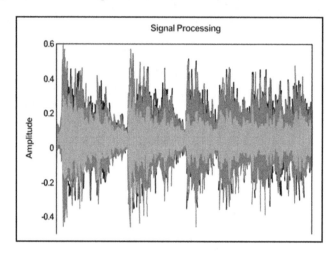

Stock market predictions

Stock market predictions are yet another use case for time series analysis. Investors can make an educated guess about stocks by analyzing data. Though non-mathematical components like the history of the company do play a art in stock market predictions, they largely depend on the historic stock market trends. We can do a trend analysis of the historic trade-in prices of different stocks and use predictive analytics to predict future prices. Such analytics need data points, that is, stock prices at each hour over a trading period. Quantitative analysts and trading algorithms make investment decisions using these data points by performing time series analysis.

The following diagram shows a time series using historic stock data to make predictions:

Time Series in Predicting Historic Stock Data

Weather forecasting

Time series analysis is a well-used process in the field of meteorology. Temperature data points obtained over a period of time help to detect the nature of possible climate changes. They consider seasonality in the data to predict weather changes like storms, hurricanes, or blizzards and then adapt precautions to mitigate the harmful side-effects.

The following shows a time series in a weather forecast:

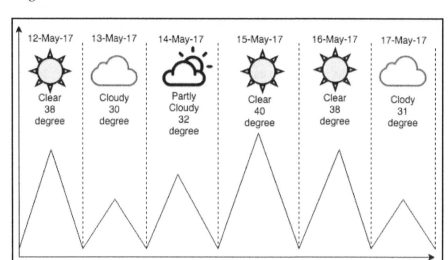

Time Series in Weather Forecast

Reconnaissance detection

We can use time series concepts to detect early signs of malware compromise or a cyber attack against a system. In the earliest phase of the attack, the malware just sniffs through the system looking for vulnerabilities. The malware goes looking for loosely open ports and peripherals, thus sniffing information about the system. These early stages of cyber attack are very similar to what the military does when it surveys a new region, looking for enemy activities. This stage in a cyber attack is called the **Reconnaissance**.

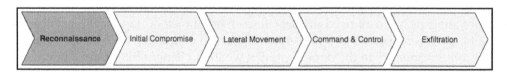

Time series analysis in cybersecurity

Computer attacks interrupt day-to-day services and cause data losses and network interruption. Time series analyses are popular machine learning methods that help to quantitatively detect anomalies or outliers in data, by either data fitting or forecasting. Time series analysis helps thwarting compromises and keep information loss to a minimum. The following graph shows the attacks mitigated on a routed platform:

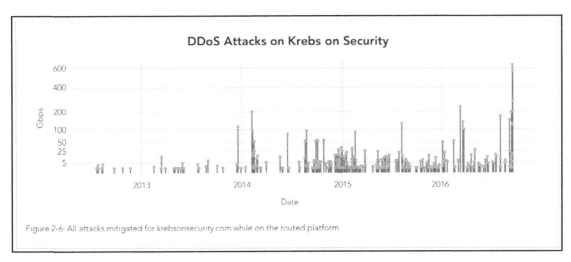

Figure 2-6: All attacks mitigated for krebsonsecurity.com while on the routed platform

Time series trends and seasonal spikes

Time series analysis can be used to detect attack attempts, like failed logins, using a time series model. Plotting login attempts identifies spikes (/) in failed logins. Such spikes are indicative of **account takeover (ATO)**.

Time series identify another cyber security use case—data exfiltration is the process in which the unauthorized transfer of data takes place from a computer system to a malicious location. Time series can identify huge network data packets being transported out of the network. Data exfiltration could be because of either an outsider compromise or an insider threat. In a later section of the chapter, we will use ensemble learning methods to identify the source of the attack.

We will learn the details of the attack in the next section. The goal of this chapter is to be able to detect reconnaissance so that we are able to prevent the system being compromised in the early stages and keep the loss of information to a minimum.

Detecting distributed denial of series with time series

Distributed denial-of-service (DDoS) is a cybersecurity menace which disrupts online services by sending an overwhelming amount of network traffic. These attacks are manually started with botnets that flood the target network. These attacks could have either of the following characteristics:

- The botnet sends a massive number of requests to the hosting servers.
- The botnet sends a high volume of random data packets, thus incapacitating the network.

Time series analysis helps identify network patterns with respect to time. Such pattern detection is done with the historic monitoring of network traffic data. It helps to identify attacks like DDoS. These attacks can be very critical if implemented. Baselining the regular traffic of a network and then overlaying the network with a compromised activity on top of it will help to detect deviations from the normal.

We will be analyzing this use case and will choose a machine learning model that will help detect such DDoS attacks before they crash the entire network.

We will work with a dataset that compromises traffic received by a website, say, `donotddos.com`. We will analyze 30 days of historic network traffic data from this website and detect whether the current traffic being received by the website is a part of any DDoS attack or not.

Before we go into the details of this use case we will analyze the `datetime` data type of Python since it will form the building block of any time series model.

Dealing with the time element in time series

This section has some short exercises to illustrate the features of time series elements:

1. Import the inbuilt `datetime` Python package, as shown:

```
from datetime import datetime
```

2. To get the current date/time which is the timestamp, do the following:

```
timestamp_now = datetime.now()
datetime(2018, 3, 14, 0, 10, 2, 17534)
```

By executing the preceding code you'll get the following output:

```
datetime.datetime(2018, 3, 14, 0, 10, 2, 17534)
```

3. You can get the difference between two timestamps by just doing the following:

```
time_difference = datetime(2018,3,14) - datetime(2015,2,13,0,59)
datetime.timedelta(1124, 82860)
```

4. You can extract the day from the preceding code by:

```
time_difference.days = 1124
```

5. You can extract the seconds by:

```
time_difference.seconds = 82860
```

6. Date times can also be added to each other.

Tackling the use case

The use case undergoes the following stages:

- We start with importing our data in a pandas data frame
- We determine that the data is properly cleansed
- We analyze the data, as per the model requirement
- We extract features from the data and analyze the features again to measure the correlation, variance, and seasonality
- We will then fit a time series model to predict whether the current data is a part of a DDoS attack or not

The following diagram sums up the entire procedure:

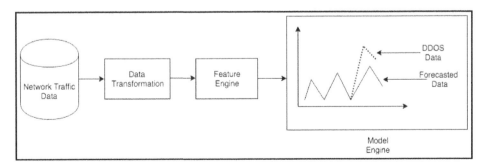

Importing packages

We import the relevant Python packages that will be needed for the visualization of this use case, as follows:

```
import pandas as p
import seaborn as sb
import numpy as n
%matplotlib inline
import matplotlib.pyplot as pl
```

Importing data in pandas

We have data in a CSV file, a text file separated by commas. While importing the data we also identify the headers in the data. Since we deal with packet capture data from the network, the columns captured are as follows:

- Sl Num: Serial number
- Time: Time of record capture
- Source: Source address or origin of the network packet
- Destination: Destination address of the network
- Volume: Data volume exchanged in **kilobyte (KB)**
- Protocol: The network protocol that is SMTP, FTP, or HTTP:

```
pdata_frame = pd.read_csv("path/to/file.csv", sep=',', index_col =
'Sl Num', names = ["Sl Num", "Time", "Source",
"Destination","Volume", "Protocol"])
```

Let's dump the first few lines of the data frame and have a look at the data. The following code displays the first 10 lines of the packet capture dataset:

```
pdata_frame.head(n=9)
```

The output of the preceding is as follows:

Sl Num	Time	Source	Destination	Volume	Protocol
1	1521039662	192.168.0.1	igmp.mcast.net	5	IGMP
2	1521039663	192.168.0.2	239.255.255.250	1	IGMP
3	1521039666	192.168.0.2	192.168.10.1	2	UDP
4	1521039669	192.168.10.2	192.168.0.8	20	DNS
5	1521039671	192.168.10.2	192.168.0.8	1	TCP

6	1521039673	192.168.0.1	192.168.0.2	1	TCP
7	1521039674	192.168.0.2	192.168.0.1	1	TCP
8	1521039675	192.168.0.1	192.168.0.2	5	DNS
9	1521039676	192.168.0.2	192.168.10.8	2	DNS

Data cleansing and transformation

Our dataset is largely clean so we will directly transform the data into more meaningful forms. For example, the timestamp of the data is in epoch format. Epoch format is alternatively known as Unix or Posix time format. We will convert this to the date-time format that we have previously discussed, as shown in the following:

```
import time
time.strftime('%Y-%m-%d %H:%M:%S', time.localtime(1521388078))

Out: '2018-03-18 21:17:58'
```

We perform the preceding operation on the Time column, add it to a new column, and call it Newtime:

```
pdata_frame['Newtime'] = pdata_frame['Time'].apply(lambda x:
time.strftime('%Y-%m-%d %H:%M:%S', time.localtime(float(x))))
```

Once we have transformed the data to a more readable format, we look at the other data columns. Since the other columns look pretty cleansed and transformed, we will leave them as is. The volume column is the next data that we will look into. We aggregate volume in the same way by the hour and plot it with the following code:

```
import matplotlib.pyplot as plt
plt.scatter(pdata_frame['time'],pdata_frame['volume'])
plt.show() # Depending on whether you use IPython or interactive mode, etc.
```

To carry out any further analysis on the data, we need to aggregate the data to generate features.

We extract the following features:

- For any source, we compute the volume of packets exchanged per minute
- For any source, we count the total number of connections received per minute

The following image shows how unprocessed data changes to data for the feature engine using data analysis:

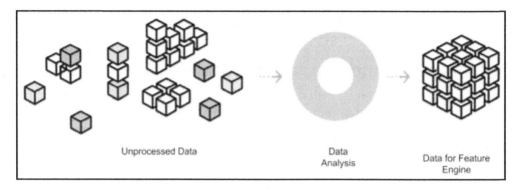

Feature computation

Since our computations are done per minute, we round off the time to the nearest minute, as shown in the following code:

```
_time = pdata_frame['Time'] #Time column of the data frame
edited_time = []
for row in pdata_frame.rows:
            arr = _time.split(':')
            time_till_mins = str(arr[0]) + str(arr[1])
            edited_time.append(time_till_mins) # the rounded off time
source = pdata_frame['Source'] # source address
```

The output of the preceding code is the time rounded off to the nearest minute, that is, 2018-03-18 21:17:58 which will become 2018-03-18 21:17:00 as shown:

```
'2018-03-18 21:17:00'
'2018-03-18 21:18:00'
'2018-03-18 21:19:00'
'2018-03-18 21:20:00'
'2018-03-19 21:17:00'
```

We count the number of connections established per minute for a particular source by iterating through the time array for a given source:

```
connection_count = {} # dictionary that stores count of connections per
minute
for s in source:
    for x in edited_time :
        if  x in connection_count :
            value = connection_count[x]
            value = value + 1
            connection_count[x] = value
        else:
            connection_count[x] = 1
new_count_df #count # date #source
```

The `connection_count` dictionary gives the number of connections. The output of the preceding code looks like:

Time	Source	Number of Connections
2018-03-18 21:17:00	192.168.0.2	5
2018-03-18 21:18:00	192.168.0.2	1
2018-03-18 21:19:00	192.168.0.2	10
2018-03-18 21:17:00	192.168.0.3	2
2018-03-18 21:20:00	192.168.0.2	3
2018-03-19 22:17:00	192.168.0.2	3
2018-03-19 22:19:00	192.168.0.2	1
2018-03-19 22:22:00	192.168.0.2	1
2018-03-19 21:17:00	192.168.0.3	20

We will decompose the data with the following code to look for trends and seasonality in the data. Decomposition of the data promotes more effective detection of an anomalous behavior, a DDoS attack, as shown in the following code:

```
from statsmodels.tsa.seasonal import seasonal_decompose
result = seasonal_decompose(new_count_df, model='additive')
result.plot()
pyplot.show()
```

The data generates a graph as follows; we are able to recognize the seasonality and trend of the data in general:

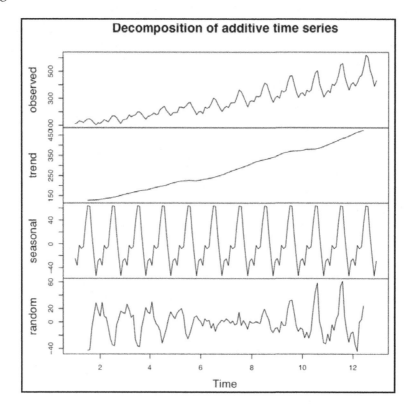

Next we find the ACF function for the data to understand the autocorrelation among the variables, with the following piece of code:

```
from matplotlib import pyplot
from pandas.tools.plotting import autocorrelation_plot
autocorrelation_plot(new_count_df)
pyplot.show()
```

Predicting DDoS attacks

Now that we have identified a seasonality, the trend in the network data will baseline the data by fitting to a stochastic model. We have already defined systematic parameters, and we will apply them next.

ARMA

This is a weak stochastic stationary process, such that, when provided with a time series X_t, ARMA helps to forecast future values with respect to current values. ARMA consists of two actions:

- The autoregression (p)
- The moving average (q)

$$X_t = c + \epsilon_t + \sum_{i=1}^{p} \varphi_i X_{t-i} + \sum_{i=1}^{q} \theta_i \epsilon_{t-i}$$

- C = Constant
- E_t = White noise
- θ = Parameters

ARIMA

ARIMA is a generalized version of ARMA. It helps us to understand the data or make predictions. This model can be applied to non-stationary sets and hence requires an initial differential step. ARIMA can be either seasonal or non-seasonal. ARIMA can be defined with (p,d,q) where:

- p= Order of the AR model
- d = Degree of the referencing
- q = Order of the moving average

$$(1 - \sum_{i=1}^{p} \phi_i L^i)(1 - L)^d X_t = \delta + (1 + \sum_{i=1}^{q} \theta_i L^i)\epsilon_t$$

Where:

- X_t = The given time series
- L = Lag operator
- E_t = Error terms
- drift is $\delta/(1 - \Sigma\phi_i)$.

ARFIMA

This is a generalized ARIMA model that allows non-integer values of the differencing parameter. It is in time series models with a long memory.

Now that we have discussed the details of each of these stochastic models, we will fit the model with the baseline network data. We will use the stats models library for the `ARIMA` stochastic model. We will pass the p, d, q values for the ARIMA model. The lag value for autoregression is set to 10, the difference in order is set to 1, and the moving average is set to 0. We use the `fit` function to fit the training/baseline data. The fitting model is shown as follows:

```
# fitting the model
model = ARIMA(new_count_df, order=(10,1,0))
fitted_model = model.fit(disp=0)
print(fitted_model.summary())
```

The preceding is the model that is fitted in the entire training set, and we can use it to find the residuals in the data. This method helps us to understand data better, but is not used in forecasts. To find the residuals in the data, we can do the following in Python:

```
# plot residual errors
residuals_train_data = DataFrame(fitted_model.resid)
residuals_train_data.plot()
pyplot.show()
```

Finally we will use the `predict()` function to predict what the current pattern in data should be like. Thus we bring in our current data, which supposedly contains the data from the DDoS attack:

- **Our training data**: Baseline network data for a period of a month
- **Our testing data**: DDoS attack data

```
from statsmodels.tsa.arima_model import ARIMA
from sklearn.metrics import mean_squared_error
ddos_predictions = list()
history = new_count_df
for ddos in range(len(ddos_data)):
    model = ARIMA(history, order=(10,1,0))
        fitted_model = model.fit(disp=0)
        output =fitted_model.forecast()
```

We can plot the error that is the difference between the forecasted DDoS free network data and the data with the network, by computing the mean square error between them, as shown in the following code:

```
pred = output[0]
ddos_predictions.append(pred)
error = mean_squared_error(ddos_data,ddos_predictions)
```

The output of the preceding code is the following plot where the dense line is the forecasted data and the dotted line is the data from the DDoS attack.

Ensemble learning methods

Ensemble learning methods are used to improve performance by taking the cumulative results from multiple models to make a prediction. Ensemble models overcome the problem of overfitting by considering outputs of multiple models. This helps in overlooking modeling errors from any one model.

Ensemble learning can be a problem for time series models because every data point has a time dependency. However, if we choose to look at the data as a whole, we can overlook time dependency components. Time dependency components are conventional ensemble methods like bagging, boosting, random forests, and so on.

Types of ensembling

Ensembling of models to derive the best model performance can happen in many ways.

Averaging

In this ensemble method, the mean of prediction results is considered from the multiple number of predictions that have been made. Here, the mean of the ensemble is dependent on the choice of ensemble; hence, their value changes from one model to another:

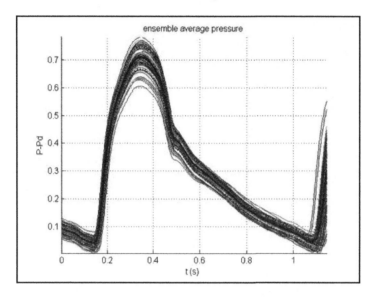

Majority vote

In this ensemble method, the forecast that gets unanimously voted by multiple models wins and is considered as the end result. For example, while classifying an email as spam, if at least three out of four emails classify a document as spam, then it is considered as spam.

The following diagram shows the classification by majority vote:

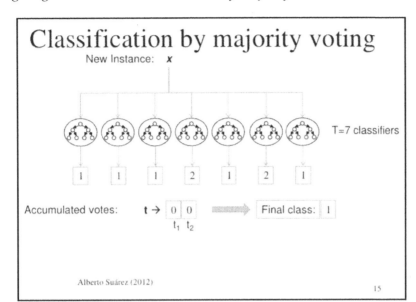

Weighted average

In this ensemble method, weights are assigned to multiple models and, while taking the average of each of these predictions, the weight is also considered. In this method, the models that have more weight receive more preference.

Types of ensemble algorithm

Let's learn more about the different types of ensemble algorithms.

Bagging

These are bootstrap aggregators where equal voting rights have been assigned to every model. The variance of these aggregators is maintained by drawing a random subset when making a decision.

Random forests are extensions of the bagging method. A random forest is a collection of decision trees that help in classification, regression, and decisions. The following shows the code for importing `RandomForestClassifier`:

```
import pandas
from sklearn import model_selection
from sklearn.ensemble import RandomForestClassifier
get_values = new_count_df.values
A =get_values[:,0:8]
B =get_values[:,8]
seed = 7
number_of_trees = 50
max_num_features = 2
kfold_crossval = model_selection.KFold(n_splits=10, random_state=seed)
model = RandomForestClassifier(n_estimators=num_trees,
max_features=max_features)
results = model_selection.cross_val_score(model, A, B, cv=kfold_crossval)
print(results.mean())
```

Boosting

Boosting is the type of ensemble learning method where each new learning model is trained by taking instances that have been misclassified by the previous learning algorithm. This process is composed of a series of weak learners, but they can classify the entire training dataset when they work together. These models often suffer from over fitting issues.

Stacking

Stacked ensemble methods have a dependency on the model's predictions. According to this model, if ensemble learning models were stacked one over the other and each learning model passes its prediction to the model on top such that the model on the top uses the predictions from the previous model layer as input.

Bayesian parameter averaging

This is a type of ensemble learning where the Bayesian parameter average model approximates the optimal classifier by taking hypotheses from hypothesis spaces and then applying Bayes' algorithm to them. Here the hypothesis spaces are sampled by using algorithms like Monte Carlo sampling, Gibbs sampling, and so on. These are also known as **Bayesian model averaging**.

Bayesian model combination

Bayesian model combination (**BMC**) is a modification to the **Bayesian model averaging** (**BMA**) model. BMC ensembles from the space of possible models. BMC provides us with great results. The performance is far better than the bagging and BMA algorithm. BMC uses cross validation methods to approximate results from the model, thus helping us select better ensembles from a collection of ensembles.

Bucket of models

This approach uses a model selection algorithm to find the best performing model for each use case. The bucket of models needs to be tested across many use cases to derive the best model by weighting and averaging. Similar to the BMC method, they choose models in the bucket by methods of cross validation. If the number of use cases are very high, the model that takes more time to train should not be taken from the selection. This selection of considering fast-learning models is also known as **landmark learning**.

Cybersecurity with ensemble techniques

Like other machine learning techniques, ensemble techniques are useful in cyber security. We will go through the same DDoS use case but, instead of using a time series model to forecast the attack, we will be using an ensemble method instead.

Voting ensemble method to detect cyber attacks

In the voting ensemble method, every model gets to make a prediction about the results of the model, and the decision on the model result is made on the majority votes or predictions made. There is another advanced level of the voting the ensemble method known as weighted voting. Here certain predictor models have more weights associated with their votes and thus get to make more privileged predictions:

1. We start by importing the respective libraries:

```
import pandas
from sklearn import model_selection
from sklearn.linear_model import LogisticRegression
from sklearn.tree import DecisionTreeClassifier
```

```
from sklearn.svm import SVC
from sklearn.ensemble import VotingClassifier
```

2. We detect a cyber attack via a voting mechanism where we use algorithms like SCV, decision tree, and logistic regression. We finally use the voting classifier to choose the best of the three. Next we create the sub-models and pass them through the DDoS dataset as follows:

```
voters = []
log_reg = LogisticRegression() # the logistic regression model
voters.append(('logistic', model1))
desc_tree = DecisionTreeClassifier() # the decision tree classifier
model
voters.append(('cart', model2))
cup_vec_mac = SVC() # the support vector machine model
voters.append(('svm', model3))
```

3. For the final voting, the voting classifier is invoked as follows:

```
# create the ensemble model
ensemble = VotingClassifier(voters)
```

4. The final model is chosen by performing a k-fold cross validation:

```
results = model_selection.cross_val_score(ensemble, X, Y, cv=kfold)
print(results.mean())
```

Summary

In this chapter, we dealt with the theory of time series analysis and ensemble learning and with real-life use cases where these methods can be implemented. We took one of the most frequent examples of cybersecurity, DoS attacks, and introduced a method that will capture them beforehand.

In the next chapter, we will learn about segregating legitimate and lousy URLs.

3
Segregating Legitimate and Lousy URLs

A recent study showed that 47% of the world's population is online right now. With the **World Wide Web (WWW)** at our disposal, we find ourselves fiddling with the various internet sites on offer. However, this exposes us to the most dangerous threat of all, because we are not able distinguish between a legitimate URL and a malicious URL.

In this chapter, we will use a machine learning approach to easily tell the difference between benign and malicious URLs. This chapter will cover the following topics:

- Understanding URLs and how they fit in the internet address scheme
- Introducing malicious URLs
- Looking at the different ways malicious URLs propagate
- Using heuristics to detect malicious URLs
- Using machine learning to detect malicious URLs

A URL stands for uniform resource locator. A URL is essentially the address of a web page located in the WWW. URLs are usually displayed in the web browser's address bar. A uniform resource locator conforms to the following address scheme:

```
scheme:[//[user[:password]@]host[:port]][/path][?query][#fragment]
```

A URL can include either the **Hypertext Transfer Protocol (HTTP)** or the **Hypertext Transfer Protocol secure (HTTPS)**. Other types of protocols include the **File Transfer Protocol (FTP)**, **Simple Mail Transfer Protocol (SMTP)**, and others, such as telnet, DNS, and so on. A URL consists of the top-level domain, hostname, paths, and port of the web address, as in the following diagram:

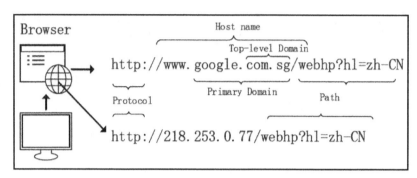

Introduction to the types of abnormalities in URLs

Lousy URLs are URLs that have been created with malicious intent. They are often the precursors to cyberattacks that may happen in the near future. Lousy URLs can hit pretty close to home, leaving each one of us very vulnerable to bad sites that we might visit on purpose or by accident.

Google often has inbuilt malicious URL detection capabilities, and the following screenshot shows what many of us have bumped into upon detecting a malicious URL:

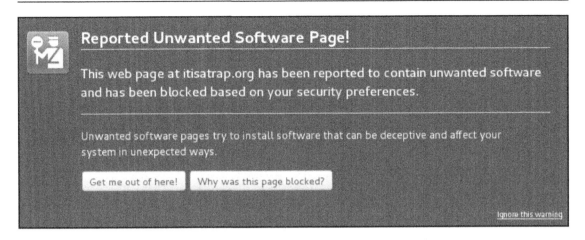

Malicious URLs lead us to bad websites that either try to sell us counterfeit products, such as medication, unsolicited products, such as watches from Rolex, and so on. These websites might sell a variety of items, such as screensavers for your computer and funny pictures.

Bad URLs may also lead to phishing sites—that is, sites that imitate real websites, such as banks and credit card company websites, but with the sole purpose of stealing credentials.

The following screenshots show a legitimate Bank of America login page and a fake Bank of America login page. The difference between the two is that the fake page has a illegitimate URL.

This is a legitimate **Bank of America** page and is not malicious:

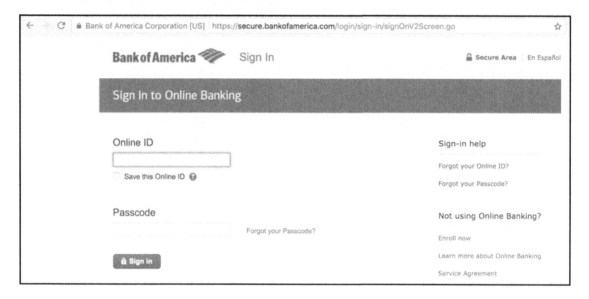

This is a fake Bank of America page, where the URL is not that of the host of Bank of America:

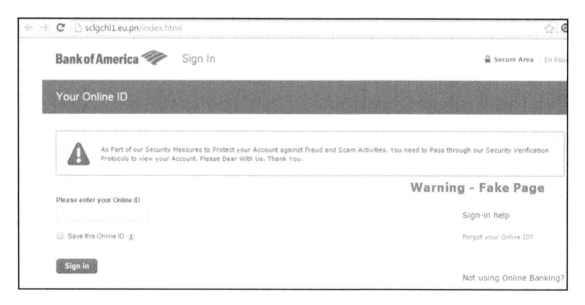

URL blacklisting

There are some traditional methods of detecting malicious URLs. Blacklists are static lists containing an exhaustive list of URLs that have been identified as being harmful. These URLs are usually created by web security companies and agencies. They can be categorized into multiple primary types, as listed in the following sections.

Drive-by download URLs

Drive-by download URLs are URLs that promote the unintended download of software from websites. They could be downloaded when a naive user first clicks on a URL, without knowing the consequences of this action. Drive-by downloads could also result from downloads that are carried out by malware that has infected a system. Drive-by downloads are the most prevalent form of attack.

The following diagram shows a drive-by download, and explains how a malicious email is first sent to the user and gets downloaded to the user's computer:

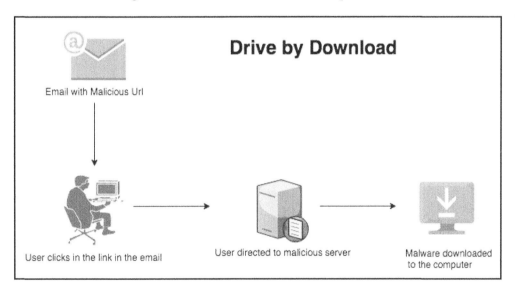

Command and control URLs

Command and control URLs are URLs that are linked to malware that connects the target computer to command and control servers. These are different from URLs that can be categorized as malicious as it is not always a virus that connects to command and control URLs via external or remote servers. The connections here are inside out:

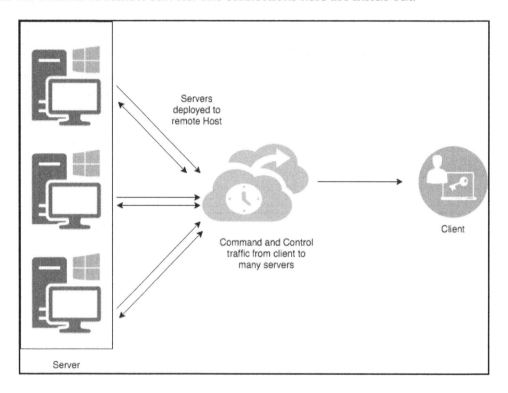

Phishing URLs

Phishing URLs are a form of attack that steals sensitive data, such as **personally identifiable information** (**PII**), by either luring the user or disguising the URL as a legitimate or trustworthy URL. Phishing is usually carried out through emails or instant messages, and directs users to fake websites by disguising the URLs as legitimate ones, as shown in the following screenshot:

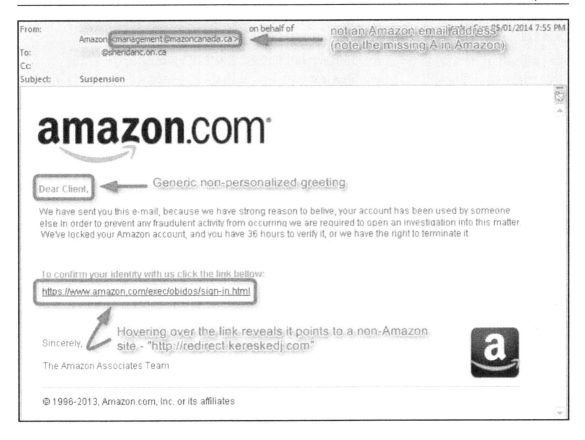

Using heuristics to detect malicious pages

We have already discussed the different kinds of URLs, such as benign URLs, spam URLs, and malicious URLs. In the following exercise, we will categorize some URLs, thereby making a prediction of the type of pages that they would redirect us to. Benign URLs always drives us to benign sites. Spam URLs either lead us to a command and control server or a spam website that tries to sell us unsolicited items. Malicious URLs lead us to sites that install some kind of malware on our systems. Since the system does not actually visit the pages of the websites that the URL points to, we are able to save a lot of resources in terms of latency and get a better performance out of our computer.

Data for the analysis

We will gather data from different sources, and will be able to create a dataset with approximately 1,000 URLs. These URLs are prelabelled in their respective classes: benign, spam, and malicious. The following screenshot is a snippet from our URL dataset:

```
http://uol.com.br,0
http://google.pl,0
http://ebay.co.uk,0
http://netflix.com,0
http://dailymotion.com,0
http://cnet.com,0
http://delta-search.com,0
http://dailymail.co.uk,0
http://rakuten.co.jp,0
http://aliexpress.com,0
http://aol.com,0
http://dce.edu,0
http://google.com,0
http://stackoverflow.com/questions/8551735/how-do-i-run-python-code-from-sublime-text-2,0
http://paypal.com.webscr.cmd.login.submit.dispatch.5885d80a13c0db1f8e263663d3faee8db2b24f7b84f1819343fd6c338b1d9d.222studio.com
http://paypal-manager-login.net/konflikt/66211165125/,1
http://paypal-manager-loesung.net/konflikt/66211165125/,1
http://paypal-manager-account.net/konflikt/66211165125/,1
http://www.paypal-manager-account.net/konflikt/6222649185/index.php,1
http://www.paypal-manager-login.net/konflikt/79235228200/index.php,1
http://paypal.com.laveaki.com.br/PayPal.com/,1
http://paypal.com.client.identifiant.compte.clefs.informations.upgarde.mon.compte.personnel.ghs56hge556rg4h6qe4th654f84e84r8e.h
http://msd2003.com/rche/index.htm,1
http://paypal-manager-loesung.net/konflikt/6624985147/index.php,1
http://eadideal.com.br/conteudos/material/66/Netzro-Login.html,1
http://tahmid.ir/user/?cmd=_home&amp;dispatch=5885d80a13c0db1f8e&amp;ee=669498ee5d0b4b381fd2bb1cceb52112,1
http://208.115.247.198/paypal.com.au.434324.fdsfsd32423423.fadfafas.3423423432fsfdafsdfsd/index1.php,1
http://www.paypal-manager-service.net/konflikt/785549116/index.php?webapps=/mpp/verkaufen,1
http://www.nervemobilization.com/update/06bb5b5bd8b1be54b78648f4993a1de1/protect.html,1
http://www.nervemobilization.com/update/15f58e7e4a736e2cd442b733e8755716/protect.html,1
http://sionaviatur.ru/wp-includes/syystemyj/index50.htm,1
```

Feature extraction

Since the data that we have is structured and prelabelled, we can move on to extract the features from the data. We will primarily extract certain lexical features, host-based features, and popularity-based features.

Lexical features

Lexical features are derived by analyzing the lexical unit of sentences. Lexical semantics are composed of full words or semiformed words. We will analyze the lexical features in the URL and extract them in accordance with the URLs that are available. We will extract the different URL components, such as the address, comprised of the hostname, the path, and so on.

We start by importing the headers, as shown in the following code:

```
from url parse import urlparse
import re
import urllib2
import urllib
from xml.dom import minidom
import csv
import pygeoip
```

Once done, we will import the necessary packages. We then tokenize the URLs. Tokenizing is the process of chopping the URL into several pieces. A token refers to the part that has been broken down into a sequence. When taken together, the tokens are used for semantic processing. Let's look at an example of tokenization using the phrase The quick brown fox jumps over the lazy dog, as shown in the following code:

```
Tokens are:
 The
 quick
 brown
 fox
 jumps
 over
 the
 lazy
 dog
```

Before we go ahead and start tokenizing URLs, we need to check whether they are IP addresses by using the following code:

```
def get_IPaddress(tokenized_words):
    count=0;
    for element in tokenized_words:
        if unicode(element).isnumeric():
            count= count + 1
        else:
            if count >=4 :
                return 1
            else:
```

```
                    count=0;
      if count >=4:
          return 1
      return 0
```

We then move on to tokenizing the URLs:

```
def url_tokenize(url):
    tokenized_word=re.split('\W+',url)
    num_element = 0
    sum_of_element=0
    largest=0
    for element in tokenized_word:
        l=len(element)
    sum_of_element+=l
```

For empty element exclusion in average length, use the following:

```
        if l>0:
            num_element+=1
            if largest<l:
                largest=l
    try:
        return [float(sum_of_element)/num_element,num_element,largest]
    except:
        return [0,num_element,largest]
```

Malicious sites that use phishing URLs to lure people are usually longer in length. Each token is separated by a dot. After researching several previous analyses of malicious emails, we search for these patterns in the tokens.

To search for these patterns of data in the tokens, we will go through the following steps:

1. We look for .exe files in the token of the data. If the token shows that the URL contains exe files pointers in the URL, we flag it, as shown in the following code:

```
def url_has_exe(url):
  if url.find('.exe')!=-1:
      return 1
  else :
      return 0
```

2. We then look for common words that are associated with phishing. We count the presence of words such as `'confirm'`, `'account'`, `'banking'`, `'secure'`, `'rolex'`, `'login'`, `'signin'`, as shown in the following code:

```
def get_sec_sensitive_words(tokenized_words):
    sec_sen_words=['confirm', 'account', 'banking', 'secure', ,
'rolex', 'login', 'signin']
    count=0
    for element in sec_sen_words:
        if(element in tokenized_words):
            count= count + 1;
    return count
```

Web-content-based features

We can also look for features that are usually found in malicious pages, such as the following:

- The count of HTML tags in the web page
- The count of hyperlinks in the web page
- The count of iframes in the web page

We can search for these features using the following code:

```
def web_content_features(url):
    webfeatures={}
    total_count=0
    try:
        source_code = str(opener.open(url))
        webfeatures['src_html_cnt']=source_code.count('<html')
        webfeatures['src_hlink_cnt']=source_code.count('<a href=')
        webfeatures['src_iframe_cnt']=source_code.count('<iframe')
```

We can also count the number of suspicious JavaScript objects, as shown in the following list:

- The count of evals
- The count of escapes
- The count of links
- The count of underescapes
- The count of `exec()` functions
- The count of search functions

We can count these objects using the following code:

```
webfeatures['src_eval_cnt']=source_code.count('eval(')
webfeatures['src_escape_cnt']=source_code.count('escape(')
webfeatures['src_link_cnt']=source_code.count('link(')
webfeatures['src_underescape_cnt']=source_code.count('underescape('
)
        webfeatures['src_exec_cnt']=source_code.count('exec(')
        webfeatures['src_search_cnt']=source_code.count('search(')
```

We can also count the number of times `html`, `hlink`, and `iframe` appear in the web feature keys, as shown in the following code:

```
for key in webfeatures:
    if(key!='src_html_cnt' and key!='src_hlink_cnt' and
key!='src_iframe_cnt'):
        total_count=total_count + webfeatures[key]
    webfeatures['src_total_jfun_cnt']=total_count
```

We also look for other web features and handle the exceptions, as shown in the following code:

```
except Exception, e:
    print "Error"+str(e)+" in downloading page "+url
    default_value=nf

    webfeatures['src_html_cnt']=default_value
    webfeatures['src_hlink_cnt']=default_value
    webfeatures['src_iframe_cnt']=default_value
    webfeatures['src_eval_cnt']=default_value
    webfeatures['src_escape_cnt']=default_value
    webfeatures['src_link_cnt']=default_value
    webfeatures['src_underescape_cnt']=default_value
    webfeatures['src_exec_cnt']=default_value
    webfeatures['src_search_cnt']=default_value
    webfeatures['src_total_jfun_cnt']=default_value

return webfeatures
```

Host-based features

Hosting services are internet services that allow users to make a website available to the World Wide Web. Oftentimes, a single server is rented out to multiple websites. Using these services, we will be able to find out the IP addresses of each of the URLs that we inspect. We will also look up the **autonomous system number (ASN)**. These numbers are a collection of IP routing prefixes that are controlled by central network operators. We use the ASN information to look for sites that have already been filed under the bad ASN category (colored in red), as shown in the following diagram:

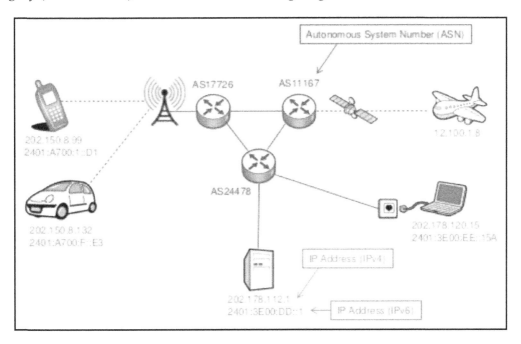

The following code helps in identifying the ASN. This number is unique, and identifies an autonomous system that exchanges routing details:

```
def getASN(host_info):
    try:
        g = pygeoip.GeoIP('GeoIPASNum.dat')
        asn=int(g.org_by_name(host_info).split()[0][2:])
        return asn
    except:
        return nf
```

Site-popularity features

We will use Alexa's website ranking system to help us discern which URLs are malicious and which are benign. Alexa ranks websites based on their popularity by looking at the number of individuals who visit the site. We use Alexa's popularity rank for each website. The basic idea for using Alexa for this purpose is that highly popular sites are usually non-malicious.

The top 10 most popular websites on Alexa are as follows:

Google	google.com	1
YouTube	youtube.com	2
Facebook	facebook.com	3
Baidu	baidu.com	4
Wikipedia	wikipedia.org	5
Reddit	reddit.com	6
Yahoo!	yahoo.com	7
Google India	google.co.in	8
Tencent QQ	qq.com	9
Amazon	amazon.com	10

The following Python function is used to detect the popularity:

```
def site_popularity_index(host_name):
    xmlpath='http://data.alexa.com/data?cli=10&dat=snbamz&url='+host_name
    try:
        get_xml= urllib2.urlopen(xmlpath) # get the xml
        get_dom =minidom.parse(get_xml) # get the dom element
        get_rank_host=find_ele_with_attribute(get_dom,'REACH','RANK')
        ranked_country=find_ele_with_attribute(get_dom,'COUNTRY','RANK')
        return [get_rank_host,ranked_country]
    except:
        return [nf,nf]
```

We will use the preceding parameters to segregate a lousy URL from a legitimate URL. A legitimate URL will have a a proper ASN, and will have a high site-popularity index. However, these are just heuristic measures to detect the the lousiness of a URL.

Using machine learning to detect malicious URLs

Since this is a classification problem, we can use several classification problems to solve this, as shown in the following list:

- Logistic regression
- Support vector machine
- Decision tree

Logistic regression to detect malicious URLs

We will be using logistic regression to detect malicious URLs. Before we deal with the model, let's look at the dataset.

Dataset

We have the data in a comma-separated file. The first column is the URL and the second column identifies the label, stating whether the URL is good or bad. The dataset looks as follows:

```
url,label
diaryofagameaddict.com,bad
espdesign.com.au,bad
iamagameaddict.com,bad
kalantzis.net,bad
slightlyoffcenter.net,bad
toddscarwash.com,bad
tubemoviez.com,bad
ipl.hk,bad
crackspider.us/toolbar/install.php?pack=exe,bad
pos-kupang.com/,bad
rupor.info,bad
svision-
online.de/mgfi/administrator/components/com_babackup/classes/fx29id1.txt,ba
d
officeon.ch.ma/office.js?google_ad_format=728x90_as,bad
sn-gzzx.com,bad
sunlux.net/company/about.html,bad
```

```
outporn.com,bad
timothycopus.aimoo.com,bad
xindalawyer.com,bad
freeserials.spb.ru/key/68703.htm,bad
deletespyware-adware.com,bad
orbowlada.strefa.pl/text396.htm,bad
ruiyangcn.com,bad
zkic.com,bad
adserving.favorit-
network.com/eas?camp=19320;cre=mu&grpid=1738&tag_id=618&nums=FGApbjFAAA,bad
cracks.vg/d1.php,bad
juicypussyclips.com,bad
nuptialimages.com,bad
andysgame.com,bad
bezproudoff.cz,bad
ceskarepublika.net,bad
hotspot.cz,bad
gmcjjh.org/DHL,bad
nerez-schodiste-zabradli.com,bad
nordiccountry.cz,bad
nowina.info,bad
obada-konstruktiwa.org,bad
otylkaaotesanek.cz,bad
pb-webdesign.net,bad
pension-helene.cz,bad
podzemi.myotis.info,bad
smrcek.com,bad
```

Model

The logistic regression model is a regression model that can be used to categorize data using a logistic function. These mostly consist of a dependent binary variable that is used to estimate the outcome of the logistic model, as shown in the following diagram:

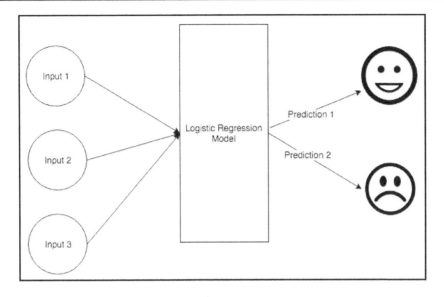

To start with our use case, we first import the respective packages using the following code:

```
import pandas as pd
import numpy as np
import random
import pickle

from sklearn.model_selection import train_test_split
from sklearn.feature_extraction.text import TfidfVectorizer
from sklearn.linear_model import LogisticRegression
```

The URL needs to undergo a degree of cleansing before we use it. We tokenize it by removing the slashes, dots, and coms, as shown in the following code. We do this because the input data needs to be converted to the binary format for logistic regression:

```
def url_cleanse(web_url):
 web_url = web_url.lower()

 urltoken = []
 dot_slash = []
 slash = str(web_url).split('/')
 for i in slash:
 r1 = str(i).split('-')

 token_slash = []
 for j in range(0,len(r1)):
 r2 = str(r1[j]).split('.')
```

```
    token_slash = token_slash + r2
    dot_slash = dot_slash + r1 + token_slash

    urltoken = list(set(dot_slash))
    if 'com' in urltoken:
    urltoken.remove('com')

    return urltoken
```

We then ingest the data and convert it to the relevant dataframes using the following code:

```
input_url = '~/data.csv'
data_csv = pd.read_csv(input_url,',',error_bad_lines=False)
data_df = pd.DataFrame(data_csv)
url_df = np.array(data_df)
random.shuffle(data_df)
y = [d[1] for d in data_df]
inputurls = [d[0] for d in data_df]
```

We now need to generate the **term frequency–inverse document frequency (TF-IDF)** from the URLs.

TF-IDF

The TF-IDF is used to measure how important a selected word is with respect to the entire document. This word is chosen from a corpus of words.

We need to generate the TF-IDF from the URLs by using the following code:

```
url_vectorizer = TfidfVectorizer(tokenizer=url_cleanse)
x = url_vectorizer.fit_transform(inputurls)
x_train, x_test, y_train, y_test = train_test_split(x, y, test_size=0.2,
random_state=42)
```

We then perform a logistic regression on the data frame, as follows:

```
l_regress = LogisticRegression() # Logistic regression
l_regress.fit(x_train, y_train)
l_score = l_regress.score(x_test, y_test)
print("score: {0:.2f} %".format(100 * l_score))
url_vectorizer_save = url_vectorizer
```

Finally we save the model and the vector in the file so that we can use it later, as follows:

```
file = "model.pkl"
with open(file, 'wb') as f:
 pickle.dump(l_regress, f)
f.close()

file2 = "vector.pkl"
with open(file2,'wb') as f2:
    pickle.dump(vectorizer_save, f2)
f2.close()
```

We will test the model we fitted in the preceding code to check whether it can predict the goodness or badness of URLs properly, as shown in the following code:

```
#We load a bunch of urls that we want to check are legit or not

urls = ['hackthebox.eu','facebook.com']
file1 = "model.pkl"

with open(file1, 'rb') as f1:
 lgr = pickle.load(f1)
f1.close()
file2 = "pvector.pkl"
with open(file2, 'rb') as f2:
 url_vectorizer = pickle.load(f2)
f2.close()
url_vectorizer = url_vectorizer
x = url_vectorizer.transform(inputurls)
y_predict = l_regress.predict(x)

print(inputurls)
print(y_predict)
```

However, there is a problem with the specified model. This is because there are URLs that could already be identified as good or bad. We do not have to classify them again. Instead, we can create a whitelist file, as follows:

```
# We can use the whitelist to make the predictions
whitelisted_url = ['hackthebox.eu','root-me.org']
some_url = [i for i in inputurls if i not in whitelisted_url]

file1 = "model.pkl"
with open(file1, 'rb') as f1:
 l_regress = pickle.load(f1)
f1.close()

file2 = "vector.pkl"
```

```
with open(file2, 'rb') as f2:
 url_vectorizer = pickle.load(f2)
f2.close()
url_vectorizer = url_vectorizer
x = url_vectorizer.transform(some_url)
y_predict = l_regress.predict(x)

for site in whitelisted_url:
 some_url.append(site)
print(some_url)
l_predict = list(y_predict)
for j in range(0,len(whitelisted_url)):
 l_predict.append('good')
print(l_predict)
```

SVM to detect malicious URLs

We will now use another machine learning approach to detect malicious URLs. **Support vector machines (SVMs)** are a popular method for classifying whether a URL is malicious or benign.

An SVM model classifies data across two or more hyperplanes. The output of the model is a hyperplane that can be used to segregate the input dataset, as shown in the following graph:

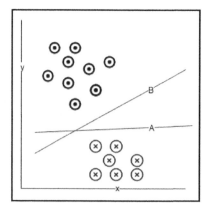

We then import the required packages. The SVM package available in the `sklearn` package (as shown in the following code) is very useful for this purpose:

```
#use SVM
from sklearn.svm import SVC
svmModel = SVC()
svmModel.fit(X_train, y_train)
#lsvcModel = svm.LinearSVC.fit(X_train, y_train)
svmModel.score(X_test, y_test)
```

Once the model is trained with the SVM classifier, we will again load the model and the feature vector to predict the URL's nature using the model, as shown in the following code:

```
file1 = "model.pkl"
with open(file1, 'rb') as f1:
  svm_model = pickle.load(f1)
f1.close()
file2 = "pvector.pkl"
with open(file2, 'rb') as f2:
  url_vectorizer = pickle.load(f2)
f2.close()

test_url = "http://www.isitmalware.com" #url to test
vec_test_url = url_vectorizer.transform([trim(test_url)])
result = svm_model.predict(vec_test_url)
print(test_url)
print(result)
```

Multiclass classification for URL classification

Multiclass classification is a type of classification that categorizes data into multiple classes. This method is different from the previous classification methods we have used so far, which all involved binary classification. One-versus-rest is one such type.

One-versus-rest

The one-versus-rest form of multiclass classifier involves training a single class with positive samples, and labeling all other classes as negative. This method requires that the base class produces a confidence with real value, as we see in binary classification where a class label is produced. The following graph displays the results of this classification style:

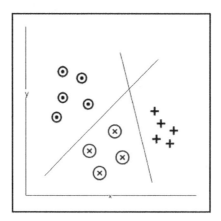

The base classifier here is logistic regression, as shown in the following code:

```
l_regress = LogisticRegression(maxIter=10, regParam=0.001,
elasticNetParam=0, tol=1E-6, fitIntercept=True )
```

We then train using the one-versus-rest classifier, as shown in the following code:

```
onvsrt = OneVsRest(classifier=lr)
onvsrtModel = onvsrt.fit(trainingUrlData)
```

We then compute the model score for the test data using the following code:

```
predictions = onvsrtModel.transform(testUrlData)
```

We then evaluate the performance of the model using the following code:

```
model_eval = MulticlassClassificationEvaluator(metricName="accuracy")
```

Finally, we compute the accuracy of the classification using the following code:

```
accuracy = model_eval.evaluate(predictions)
```

You might have noticed that we have not yet discussed classifying URLs using the decision tree method. We will be delving into this topic later in the chapter on decision trees.

Summary

In this chapter, we were introduced to the detection of the different types of abnormalities in URLs, including URL blacklisting. We also learned about how to use heuristics to detect malicious pages, including using the data for the analysis and extraction of different features. This chapter also taught us how machine learning and logistic regression is used to detect malicious URLs.

We also learned about using multiclass classification, along with SVM, to detect malicious URLs. In the next chapter, we will learn about the different types of CAPTCHAs.

Knocking Down CAPTCHAs 4

CAPTCHA is short for **Completely Automated Public Turing test to tell Computers and Humans Apart**. These are tests that verify whether a computing system is being operated by a human or a robot.

CAPTCHAs were built in such a way that they would need human mediation to be administered to computing systems as a part of the authentication system to ensure system security and hence prevention of unwanted looses for organizations.

Apart from summarizing how CAPTCHA works, this chapter also covers the following topics:

- Characteristics of CAPTCHAs
- Using artificial intelligence to crack CAPTCHAs
- Types of CAPTCHA
- Solving CAPTCHAs with neural networks

The following screenshot shows a CAPTCHA image that is used for verification:

Characteristics of CAPTCHA

Cracking CAPTCHA is difficult and the algorithm driving it is patented. However, it was made public because CAPTCHAs are just not a novel algorithm but a difficult case of artificial intelligence. Hence, reverse engineering it is challenging.

Deciphering CAPTCHAs require three primary capabilities. When the following capabilities are used in sync, it is then that deciphering a CAPTCHA becomes difficult. The three capabilities are as follows:

- **Capacity of consistent image recognition**: No matter what shape or size an alphabet appears, the human brain can automatically identify the characters.
- **Capacity of image segmentation**: This is the capability to segregate one character from the other.
- **Capacity to parse images**: Context is important for identifying a CAPTCHA, because often it is required to parse the entire word and derive context from the word.

Using artificial intelligence to crack CAPTCHA

Recently, one of the popular ways of benchmarking artificially intelligent systems is its capability to detect CAPTCHA images. The notion lies that if an AI system can crack a CAPTCHA, then it can be used to solve other complicated AI problems. An artificially intelligent system cracks CAPTCHA by either image recognition or by text/character recognition. The following screenshot shows a CAPTCHA image along with a deciphered image:

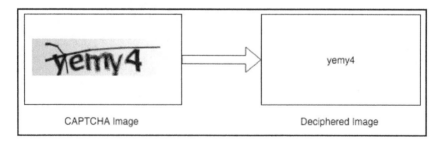

CAPTCHA Image   Deciphered Image

Types of CAPTCHA

The different types of CAPTCHA available are as follows:

- **Reading-based CAPTCHA**: These are visual preceptors. They include text recognizers and image detectors. These are difficult to crack, but the downside is that they cannot be accessed by visually impaired persons.
- **Speech recognition-based CAPTCHA**: These are audio CAPTCHAs. Like visual CAPTCHAs, they are complicated audio representations of a jumble of words with or without context.
- **Graphical CAPTCHA**: These are sophisticated forms of visual CAPTCHA. Graphical CAPTCHA is also almost impossible to crack by software.
- **Smart CAPTCHA**: When CAPTCHAs are fused with JavaScript, their complexity increases exponentially. Malicious bots find it difficult to parse JavaScript.
- **MAPTCHA**: These are mathematical CAPTCHAs. However, they require cognitive intelligence to crack.
- **Logic/trivia**: CAPTCHA often asks logical questions and puzzles. However, little is known about the amount of resistance that CAPTCHA provides.

The following screenshot shows the different CAPTCHAs:

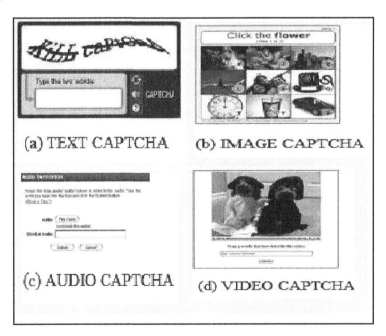

There are also other types of CAPTCHAs available, as shown here:

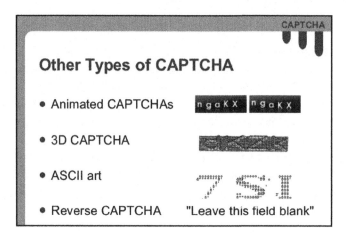

reCAPTCHA

reCAPTCHA is a free security service that protects your websites from spam and abuse. It is designed to distinguish between actual human computer users and malicious bots.

reCAPTCHAs were originally decided to identify words that are usually failed to be recognized by the **OCR** short for **optical character recognition**. Such words do not match to any words in the dictionary, as OCRs have not deciphered them properly, and are transferred to become CAPTCHAs, where multiple people submit their notion of the word.

No CAPTCHA reCAPTCHA

The following screenshot shows the image of a cat, and humans are asked to identify images with the same theme:

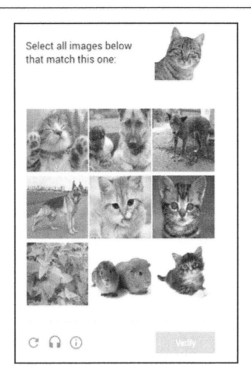

Breaking a CAPTCHA

Cyber criminals break CAPTCHAs for **account takeover (ATO)** purposes. ATO is a method of credential theft where the malicious agent takes over the account/profile of the victim leading to unauthorized activities.

Credential stuffing is one way to carry over an ATO; here, passwords collected from different places or previous attacks are used to break into many sites. This form of ATO may or may not require CAPTCHA. Here, fraudsters use the propensity that the victim may reuse a password.

For the preceding case, if there are CAPTCHAs that need to be cracked, then one of the following methods are adopted:

- **Use of human labor to crack the CAPTCHA**: Malicious agents often use cheap human labor to decode CAPTCHA. Human agents are made to solve CAPTCHAs and get paid either on an hourly rate or by the number of CAPTCHAs they solve. The workforce is tactically selected from the under-developed countries, and together they are able to solve hundreds of CAPTCHAs per hour. A study from the University of California at San Diego suggested that it takes approximately $1,000 to solve one million CAPTCHAs. Often, malicious owners repost CAPTCHAs to sites that get lots of human traffic and get them solved there.

  Malicious agents often make use of the insecure implementation used by website owners. In many cases, the session ID of a solved CAPTCHA can be used to bypass existing unsolved CAPTCHAs.

- **Use of brute force to crack CAPTCHA**: These are attacks where machines try all combinations of alpha-numeric characters until they are able to crack CAPTCHA.

Solving CAPTCHAs with a neural network

We will be using a **convolutional neural network** (**CNN**) to detect CAPTCHAs. We will the theory behind the model shortly. Before we proceed, we will discuss the library called **OpenCV**, which is used to read images for image processing in this NN system that we develop. The following diagram shows how a CAPTCHA image is formed into a deciphered image by a CNN:

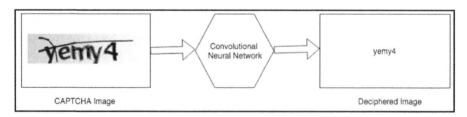

Dataset

We download CAPTCHA in the form of `.png` files from the research gate database. A total of 1,070 PNG images are gathered and divided in the training and testing datasets in a ratio of 7:3.

Packages

We will require the following packages to create our code that will decipher CAPTCHAs:

- `numpy`
- `imutils`
- `sklearn`
- `tensorflow`
- `keras`

Theory of CNN

CNNs are a class of **feedforward neural network (FFNN)**. In deep learning, a CNN, or ConvNet, is a class of deep FFNN, most commonly applied to analyzing visual imagery.

CNNs use a variation of multilayer perceptrons designed to require minimal preprocessing. They are also known as **shift invariant** or **space invariant artificial neural networks (SIANNs)**, based on their shared-weights architecture and translation invariance characteristics.

Convolutional networks were inspired by biological processes in that the connectivity pattern between neurons resembles the organization of the animal visual cortex. Individual cortical neurons respond to stimuli only in a restricted region of the visual field known as the **receptive field**. The receptive fields of different neurons partially overlap such that they cover the entire visual field.

CNNs use relatively little pre-processing compared to other image classification algorithms. This means that the network learns the filters that in traditional algorithms were hand-engineered. This independence from prior knowledge and human effort in feature design is a major advantage.

They have applications in image and video recognition, recommender systems, image classification, medical image analysis, and **natural language processing (NLP)**.

Model

The model works in the following stages:

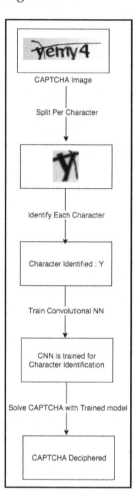

Code

In the first step, we will write a machine learning system using image-processing techniques that will be able to read letters from images.

We import the relevant packages; cv2 is the respective OpenCV package, as shown in the following code:

```
import os
import os.path
import cv2
import glob
import imutils
```

We read in the images, but we will output the respective letters in the images:

```
CAPTCHA_IMAGES_PATH = "input_captcha_images"
LETTER_IMAGES_PATH = "output_letter_images"
```

We list all of the CAPTCHA images that are present in the input folder and loop over all of the images:

```
captcha_images = glob.glob(os.path.join(CAPTCHA_IMAGES_PATH, "*"))
 counts = {}
 for (x, captcha_images) in enumerate(captcha_image_files):
 print("[INFO] processing image {}/{}".format(x + 1,
len(captcha_image_files)))
filename = os.path.basename(captcha_image_file)
captcha_correct_text = os.path.splitext(filename)[0]
```

After loading the image, we convert it into grayscale and add extra padding to the image:

```
text_image = cv2.imread(captcha_image_file)
text_to_gray = cv2.cvtColor(text_image, cv2.COLOR_BGR2GRAY)
text_to_gray = cv2.copyMakeBorder(gray, 8, 8, 8, 8, cv2.BORDER_REPLICATE)
```

The image is converted into pure black and white, and the contours of the image are also found:

```
image_threshold = cv2.threshold(gray, 0, 255, cv2.THRESH_BINARY_INV |
cv2.THRESH_OTSU)[1]

image_contours = cv2.findContours(image_threshold.copy(),
cv2.RETR_EXTERNAL, cv2.CHAIN_APPROX_SIMPLE)
```

We need to check which version of OpenCV this is compatible with:

```
image_contours = image_contours[0] if imutils.is_cv2() else
image_contours[1]
letterImage_regions = []
```

We loop through the image and get the contours on all of the sides with the corresponding rectangle where the contour is present:

```
for image_contours in image_contours:
    (x_axis, y_axis, wid, hig) = cv2.boundingRect(image_contours)
```

We compare the width and height to detect the corresponding letters:

```
if wid / hig > 1.25:
half_width = int(wid / 2)
letterImage_regions.append((x_axis, y_axis, half_width, hig))
letterImage_regions.append((x_axis + half_width, y_axis, half_width, hig))
else:
letterImage_regions.append((x_axis, y_axis, wid, hig))
```

If we detect more or less than five character access in the image provided, we ignore it, as it means that we have not cracked the CAPTCHA:

```
if len(letterImage_regions) != 5:
 continue

letterImage_regions = sorted(letterImage_regions, key=lambda x: x_axis[0])
```

We individually save all of the letters:

```
for letterboundingbox, letter_in_text in zip(letterImage_regions,
captcha_correct_text):
x_axis, y_axis, wid, hig = letterboundingbox

letter_in_image = text_to_gray[y_axis - 2:y_axis + hig + 2, x_axis -
2:x_axis + wid + 2]
```

Finally, we save the image in the respective folder, as shown:

```
save_p = os.path.join(LETTER_IMAGES_PATH, letter_in_text)

if not os.path.exists(save_p):
 os.makedirs(save_p)

c = counts.get(letter_in_text, 1)
p = os.path.join(save_p, "{}.png".format(str(c).zfill(6)))
cv2.imwrite(p, letter_in_image)
counts[letter_in_text] = c + 1
```

Training the model

This section explains about training the neural network model to identify each character.

We start by importing the desired packages for the purpose. The label binarizor class is used to convert a vector into one-hot encoding in one step. The `model_selection` import, `train_test_split`, is used to split into test and train sets. Several other `keras` packages are used for training the model:

```
import cv2
import pickle
import os.path
import numpy as np
from imutils import paths
from sklearn.preprocessing import LabelBinarizer
from sklearn.model_selection import train_test_split
from keras.models import Sequential
from keras.layers.convolutional import Conv2D, MaxPooling2D
from keras.layers.core import Flatten, Dense
from helpers import resize_to_fit
```

We need to initialize and look over the input CAPTCHAs. After converting the images into grayscale, we make sure that they fit in 20 x 20 pixels. We grab the letter and the name of letter and add the letter and name to our training set, as shown:

```
LETTER_IMAGES_PATH = "output_letter_images"
MODEL = "captcha.hdf5"
MODEL_LABELS = "labels.dat"

dataimages = []
imagelabels = []

for image_file in paths.list_images(LETTER_IMAGES_PATH):

  text_image = cv2.imread(image_file)
  text_image = cv2.cvtColor(text_image, cv2.COLOR_BGR2GRAY)

text_image = resize_to_fit(text_image, 20, 20)
text_image = np.expand_dims(text_image, axis=2)
text_label = image_file.split(os.path.sep)[-2]

dataimages.append(text_image)
  imagelabels.append(text_label)
```

We scale the pixel intensities to the range *[0, 1]* to improve training:

```
dataimages = np.array(dataimages, dtype="float") / 255.0
imagelabels = np.array(imagelabels)
```

We again split the training data into train and test sets. We then convert the letter labels to one into one-hot encoding. One-hot encodings make it easy for Keras with:

```
(X_train_set, X_test_set, Y_train_set, Y_test_set) =
train_test_split(dataimages, imagelabels, test_size=0.25, random_state=0)

lbzr = LabelBinarizer().fit(Y_train_set)
Y_train_set = lbzr.transform(Y_train_set)
Y_test_set = lbzr.transform(Y_test_set)

with open(MODEL_LABELS, "wb") as f:
 pickle.dump(lbzr, f)
```

Finally, we build the neural network. Both the first and the second convolutional layer have max pooling, as shown in the following code:

```
nn_model = Sequential()

nn_model.add(Conv2D(20, (5, 5), padding="same", input_shape=(20, 20, 1),
activation="relu"))
nn_model.add(MaxPooling2D(pool_size=(2, 2), strides=(2, 2)))

nn_model.add(Conv2D(50, (5, 5), padding="same", activation="relu"))
nn_model.add(MaxPooling2D(pool_size=(2, 2), strides=(2, 2)))
```

The hidden layer has 500 nodes, and every output layer has 32 possibilities, which means one for each alphabet.

Keras will build the TensorFlow model in the background and hence train the neural network:

```
nn_model.add(Flatten())
nn_model.add(Dense(500, activation="relu"))

nn_model.add(Dense(32, activation="softmax"))

nn_model.compile(loss="categorical_crossentropy", optimizer="adam",
metrics=["accuracy"])

nn_model.fit(X_train_set, Y_train_set, validation_data=(X_test_set,
Y_test_set), batch_size=32, epochs=10, verbose=1)

nn_model.save(MODEL)
```

Testing the model

Finally, we test the model such that we have built a machine learning solution that is able to crack the CAPTCHA:

```
from keras.models import load_model
from helpers import resize_to_fit
from imutils import paths
import numpy as np
import imutils
import cv2
import pickle
```

We load up the model labels and the neural network to test whether the model is able to read from the test set:

```
MODEL = "captcha.hdf5"
MODEL_LABELS = "labels.dat"
CAPTCHA_IMAGE = "generated_captcha_images"

with open(MODEL_LABELS, "rb") as f:
 labb = pickle.load(f)

model = load_model(MODEL)
```

We get some CAPTCHA images from different authentication sites to see whether the model is working:

```
captcha_image_files = list(paths.list_images(CAPTCHA_IMAGE))
captcha_image_files = np.random.choice(captcha_image_files, size=(10,),
replace=False)

for image_file in captcha_image_files:
 # grayscale
 image = cv2.imread(image_file)
 image = cv2.cvtColor(image, cv2.COLOR_BGR2GRAY)

#extra padding
 image = cv2.copyMakeBorder(image, 20, 20, 20, 20, cv2.BORDER_REPLICATE)

# threshold
 thresh = cv2.threshold(image, 0, 255, cv2.THRESH_BINARY_INV |
cv2.THRESH_OTSU)[1]

#contours
 contours = cv2.findContours(thresh.copy(), cv2.RETR_EXTERNAL,
cv2.CHAIN_APPROX_SIMPLE)
```

```
#different OpenCV versions
contours = contours[0] if imutils.is_cv2() else contours[1]

letter_image_regions = []
```

We loop through each of the four contours and extract the letter:

```
for contour in contours:
 (x, y, w, h) = cv2.boundingRect(contour)

if w / h > 1.25:

half_width = int(w / 2)
 letter_image_regions.append((x, y, half_width, h))
 letter_image_regions.append((x + half_width, y, half_width, h))
 else:

letter_image_regions.append((x, y, w, h))
```

We sort the detected letter images from left to right. We make a list of predicted letters:

```
letter_image_regions = sorted(letter_image_regions, key=lambda x: x[0])

output = cv2.merge([image] * 3)
 predictions = []

for letter_bounding_box in letter_image_regions:

 x, y, w, h = letter_bounding_box

letter_image = image[y - 2:y + h + 2, x - 2:x + w + 2]

letter_image = resize_to_fit(letter_image, 20, 20)

letter_image = np.expand_dims(letter_image, axis=2)
 letter_image = np.expand_dims(letter_image, axis=0)

prediction = model.predict(letter_image)

letter = labb.inverse_transform(prediction)[0]
 predictions.append(letter)
```

We finally match the images that we predicted with the actual letters in the image with the list created from the predicted images:

```
cv2.rectangle(output, (x - 2, y - 2), (x + w + 4, y + h + 4), (0, 255, 0),
1)
  cv2.putText(output, letter, (x - 5, y - 5), cv2.FONT_HERSHEY_SIMPLEX,
0.55, (0, 255, 0), 2)

captcha_text = "".join(predictions)
  print("CAPTCHA text is: {}".format(captcha_text))

cv2.imshow("Output", output)
  cv2.waitKey()
```

This is the output:

Summary

In this chapter, we learned about the different characteristics and types of CAPTCHA. Artificial Intelligence can be used to crack CAPTCHA, wherein we see how a CAPTCHA image can be converted into a deciphered image. We also saw how cyber criminals break CAPTCHAs for ATO purposes.

We also learned about the theory on CNN, which is a class of deep FFNN, most commonly applied to analyzing visual imagery.

In the next chapter, we will learn about using data science to catch email frauds and spam.

5

Using Data Science to Catch Email Fraud and Spam

Fraudulent emails are deceptive measures that are taken up by goons for personal gain in order to lure in innocent people. They are used to scam and defraud people. The emails usually involve offers that are too good to be true, and they are targeted towards naive individuals.

In this chapter, we will describe how spam emails work, and we will list a few machine learning algorithms that can mitigate the problem. The chapter will be divided into the following sub-sections:

- Fraudulent emails and spoofs
- Types of email fraud
- Spam detection using the Naive Bayes algorithm
- Featurization techniques that convert text-based emails into numeric values
- Spam detection with logistic regression

Email spoofing

Email spoofing involves masquerading as someone else in an email. The most common method of spoofing has the same sender's name, but masks the ID. In other words, the sender ID is forged. Email spoofing is possible when there are no valid methods for authenticating the sender's ID. A simple mail transfer protocol email consists of the following details:

```
Mail From:
Receipt to:
Sender's ID:
```

The following screenshot shows an email from **PayPal** for updating an account:

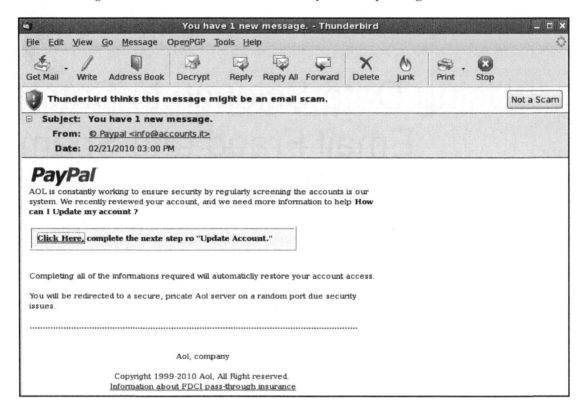

Bogus offers

There are also emails that try to sell us different commodities. They often include offers that seem too good to be true.

These offers could include items available before their actual release dates, such as the iPhone X, available one month prior to its release by Apple. Such availability offers play off the greed factor in human brains, allowing a person to procure and flaunt an item before its release.

These bogus offers might also try to sell items at ridiculously low prices, such as a Rolex watch at 100 bucks. Ultimately, the goal of such an offer is to steal credit card information or to lure users into buying products that will never be shipped to them.

Some examples of bogus email offers are as follows:

From: DesignerWatches by LR ████████████
To: ██████████████
Cc:
Subject: Start Black Friday today

LR Luxury Replicas

BLACK FRIDAY EVERY DAY UNTIL FRIDAY NOVEMBER 23RD!

The best quality watch replications on PLANET EARTH!
The lowest priced high-end watches on the INTERNET!

~~$131.00~~   Now $89.00

ROLEX OYSTER PERPETUAL DATEJUST

Model # RX459
Gender Men
Availability: INSTOCK - SHIPS WITHIN 24 HOURS

www.LRblackfridaytoday.com

BLACK FRIDAY HAS STARTED!
Black Friday Every day until November 23rd!
All items reduced by 25-50% as of TODAY

Over 25,000 exact watch-copies have been reduced until Friday November 23rd
There plenty of time to get the watch of your dreams but we recommend doing it as soon as possible.
This will ensure INSTOCK availability and fast delivery.

NOTE: BLACK FRIDAY PRICES ARE AVAILABLE ON INSTOCK ITEMS ONLY!
Currently every watch-model is INSTOCK and ready to ship within 1 hour

THESE ARE NOT CHEAP CHINA KNOCK-OFFS:

These are hand crafted high-end watch-copies.
These are made using identical parts and materials
These are tested inside and out to be identical.
There is no difference between our watch-copies and the originals!

http://lrblackfridaytoday.com

Requests for help

You may see emails with requests for help; there are usually awards associated with the requests. The rewards can range from artifacts to large sums of money or treasures. These types of emails are also known as **advance fee scams**. This type of scam dates back to the medieval times. The scam is not limited to only one payment; if the victim makes the payment for the first bait, they are usually lured into making several other payments.

A very popular email scam that prevailed during the early 2000s was that of the Nigerian prince. The messages were received via email or fax and were tagged as urgent. The sender was supposedly a member of Nigerian royalty that needed thousand of dollars, but promised to pay it back as soon as possible.

Types of spam emails

Spam emails are economical methods of commercial advertisement, wherein unsolicited emails are sent to recipients, asking them to buy forged items. They are money-making schemes, meant to target masses of people with very little investment.

Spam emails can be divided into the following broad categories.

Deceptive emails

Deceptive emails are the most common method of deceiving people. Phishing emails are sent by fraudsters. They impersonate legitimate sources and lure users into entering their user IDs and credentials, by asking them to log in. These emails use threats to trap vulnerable people.

A typical example of such a scam involves scammers sending emails by mimicking legitimate PayPal agents that send emails with links to reset passwords. The reason listed would be sudden account balance discrepancies.

The more legitimate the email looks, the higher the chances are of people falling prey to it. The onus is on the user to test the validity of any such email. Particularly, they need to look out for a redirect when the link is clicked. Other suspicious aspects can include email addresses, grammar, and any other semantics associated with the email.

The following screenshot shows a classic example of a deceptive email:

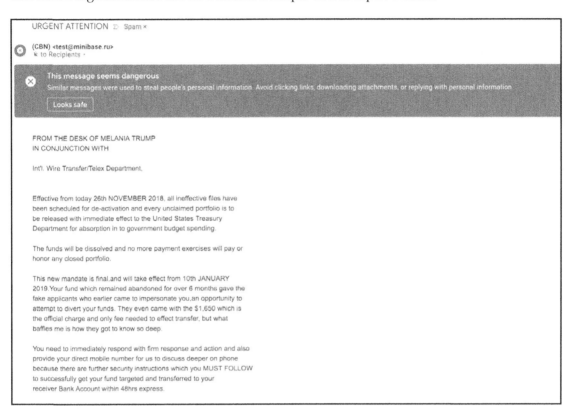

CEO fraud

CEO fraud is a form of **spear phishing,** where the top executives of an organization are the target. They suffer from account takeovers due to stolen login credentials.

Once the account takeover is successful, the business's emails are compromised, and the top executives' business emails are used to send wire transfers or at least to initiate one. Such types of attacks are also know as **whaling attacks**.

These attacks often happen due to a lack of security awareness among the executives, who do not have time to commit to security awareness training. Hence, there should be security training that is especially meant for CEOs and CXOs.

Often, organizational policies need to be revamped, in order to prevent such attacks. Authentication and authorization at stages should be a compulsory:

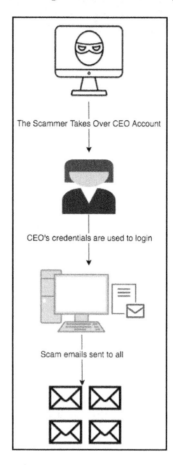

Pharming

Pharming is a more sophisticated form of phishing attack, wherein the **domain name system** (**DNS**) cache is tampered with. These attacks are more sure-fire ways to propagate scams, as basic security training classes have made users less vulnerable to phishing attacks. Before we move on to the details of how an attack works, we will explain how the DNS server works. The DNS server translates all of the website addresses into numerical forms, so that they can easily be mapped. The IP address for Microsoft (`https://www.microsoft.com/en-in/`) is as follows:

```
Checking Domain Name

Domain Name: microsoft.com
Top Level Domain: COM (Commercial TLD)

DNS Lookup
IP Address: 40.76.4.15

Geolocation: US (United States), VA, Virginia, 23917 Boydton - Google Maps

Reverse DNS entry: not found
Domain Check
Domain Name: microsoft.com
Top Level Domain: COM (Commercial TLD)

Domain Name: MICROSOFT.COM
Registry Domain ID: 2724960_DOMAIN_COM-VRSN
Registrar WHOIS Server: whois.markmonitor.com
Registrar URL: http://www.markmonitor.com
Updated Date: 2014-10-09T16:28:25Z
Creation Date: 1991-05-02T04:00:00Z
Registry Expiry Date: 2021-05-03T04:00:00Z
Registrar: MarkMonitor Inc.
Registrar IANA ID: 292
Registrar Abuse Contact Email: abusecomplaints@markmonitor.com
Registrar Abuse Contact Phone: +1.2083895740
Domain Status: clientDeleteProhibited
https://icann.org/epp#clientDeleteProhibited
Domain Status: clientTransferProhibited
https://icann.org/epp#clientTransferProhibited
Domain Status: clientUpdateProhibited
https://icann.org/epp#clientUpdateProhibited
Domain Status: serverDeleteProhibited
https://icann.org/epp#serverDeleteProhibited
Domain Status: serverTransferProhibited
https://icann.org/epp#serverTransferProhibited
Domain Status: serverUpdateProhibited
```

```
https://icann.org/epp#serverUpdateProhibited
Name Server: NS1.MSFT.NET
Name Server: NS2.MSFT.NET
Name Server: NS3.MSFT.NET
Name Server: NS4.MSFT.NET
DNSSEC: unsigned
URL of the ICANN Whois Inaccuracy Complaint Form:
https://www.icann.org/wicf/
>>> Last update of whois database: 2018-12-14T04:12:27Z <<<
```

In a pharming attack, rather than obfuscating a URL, a pharmer attacks the DNS server and changes the IP address associated with a website. Hence, the attacker is able to redirect all of the traffic to the website to a new, malicious location. The user is not aware of this, because they have typed the website address into the browser correctly.

To combat these attacks, companies advise users/employees to visit only HTTPS sites or sites with proper certificates. There are many types of antivirus software that can prevent you from falling prey to pharming attacks, but not every user wants to spend money on antivirus programs, especially in developing countries.

Dropbox phishing

Although we have discussed methods more sophisticated than phishing to lure in users, phishing simply works well for certain sites, especially cloud storage sites.

With the volume of data rapidly expanding, people have resorted to cloud storage. Every day, millions of users back up their content by uploading it to sites such as Dropbox. Phishing often takes advantage of such individual services.

Attackers create fake sign-in pages for Dropbox as a part of credential harvesting. They then use the stolen credentials to log in to legitimate sites and steal user data.

Google Docs phishing

A Google Docs phishing attack is very similar to the attack described in the preceding section. Google Drive is a massive store of information, ranging from spreadsheets to images and documents. A simple fake login is an easy win for fraudsters.

To combat such attacks, Google have set up two-factor authentication to allow users to get into their accounts. However, the onus is on the user to enable this form of two-factor authentication. A simple download of the Google Authenticator app solves the problem.

Spam detection

We will now deal with a hands-on exercise of separating spam emails a set of non-spam, or ham, emails. Unlike manual spam detectors, where users mark email as spam upon manual verification, this method uses machine learning to distinguish between spam and ham emails. The stages of detection can be illustrated as follows:

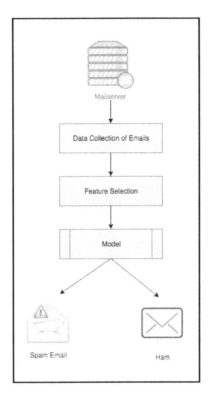

Types of mail servers

Mail servers are meant to receive email items, and they consist of a return path. The path bounces an email off to the ID mentioned in the return path. Mail servers are equivalent to the neighborhood mailman. All emails pass through a series of servers called **mail-servers** through series of processes.

The different types of mail servers are as follows:

- **POP3 email servers**: **Post Office Protocol 3 (POP3)** is a type of email server used by **internet service providers (ISP)**. These servers store emails in remote servers. When the emails are opened by the users, they are fetched from the remote servers and are stored locally in the user's computer/machine. The external copy of the email is then deleted from the remote server.

- **IMAP email servers**: **Internet Message Access Protocol (IMAP)** is a variation of a POP3 type of server. IMAP email servers are mainly used for business purposes, and allow for organizing, previewing, and deleting emails. After the emails are organized, they can be transferred to the user's computer. A copy of the email will still reside in the external server, unless the business user decides to explicitly delete it.

- **SMTP email servers**: These work hand in hand with the POP3 and IMAP servers. They help with sending emails to and fro, from the server to the user. The following diagram illustrates the SMTP process:

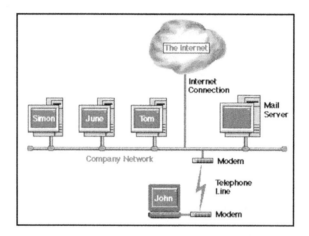

Data collection from mail servers

We will use the Kaggle dataset in the following example. The data is similar to the data gathered in a mail server. An intelligent way to gather spam email is to collect data from mail servers that have been shut down. Since the email accounts associated with such mail servers perpetually do not exist, it can be assumed that any emails sent to these email accounts are spam emails.

The following screenshot shows a snippet of actual Kaggle data, taken from `https://www.`
`kaggle.com/uciml/sms-spam-collection-dataset`:

	ham	87%				
	spam	13%	5169	43	10	5
			unique values	unique values	unique values	unique values
1	ham		Go until jurong point, crazy.. Available only in bugis n great world la e buffet... Cine there got amore wat...			
2	ham		Ok lar... Joking wif u oni...			
3	spam		Free entry in 2 a wkly comp to win FA Cup final tkts 21st May 2005. Text FA to 87121 to receive entry question(std txt rate)T&C's apply 08452810075over18's			
4	ham		U dun say so early hor... U c already then say...			
5	ham		Nah I don't think he goes to usf, he lives around here			

We have modified the data to add labels (0 is ham and 1 is spam), as follows:

Spam/Ham	Email	Label
Ham	Your electricity bill is	0
Ham	Mom, see you this friday at 6	0
Spam	Win free iPhone	1
Spam	60% off on Rolex watches	1
Ham	Your order `#RELPG4513`	0
Ham	OCT timesheet	0

Using the Naive Bayes theorem to detect spam

The Naive Bayes theorem is a classification technique. The basis of this algorithm is Bayes' theorem; the basic assumption is that the predictor variables are independent of each other.

Bayes' theorem is mathematically expressed as follows:

$$P(A \mid B) = \frac{P(B \mid A)\,P(A)}{P(B)},$$

where A and B are events and $P(B) \neq 0$.

- $P(A)$ and $P(B)$ are the probabilities of observing A and B without regard to each other.
- $P(A \mid B)$, a conditional probability, is the probability of observing event A given that B is true.
- $P(B \mid A)$ is the probability of observing event B given that A is true.

It essentially gives us a trick for calculating conditional probabilities, in situations where it wouldn't be feasible to directly measure them. For instance, if you wanted to calculate someone's chance of having cancer, given their age, instead of performing a nationwide study, you can just take existing statistics about age distribution and cancer and plug them into Bayes' theorem.

However, it is recommended to go back and try to understand later as the failure to understand Bayes' theorem is the root of many logical fallacies.

For our problem, we can set A to the probability that the email is spam and B as the contents of the email. If $P(A|B) > P(\neg A|B)$, then we can classify the email as spam; otherwise, we can't. Note that, since Bayes' theorem results in a divisor of $P(B)$ in both cases, we can remove it from the equation for our comparison. This leaves the following: $P(A)*P(B|A) > P(\neg A)*P(B|\neg A)$. Calculating $P(A)$ and $P(\neg A)$ is trivial; they are simply the percentages of your training set that are spam or not spam. The following block diagram shows how to build a Naive Bayes classifier:

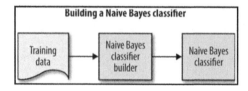

The following code shows the training data:

```
#runs once on training data
def train:
    total = 0
    numSpam = 0
    for email in trainData:
        if email.label == SPAM:
            numSpam += 1
        total += 1
    pA = numSpam/(float)total
    pNotA = (total — numSpam)/(float)total
```

The most difficult part is calculating *P(B|A)* and *P(B|¬A)*. In order to calculate these, we are going to use the **bag of words model**. This is a pretty simple model that treats a piece of text as a bag of individual words, paying no attention to their order. For each word, we calculate the percentage of times it shows up in spam emails, as well as in non-spam emails. We call this probability *P(B_i|A_x)*. For example, in order to calculate *P(free | spam)*, we would count the number of times the word free occurs in all of the spam emails combined and divide this by the total number of words in all of the spam emails combined. Since these are static values, we can calculate them in our training phase, as shown in the following code:

```
#runs once on training data
def train:
    total = 0
    numSpam = 0
    for email in trainData:
        if email.label == SPAM:
            numSpam += 1
        total += 1
        processEmail(email.body, email.label)
    pA = numSpam/(float)total
    pNotA = (total — numSpam)/(float)total

#counts the words in a specific email
def processEmail(body, label):
    for word in body:
        if label == SPAM:
            trainPositive[word] = trainPositive.get(word, 0) + 1
            positiveTotal += 1
        else:
            trainNegative[word] = trainNegative.get(word, 0) + 1
            negativeTotal += 1

#gives the conditional probability p(B_i | A_x)
def conditionalWord(word, spam):
```

```
    if spam:
        return trainPositive[word]/(float)positiveTotal
    return trainNegative[word]/(float)negativeTotal
```

To get $p(B|A\_x)$ for an entire email, we simply take the product of the $p(B\_i|A\_x)$ value for every word i in the email. Note that this is done at the time of classification and not when initially training:

```
#gives the conditional probability p(B | A_x)
def conditionalEmail(body, spam):
    result = 1.0
    for word in body:
        result *= conditionalWord(word, spam)
    return result
```

Finally, we have all of the components that are required to put it all together. The final piece that we need is the classifier, which gets called for every email, and which uses our previous functions to classify the emails:

```
#classifies a new email as spam or not spam
def classify(email):
    isSpam = pA * conditionalEmail(email, True) # P (A | B)
    notSpam = pNotA * conditionalEmail(email, False) # P(¬A | B)
    return isSpam > notSpam
```

However, there are some changes that you'd need to make in order to make it work optimally and bug free.

Laplace smoothing

One thing that we haven't mentioned is what happens if a word in the email that you're classifying wasn't in your training set. In order to handle this case, we would need to add a smoothing factor. This is best demonstrated in the following modified code, where the smoothing factor, alpha, is added:

```
#gives the conditional probability p(B_i | A_x) with smoothing
def conditionalWord(word, spam):
    if spam:
        return
(trainPositive.get(word,0)+alpha)/(float)(positiveTotal+alpha*numWords)
    return
(trainNegative.get(word,0)+alpha)/(float)(negativeTotal+alpha*numWords)
```

Featurization techniques that convert text-based emails into numeric values

Spam data is in a text format, and we can use machine learning algorithms to transform this data into meaningful mathematical parameters. In the following sections, we will discuss many such parameters.

Log-space

Our current implementation relies heavily on floating point multiplication. To avoid all of the potential issues with multiplying very small numbers, one usually performs a logarithm on the equation, to transform all of the multiplication into addition. I didn't implement this in my sample code, but it is strongly recommended in practice.

TF-IDF

Overall, the bag of words model for text classification is fairly naive and could be upon by something else, such as `tf-idf`.

N-grams

Another improvement that we could make is to not just count individual words. N-grams is a technique in which we consider sets of N consecutive words and use them to calculate the probabilities. This makes sense, because in English, the 1-gram *good* conveys something different than the 2-gram *not good*.

Tokenization

One interesting thing to play around with is how to classify distinct words. For instance, are Free, free, and FREE the same words? What about punctuation?

Please note that the sample code is written for optimal teaching, instead of for performance. There are some clear, trivial changes that could drastically improve its performance.

Logistic regression spam filters

In this part of this chapter, we will deal with logistic regression, using it to detect spam emails. The use of logistic regression to detect spam is a fairly unconventional method.

Logistic regression

This a regression method that is used for prediction. Logistic regression helps us to understand the relationships that exist between a dependent variable and independent variables.

The equation of a logistic regression is as follows:

$$f(x) = \frac{1}{1 + e^{-\beta x}}$$

A logistic regression graph is depicted as follows:

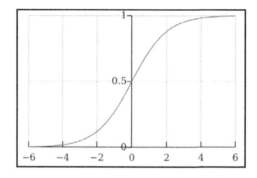

Dataset

We will ingest the SMS spam dataset for this use case. This dataset is available from Federal University in Sao Carlos, Brazil.

The link to the dataset is as follows: `https://archive.ics.uci.edu/ml/datasets/SMS+Spam+Collection`.

The dataset consists of a collection of 425 items from the Grumbletext website. Grumbletext is a site in the UK where users manually report spam text messages. In addition to the spam text messages, 3,375 SMS messages that were randomly chosen from the **National University of Singapore SMS Corpus** (**NSC**) have also been added to the dataset. Another 450 benign SMS messages were collected from Caroline Tag's PhD thesis, available at `http://etheses.bham.ac.uk/253/1/Tagg09PhD.pdf`.

The dataset is divided into training and testing data, and, for featurization, the `tf-idf` method is used.

The dataset looks as follows:

```
●●●                                    SMSSpamCollection ˅
ham      Go until jurong point, crazy.. Available only in bugis n great world la e buffet... Cine there got amore wat...
ham      Ok lar... Joking wif u oni...
spam     Free entry in 2 a wkly comp to win FA Cup final tkts 21st May 2005. Text FA to 87121 to receive entry question(std txt rate)T&C's apply
08452810075over18's
ham      U dun say so early hor... U c already then say...
ham      Nah I don't think he goes to usf, he lives around here though
spam     FreeMsg Hey there darling it's been 3 week's now and no word back! I'd like some fun you up for it still? Tb ok! XxX std chgs to send,
£1.50 to rcv
ham      Even my brother is not like to speak with me. They treat me like aids patent.
ham      As per your request 'Melle Melle (Oru Minnaminunginte Nurungu Vettam)' has been set as your callertune for all Callers. Press *9 to copy
your friends Callertune
spam     WINNER!! As a valued network customer you have been selected to receivea £900 prize reward! To claim call 09061701461. Claim code KL341.
Valid 12 hours only.
spam     Had your mobile 11 months or more? U R entitled to Update to the latest colour mobiles with camera for Free! Call The Mobile Update Co
FREE on 08002986030
ham      I'm gonna be home soon and i don't want to talk about this stuff anymore tonight, k? I've cried enough today.
spam     SIX chances to win CASH! From 100 to 20,000 pounds txt> CSH11 and send to 87575. Cost 150p/day, 6days, 16+ TsandCs apply Reply HL 4 info
spam     URGENT! You have won a 1 week FREE membership in our £100,000 Prize Jackpot! Txt the word: CLAIM to No: 81010 T&C www.dbuk.net LCCLTD
POBOX 4403LDNW1A7RW18
ham      I've been searching for the right words to thank you for this breather. I promise i wont take your help for granted and will fulfil my
promise. You have been wonderful and a blessing at all times.
ham      I HAVE A DATE ON SUNDAY WITH WILL!!
spam     XXXMobileMovieClub: To use your credit, click the WAP link in the next txt message or click here>> http://wap. xxxmobilemovieclub.com?
n=QJKGIGHJJGCBL
ham      Oh k...i'm watching here:)
```

Python

We will start by importing the relevant packages. The `pandas` package will be used to enable data frame capabilities. The `sklearn` package will be used to divide the data into training and testing datasets. We will also use the logistic regression available in `sklearn`:

```python
import pandas as pd
import numpy as np
from sklearn.feature_extraction.text import TfidfVectorizer
from sklearn.linear_model.logistic import LogisticRegression
from sklearn.model_selection import train_test_split, cross_val_score
```

We import SMSSpamCollectiondataSet using pandas, as follows:

```
dataframe = pd.read_csv('SMSSpamCollectionDataSet',
delimiter='\t',header=None)

X_train_dataset, X_test_dataset, y_train_dataset, y_test_dataset =
train_test_split(dataframe[1],dataframe[0])
```

The data is transformed to fit the logistic regression model:

```
vectorizer = TfidfVectorizer()
X_train_dataset = vectorizer.fit_transform(X_train_dataset)
classifier_log = LogisticRegression()
classifier_log.fit(X_train_dataset, y_train_dataset)
```

The test dataset is used to predict the accuracy of the model:

```
X_test_dataset = vectorizer.transform( ['URGENT! Your Mobile No 1234 was
awarded a Prize', 'Hey honey, whats up?'] )

predictions_logistic = classifier.predict(X_test_dataset)
print(predictions)
```

Results

The logistic regression for the proceeding code will output the predicted value, where 0 is ham and 1 is spam.

Summary

In this chapter, we studied email spoofing and the different types of spam emails, including deceptive emails, CEO pharming, and Dropbox phishing. We also covered spam detection, as well as using the Naive Bayes theorem to detect spam. This chapter covered the logistic regression spam filter, including datasets and Python.

In the next chapter, you will learn about efficient network anomaly detection with k-means.

6
Efficient Network Anomaly Detection Using k-means

Network attacks are on the rise, and a lot of research work has been done to thwart the negative effects from such attacks. As discussed in the previous chapters, we identify attacks as any unauthorized attempt to do the following:

- Get hold of information
- Modify information
- Disrupt services
- Perform distributed denial of service to and from the server where information is stored
- Exploit using malware and viruses
- Privilege escalation and credential compromise

Network anomalies are unlike regular network infections by viruses. In such cases, network anomalies are detected by identifying non-conforming patterns in the network data. Not just network intrusion detection, such methods can also be used for other forms of outlier detection such as credit fraud, traffic violation detection, and customer churn detection.

This chapter will cover the following topics:

- Stages of a network attack
- Dealing with lateral movement
- Understanding how Windows activity logs can help detect network anomalies
- How to ingest large volume of Microsoft activity logs
- Writing a simple novelty model that will detect anomalies in the network
- Work of a sophisticated model that will use k-means to detect network anomalies

Stages of a network attack

Before moving on to methods of intrusion detection, we will deal with multiple methods of network threats. To understand the details of network anomaly, we will discuss the six stages of cyber attacks.

Phase 1 – Reconnaissance

This is the very first stage of a network attack, where the vulnerabilities and potential targets are identified. Once the assessing of the vulnerabilities and the measure of the defenses are done, a weapon is chosen, and it could vary from being a phishing attack, a zero-day attack, or some other form of malware attack.

Phase 2 – Initial compromise

During this phase of the attack, the first compromise happens, such as the dropping of a spear-phishing email or bypassing of network firewalls.

Phase 3 – Command and control

Once the initial compromise has been done, a connection to the homing device also known as the **command and control server** is made. Usually, this stage requires a user to install a **Remote-Qaccess Trojan (RAT)**, which sets up a remote connection to the command and control server or the botnet.

Phase 4 – Lateral movement

This stage of the network attack follows when a solid connection with the command and control server is already established for quite some time without being noticed. The command and control server gives orders in the form of hidden codes to laterally spread across multiple devices that are in the same network.

Phase 5 – Target attainment

When the malware has established a lateral connection with multiple devices in the network, it will carry several orders for unsolicited authorization, privilege escalation, and account compromise.

Phase 6 – Ex-filtration, corruption, and disruption

In this final stage of attack, the escalated permissions are used to transfer data out of the network, also known as **ex-filtration**. They steal sensitive data from the organization and corrupt critical resources. Often, the disruption could also include deleting entire file systems.

Dealing with lateral movement in networks

We will deal with network anomaly detection with respect to lateral movement in much more detail in this chapter. Lateral movement enables attackers to compromise systems within the same network with an east-to-west movement. Lateral movement enables attackers to search for the key data and assets that are ultimately the target of their attack campaigns.

Lateral movement is not limited to a single victim within a network and enables spreading of the malware infestations across the servers and domain controllers, hence compromising the network in its entirety. Lateral movement attacks are the key differentiators that distinguish between the current complicated targeted attacks and the older comparatively simplistic attacks such as zero-day attacks.

Lateral movement moves across the network to gain privileges within the network and grant various accesses to the command and control servers. Such access includes but is not limited to endpoints such as confidential documents, **personally identifiable information (PII)** documents, files stored in computers, files stored in shared network areas, and more. Lateral movement also includes the use of sophisticated tools used by network administrators.

This diagram shows the most common way that network intrusion spreads within an organization:

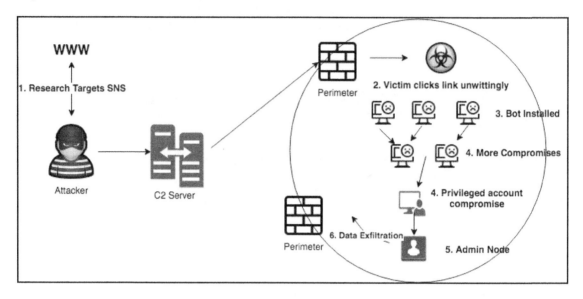

Using Windows event logs to detect network anomalies

We will use Windows event logs to detect lateral movement in the first pass of detecting network anomalies. We will use **Windows Active Directory** logs for the purpose of the experiment. Active Directory is a Microsoft product that provides a directory service for network domains. Active Directory services include a wide range of directory-based identity-related services.

Active Directory stores all sorts of authorization and authentication logs using **lightweight directory access protocol (LDAP)**. Active Directory logs a host of processes such as log-on events. In other words, when someone logs on to a computer and lockout events, that is, when someone enters wrong passwords and is unable to login. The following diagram shows the Active Directory logs along with the different processes:

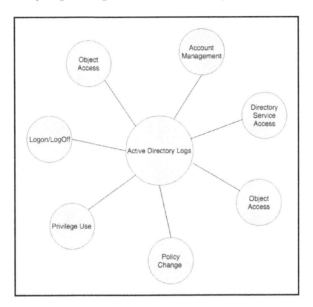

We will discuss each of these types so that we can establish how each of these are related to network anomaly detection.

Logon/Logoff events

These correspond to audit logon/logoff events, which are logon sessions or attempts to log on to the local computer.

The following diagram describes interactive logon and network logon on the file server:

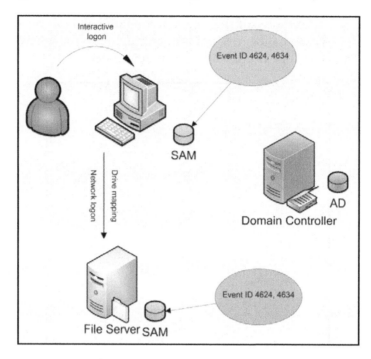

Account logon events

The account logon events consists of account authentication activities such as credential validation, Kerberos authentication, and grating a service ticket. These are mostly logged on by the domain controller server:

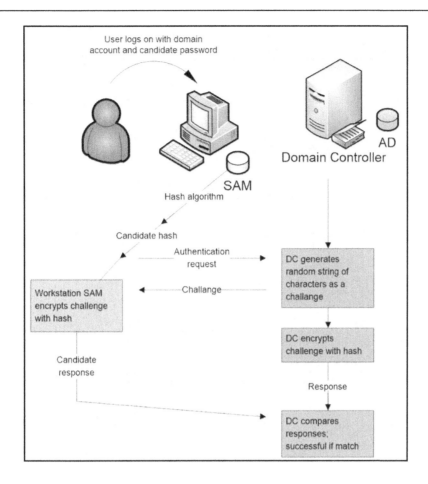

Object access events

These events track the permissions and objects that are accessed within the local computer or server such as file handle manipulation, file share access, and certification services.

The following diagram describes how the object access events works:

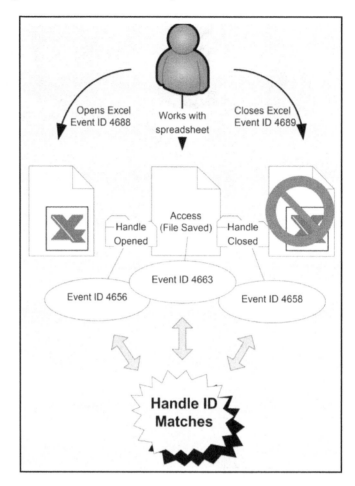

Account management events

Account management logs keeps track of activities such as account creation, account enabling, account change, and password reset attempts, and so on.

Active directory events

A sample active directory log 2008 looks as follows:

```
Log Name: Security
Source: Microsoft-Windows-Security-Auditing
Date: 10/28/2008 6:17:28 PM
Event ID: 4768
Task Category: Kerberos Authentication Service
Level: Information
Keywords: Audit Success
User: N/A
Computer: Lab2008.acme.ru
Description:
A Kerberos authentication ticket (TGT) was requested.

Account Information:
        Account Name:          Fred
        Supplied Realm Name:   ACME
        User ID:               ACME\Fred

Service Information:
        Service Name:          krbtgt
        Service ID:            ACME\krbtgt

Network Information:
        Client Address:        ::1
        Client Port:           0

Additional Information:
        Ticket Options:        0x40810010
        Result Code:           0x0
        Ticket Encryption Type: 0x17
        Pre-Authentication Type: 2

Certificate Information:
        Certificate Issuer Name:
        Certificate Serial Number:
        Certificate Thumbprint:

Certificate information is only provided if a certificate was used for pre-authentication.
Pre-
authentication types, ticket options, encryption types and result codes are defined in RFC 4120.
```

Active Directory columns involves having an event ID, an event description, the source of the log and the destination, the network information, the name of the local computer, the log source name, and many more.

For the purposes of the experiment, we will use the following event IDs:

Event ID	Event Description
4624	An account was successfully logged on.
4768	A Kerberos authentication ticket (TGT) was requested.
4769	A Kerberos service ticket was requested.
4672	Special privileges was assigned to a new logon.
4776	The domain controller attempted to validate the credentials for an account.
4663	An attempt was made to access an object.

We need to keep an account of source and destination for the preceding event IDs. We keep track of user IDs, multiple user logons, and network preferences.

Ingesting active directory data

An **active directory** (**AD**) is usually ingested through Flume and the data gets stored in HDFS.

The following diagram explains how the ingestion works:

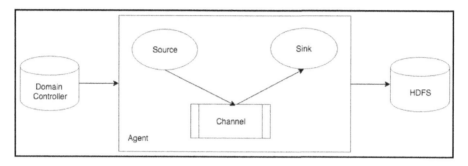

Data parsing

We need to transform data in a format that is easily and readily readable by the feature generator. The columns that we generate comprise the following:

- startTimeISO
- Type of Windows event
- Destination name or IP
- Destination SecurityID
- Destination username
- Source log on type
- Source name or IP
- Destination NtDomain
- Destination service security ID
- Destination service name

- Source username
- Privileges
- Source host name
- Destination port
- AD profile path
- AD script path
- AD user workstation
- Source log on ID
- Source security ID
- Source NtDomain

Modeling

This is a simple model that stocks in historical data features (the ones listed in the *Data parsing* section) that are associated with Windows logs. When a new feature parameter comes in, we see whether this is a new one by comparing to the historical data. Historical data could include AD logs with res to the features from over a year ago. The AD event that we will use for this purpose is 4672.

For the purposes of a use case, we will only choose the privilege feature. A list of privileges could be as follows:

- SeSecurityPrivilege
- SeTakeOwnershipPrivilege
- SeLoadDriverPrivilege
- SeBackupPrivilege
- SeRestorePrivilege
- SeDebugPrivilege
- SeSystemEnvironmentPrivilege
- SeImpersonatePrivilege

We store in the historical database all privileges that the user account had in the past year, such as the write privilege and the read privilege. When a new privilege is seen to be invoked by the user account, we raise an anomaly alarm. To score the severity of the anomaly, we check how many other people have access to the newly observed privilege. A rarity score is associated with it accordingly. The total number of privileges used by the user account in the entire day is also counted and the final score is the function of the total and the rarity score:

```python
import sys
import os
sys.path.append('.')
sys.path.insert(0, os.getcwd())
sys.path.append('/usr/lib/python2.6/site-packages')

import math

#history of privileges used

input_path_of_file_hist = "/datasets/historical.data"
data_raw_hist = sc.textFile(input_path_of_file_hist, 12)

#for each privilge a rarity map is present

rarity_map = {}
input_path_of_file_rare = "/datasets/rare.data"
data_raw_rare = sc.textFile(input_path_of_file_rare, 12)
arr = data_raw_rare.split(',')
privilege = arr[0]
rarityscore = arr[1]
rarity_map[privilege] = rarityscore


priv_hist = {}
FOREACH line in data_raw_hist :
 if line in priv_hist:
 do_nothing = 1
 else:
 priv_hist[line] = 1


input_path_of_file_curr = "/datasets/current.data"
data_raw_curr = sc.textFile(input_path_of_file_curr, 12)

num_lines = sum(1 for line in open(input_path_of_file_curr))

FOREACH line in data_raw_curr :
 if line in priv_hist
```

```
print "i dont care this is privilege is old"
else:
print "new activity detected"
C = computeScore()
score = C.compute(line,num_lines)
```

For every new activity detected in the network, we compute the score on a scale of 1 to 10 to measure the degree of malicious behavior. There are two classes that would be doing this. The first script calls the score computation script to generate the final score:

```
class computeScore:
    def __init__(self,userandkey,rarity):
        self.userandkey = userandkey
        self.anomaly_score = 0


  def compute(line,num_lines)
  total=num_lines
    itemrarity = rarity_map[line]
  T = NoxScoring()
  anomaly_score = T.threat_anomaly_score(int(itemrarity),int(total))
  return anomaly_score
```

This script is used to generate the relevant score when a newly observed privilege is seen:

```
class NoxScoring():
    def __init__(self):
        self.item_rarirty_table = []
  self.item_rarirty_table.append([.8,1,0.1])
        self.item_rarirty_table.append([.7,.8,0.2])
        self.item_rarirty_table.append([.6,.7,0.3])
        self.item_rarirty_table.append([.5,.6, 0.4])
        self.item_rarirty_table.append([.4,.5, 0.5])
        self.item_rarirty_table.append([.3, .4, 0.6])
        self.item_rarirty_table.append([.2, .3, 0.7])
        self.item_rarirty_table.append([.1, .2, 0.8])
        self.item_rarirty_table.append([.001, .1, 0.9])
        self.item_rarirty_table.append([0, .001, 1])

    def threat_anomaly_score(self,rarityscore,totalusers):
  if rarityscore is None :
            age = .9
  else :
    age = float(rarityscore) / float(totalusers)

        for row in self.item_rarirty_table:
            if (age>=row[0]) and (age<row[1]):
                score = row[2]
```

```
                return score
        return score

    def combine_threat_score(self,score,correlationscore):
        combined_score = score * 1
        return combined_score

#if __name__=='__main__':
# T = NoxScoring()
# print T.threat_anomaly_score(43,473)
```

This simplistic model can be easily used to detect newly observed document (object) access, newly seen servers in the system, or even newly added users.

Detecting anomalies in a network with k-means

In various network attacks, the malware floods the network with traffic. They use this as a means to get unauthorized access. Since network traffic usually is massive by volume, we will be using the k-means algorithm to detect anomalies.

K-means are suitable algorithms for such cases, as network traffic usually has a pattern. Also, network threats do not have labeled data. Every attack is different from the other. Hence, using unsupervised approaches is the best bet here. We will be using these methods to detect batches of traffic that stand out from the rest of the network traffic.

Network intrusion data

We will be using the KDD Cup 1999 data for this use case. The data is approximately 708 MB in size and contains 4.9 million network connections. The data comprises of information such as the following:

- Bytes sent
- Log-in attempts
- TCP errors
- Source bytes
- Destination bytes

The data contains 38 features in total. The features are categorized into both categorical and numerical data. The data collections also come with labels that help determine the purity of the clusters once the clustering algorithm has been applied.

The following is the list of all available features:

```
back,buffer_overflow,ftp_write,guess_passwd,imap,ipsweep,land,loadmodule,mu
ltihop,neptune,nmap,normal,perl,phf,pod,portsweep,rootkit,satan,smurf,spy,t
eardrop,warezclient,warezmaster.
duration: continuous.
protocol_type: symbolic.
service: symbolic.
flag: symbolic.
src_bytes: continuous.
dst_bytes: continuous.
land: symbolic.
wrong_fragment: continuous.
urgent: continuous.
hot: continuous.
num_failed_logins: continuous.
logged_in: symbolic.
num_compromised: continuous.
root_shell: continuous.
su_attempted: continuous.
num_root: continuous.
num_file_creations: continuous.
num_shells: continuous.
num_access_files: continuous.
num_outbound_cmds: continuous.
is_host_login: symbolic.
is_guest_login: symbolic.
count: continuous.
srv_count: continuous.
serror_rate: continuous.
srv_serror_rate: continuous.
rerror_rate: continuous.
srv_rerror_rate: continuous.
same_srv_rate: continuous.
diff_srv_rate: continuous.
srv_diff_host_rate: continuous.
dst_host_count: continuous.
dst_host_srv_count: continuous.
dst_host_same_srv_rate: continuous.
dst_host_diff_srv_rate: continuous.
dst_host_same_src_port_rate: continuous.
dst_host_srv_diff_host_rate: continuous.
dst_host_serror_rate: continuous.
dst_host_srv_serror_rate: continuous.
```

```
dst_host_rerror_rate: continuous.
dst_host_srv_rerror_rate: continuous.
```

Coding the network intrusion attack

We start with importing the relevant packages that will be used. Since the data is very big, we may choose to use Spark.

Spark is an open source distributed cluster-computing system that is used for handling big data:

```
import os
import sys
import re
import time
from pyspark import SparkContext
from pyspark import SparkContext
from pyspark.sql import SQLContext
from pyspark.sql.types import *
from pyspark.sql import Row
# from pyspark.sql.functions import *
%matplotlib inline
import matplotlib.pyplot as plt
import pandas as pd
import numpy as np
import pyspark.sql.functions as func
import matplotlib.patches as mpatches
from operator import add
from pyspark.mllib.clustering import KMeans, KMeansModel
from operator import add
from pyspark.mllib.tree import DecisionTree, DecisionTreeModel
from pyspark.mllib.util import MLUtils
from pyspark.mllib.regression import LabeledPoint
import itertools
```

We start by loading the entire dataset:

```
input_path_of_file = "/datasets/kddcup.data"
data_raw = sc.textFile(input_path_of_file, 12)
```

Since the data is associated with the label, we write a function that will separate the label from the feature vector:

```
def parseVector(line):
  columns = line.split(',')
  thelabel = columns[-1]
  featurevector = columns[:-1]
```

```
   featurevector = [element for i, element in enumerate(featurevector) if i
not in [1, 2, 3]]
   featurevector = np.array(featurevector, dtype=np.float)
   return (thelabel, featurevector)

labelsAndData = raw_data.map(parseVector).cache()
thedata = labelsAndData.map(lambda row: row[1]).cache()
n = thedata.count()

len(data.first())
```

The output for n, that is, the number of connections, is as follows:

```
4898431

38
```

We use the k-mean algorithm from the MLLIB package. The initial choice here is to use two clusters, because first we need to understand the data:

```
time1 = time.time()
k_clusters = KMeans.train(thedata, 2, maxIterations=10, runs=10,
initializationMode="random")

print(time.time() - time1)
```

We will display how these features look. Since the dataset is huge, we will randomly choose three out of the 38 features and display some portions of the data:

```
def getFeatVecs(data):
 n = thedata.count()
 means = thedata.reduce(add) / n
 vecs_ = thedata.map(lambda x: (x - means)**2).reduce(add) / n
 return vecs_

vecs_ = getFeatVecs(data)
```

On displaying the vectors, we see that there is a lot variance in the data:

```
print vecs_

array([  5.23205909e+05,   8.86292287e+11,   4.16040826e+11,
5.71608336e-06,   1.83649380e-03,   5.20574220e-05,           2.19940474e-01,
5.32813401e-05,   1.22928440e-01,           1.48724429e+01,   6.81804492e-05,
6.53256901e-05,           1.55084339e+01,   1.54220970e-02,   7.63454566e-05,
1.26099403e-03,   0.00000000e+00,   4.08293836e-07,           8.34467881e-04,
4.49400827e+04,   6.05124011e+04,           1.45828938e-01,   1.46118156e-01,
5.39414093e-02,           5.41308521e-02,   1.51551218e-01,   6.84170094e-03,
```

```
1.97569872e-02,    4.09867958e+03,   1.12175120e+04,         1.69073904e-01,
1.17816269e-02,    2.31349138e-01,        1.70236904e-03,   1.45800386e-01,
1.46059565e-01,         5.33345749e-02,   5.33506914e-02])
```

The mean shows that a small portion of the data has great variance. Sometimes, this could be an indication of anomalies, but we do not want to jump to a conclusion so soon:

```
mean = thedata.map(lambda x: x[1]).reduce(add) / n
print(thedata.filter(lambda x: x[1] > 10*mean).count())
```

```
4499
```

We want to identify the features that vary the most and to be able to plot them:

```
indices_of_variance = [t[0] for t in sorted(enumerate(vars_), key=lambda x:
x[1])[-3:]]
dataprojected = thedata.randomSplit([10, 90])[0]
# separate into two rdds
rdd0 = thedata.filter(lambda point: k_clusters.predict(point)==0)
rdd1 = thedata.filter(lambda point: k_clusters.predict(point)==1)

center_0 = k_clusters.centers[0]
center_1 = k_clusters.centers[1]
cluster_0 = rdd0.take(5)
cluster_1 = rdd1.take(5)

cluster_0_projected = np.array([[point[i] for i in indices_of_variance] for
point in cluster_0])
cluster_1_projected = np.array([[point[i] for i in indices_of_variance] for
point in cluster_1])

M = max(max(cluster1_projected.flatten()),
max(cluster_0_projected.flatten()))
m = min(min(cluster1_projected.flatten()),
min(cluster_0_projected.flatten()))

fig2plot = plt.figure(figsize=(8, 8))
pltx = fig2plot.add_subplot(111, projection='3d')
pltx.scatter(cluster0_projected[:, 0], cluster0_projected[:, 1],
cluster0_projected[:, 2], c="b")
pltx.scatter(cluster1_projected[:, 0], cluster1_projected[:, 1],
cluster1_projected[:, 2], c="r")
pltx.set_xlim(m, M)
pltx.set_ylim(m, M)
pltx.set_zlim(m, M)
pltx.legend(["cluster 0", "cluster 1"])
```

The graph we get from the preceding is as follows:

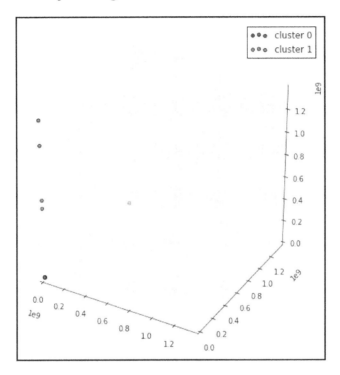

We see that the number of elements in cluster 1 is far more than that of the number of elements in cluster 2. Cluster 0 has its elements far from the center of the data, which is indicative of the imbalance in the data.

Model evaluation

At this point, we evaluate the goodness of the model and, to do, this we will be using the **sum of squared errors** method.

Sum of squared errors

In statistics, the sum of squared errors is a method that measures the difference between the predicted value from the model and the actual value that has been noted. This is also known as the **residual**. For clustering, this is measured as the distance of the projected point from the center of the cluster.

We will be using the Euclidean distance, that is, the distance between two points in a straight line as a measure to compute the sum of the squared errors.

We define the Euclidean distance as follows:

```
def euclidean_distance_points(x1, x2):
 x3 = x1 - x2
 return np.sqrt(x3.T.dot(x3))
```

We will call this preceding function to compute the error:

```
from operator import add
tine1 = time.time()

def ss_error(k_clusters, point):
 nearest_center = k_clusters.centers[k_clusters.predict(point)]
 return euclidean_distance_points(nearest_center, point)**2

WSSSE = data.map(lambda point: ss_error(k_clusters, point)).reduce(add)
print("Within Set Sum of Squared Error = " + str(WSSSE))
print(time.time() - time1)
```

```
Within Set Sum of Squared Error = 3.05254895755e+18
15.861504316329956
```

Since the data is already labeled, we will once check how these labels sit in with the two clusters that we have generated:

```
clusterLabel = labelsAndData.map(lambda row: ((k_clusters.predict(row[1]),
row[0]), 1)).reduceByKey(add)

for items in clusterLabe.collect():
 print(items)
```

```
((0, 'rootkit.'), 10)
((0, 'multihop.'), 7)
((0, 'normal.'), 972781)
((0, 'phf.'), 4)
```

```
((0, 'nmap.'), 2316)
((0, 'pod.'), 264)
((0, 'back.'), 2203)
((0, 'ftp_write.'), 8)
((0, 'spy.'), 2)
((0, 'warezmaster.'), 20)
((1, 'portsweep.'), 5)
((0, 'perl.'), 3)
((0, 'land.'), 21)
((0, 'portsweep.'), 10408)
((0, 'smurf.'), 2807886)
((0, 'ipsweep.'), 12481)
((0, 'imap.'), 12)
((0, 'warezclient.'), 1020)
((0, 'loadmodule.'), 9)
((0, 'guess_passwd.'), 53)
((0, 'neptune.'), 1072017)
((0, 'teardrop.'), 979)
((0, 'buffer_overflow.'), 30)
((0, 'satan.'), 15892)
```

The preceding labels confirms the imbalance in the data, as different types of labels have got clustered in the same cluster.

We will now cluster the entire data and, for that, we need to choose the right value of k. Since the dataset has 23 labels, we can choose K=23, but there are other methods to compute the value of K. The following section describes them.

Choosing k for k-means

There is no algorithm that actually derives the exact value of k to be used in a k-means algorithm. The user runs the k-means for various values of k and finds the one that is optimum. An accurate estimate for k can be made with the following method.

Here, the mean distance is computed between the cluster elements and the cluster centroid. By logic, if we increase the value of k, that is, increase the number of clusters in the data, the number of data points within a cluster decreases. Hence, if the value of k is equal to the number of total data points, the sum squared error is 0, as the centroid is the same as the data point.

Hence, in the elbow method, the errors are plotted for every value of the chosen k and generated error generated. When the plot sees a sharp shift in the rate of decrease in the error, we know we have gone too far.

The following graph shows how the elbow method works:

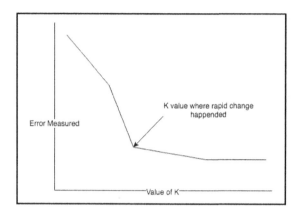

Apart from the preceding, there are other methods of detecting the value of k, such as the k-cross validation method, the silhouette method, and the G-means algorithm.

We will be using the elbow method to detect the number of clusters:

```
k_values = range(5, 126, 20)

def clustering_error_Score(thedata, k):
 k_clusters = KMeans.train(thedata, k, maxIterations=10, runs=10,
initializationMode="random")
# WSSSE = thedata.map(lambda point: error(k_clusters, point)).reduce(add)
 WSSSE = k_clusters.computeCost(thedata)
 return WSSSE

k_scores = [clustering_error_Score(thedata, k) for k in k_values]
for score in k_scores:
 print(k_score)

plt.scatter(k_values, k_scores)
plt.xlabel('k')
plt.ylabel('k_clustering score')
```

The output plot appears as follows:

```
203180867410.17664
197212695108.3952
168362743810.1947
197205266640.06128
197208496981.73676
197204082381.91348
168293832370.86035
```

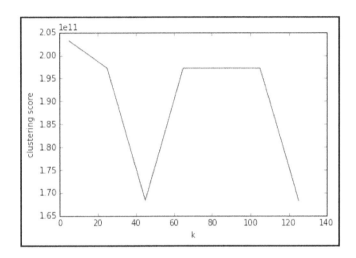

Normalizing features

In k-means clustering, since all data points are not measured on the same scale, they have a high variance. This leads to clusters being less spherical. The uneven variance leads to putting to more weights on variables that will have a lower variance.

To fix this bias, we need to normalize our data, specially because we use Euclidean distance that ends up influencing clusters that have variables with a bigger magnitude. We fix this by standardizing the score of all variables. This is achieved by subtracting the average of the variable's value from each value and followed by a division with standard deviation.

We normalize our data using this same calculation:

```
def normalize(thedata):

 n = thedata.count()
 avg = thedata.reduce(add) / n

 var = thedata.map(lambda x: (x - avg)**2).reduce(add) / n
 std = np.sqrt(var)

 std[std==0] = 1

 def normalize(val):
  return (val - avg) / std
  return thedata.map(normalize)

normalized = normalize(data).cache()
print(normalized.take(2))
print(thedata.take(2))
```

The output looks as follows:

```
[array([ -6.68331854e-02, -1.72038228e-03, 6.81884351e-02,
  -2.39084686e-03, -1.51391734e-02, -1.10348462e-03,
  -2.65207600e-02, -4.39091558e-03, 2.44279187e+00,
  -2.09732783e-03, -8.25770840e-03, -4.54646139e-03,
  -3.28458917e-03, -9.57233922e-03, -8.50457842e-03,
  -2.87561127e-02, 0.00000000e+00, -6.38979005e-04,
  -2.89113034e-02, -1.57541507e+00, -1.19624324e+00,
  -4.66042614e-01, -4.65755574e-01, -2.48285775e-01,
  -2.48130352e-01, 5.39733093e-01, -2.56056520e-01,
  -2.01059296e-01, -3.63913926e+00, -1.78651044e+00,
  -1.83302273e+00, -2.82939000e-01, -1.25793664e+00,
  -1.56668488e-01, -4.66404784e-01, -4.65453641e-01,
  -2.50831829e-01, -2.49631966e-01]), array([ -6.68331854e-02,
 -1.77667956e-03, 5.32451452e-03,
  -2.39084686e-03, -1.51391734e-02, -1.10348462e-03,
  -2.65207600e-02, -4.39091558e-03, 2.44279187e+00,
  -2.09732783e-03, -8.25770840e-03, -4.54646139e-03,
  -3.28458917e-03, -9.57233922e-03, -8.50457842e-03,
  -2.87561127e-02, 0.00000000e+00, -6.38979005e-04,
  -2.89113034e-02, -1.57069789e+00, -1.19217808e+00,
  -4.66042614e-01, -4.65755574e-01, -2.48285775e-01,
  -2.48130352e-01, 5.39733093e-01, -2.56056520e-01,
  -2.01059296e-01, -3.62351937e+00, -1.77706870e+00,
  5.98966843e-01, -2.82939000e-01, 8.21118739e-01,
  -1.56668488e-01, -4.66404784e-01, -4.65453641e-01,
  -2.50831829e-01, -2.49631966e-01])]
```

```
[array([ 0.00000000e+00, 2.15000000e+02, 4.50760000e+04,
  0.00000000e+00, 0.00000000e+00, 0.00000000e+00,
  0.00000000e+00, 0.00000000e+00, 1.00000000e+00,
  0.00000000e+00, 0.00000000e+00, 0.00000000e+00,
  0.00000000e+00, 0.00000000e+00, 0.00000000e+00,
  0.00000000e+00, 0.00000000e+00, 0.00000000e+00,
  0.00000000e+00, 1.00000000e+00, 1.00000000e+00,
  0.00000000e+00, 0.00000000e+00, 0.00000000e+00,
  0.00000000e+00, 1.00000000e+00, 0.00000000e+00,
  0.00000000e+00, 0.00000000e+00, 0.00000000e+00,
  0.00000000e+00, 0.00000000e+00, 0.00000000e+00,
  0.00000000e+00, 0.00000000e+00, 0.00000000e+00,
  0.00000000e+00, 0.00000000e+00]), array([ 0.00000000e+00, 1.62000000e+02,
4.52800000e+03,
  0.00000000e+00, 0.00000000e+00, 0.00000000e+00,
  0.00000000e+00, 0.00000000e+00, 1.00000000e+00,
  0.00000000e+00, 0.00000000e+00, 0.00000000e+00,
  0.00000000e+00, 0.00000000e+00, 0.00000000e+00,
  0.00000000e+00, 0.00000000e+00, 0.00000000e+00,
  0.00000000e+00, 2.00000000e+00, 2.00000000e+00,
  0.00000000e+00, 0.00000000e+00, 0.00000000e+00,
  0.00000000e+00, 1.00000000e+00, 0.00000000e+00,
  0.00000000e+00, 1.00000000e+00, 1.00000000e+00,
  1.00000000e+00, 0.00000000e+00, 1.00000000e+00,
  0.00000000e+00, 0.00000000e+00, 0.00000000e+00,
  0.00000000e+00, 0.00000000e+00])]
```

We now build the model once again with the normalized data for different values of k. The values start from k = 60 to 110, with a leap of 10:

```
k_range = range(60, 111, 10)

k_scores = [clustering_error_Score(normalized, k) for k in k_range]
for kscore in k_scores:
 print(kscore)

plt.plot(k_range, kscores)
```

The elbow graph shows a far better pattern:

```
13428.588817861917
26586.44539596379
18520.0580113469
10282.671313141745
12240.257631897006
12229.312684687848
```

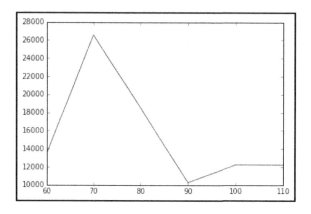

What we do next is we take a small sample of data from the given dataset and perform k-means clustering twice:

- Once with normalization
- Once without normalization

We compare the results of the clusters:

- Before normalization, the result appears as follows:

```
#before norm
K_norm = 90

var = getVariance(thedata)
indices_of_variance = [t[0] for t in sorted(enumerate(var),
key=lambda x: x[1])[-3:]]

dataprojected = thedata.randomSplit([1, 999])[0].cache()

kclusters = KMeans.train(thedata, K_norm, maxIterations=10,
runs=10, initializationMode="random")

listdataprojected = dataprojected.collect()
projected_data = np.array([[point[i] for i in indices_of_variance]
```

```
for point in listdataprojected])
klabels = [kclusters.predict(point) for point in listdataprojected]

Maxi = max(projected_data.flatten())
mini = min(projected_data.flatten())

figs = plt.figure(figsize=(8, 8))
pltx = figs.add_subplot(111, projection='3d')
pltx.scatter(projected_data[:, 0], projected_data[:, 1],
projected_data[:, 2], c=klabels)
pltx.set_xlim(mini, Maxi)
pltx.set_ylim(mini, Maxi)
pltx.set_zlim(mini, Maxi)
pltx.set_title("Before normalization")
```

The plot looks like this:

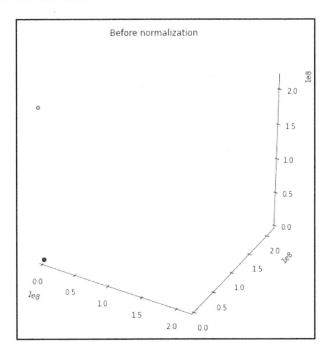

- After normalization, it looks as follows:

```
#After normalization:

kclusters = KMeans.train(normalized, K_norm, maxIterations=10,
runs=10, initializationMode="random")
```

```
dataprojected_normed = normalize(thedata, dataprojected).cache()
dataprojected_normed = dataprojected_normed.collect()
projected_data = np.array([[point[i] for i in indices_of_variance]
for point in dataprojected_normed])
klabels = [kclusters.predict(point) for point in
dataprojected_normed]

Maxi = max(projected_data.flatten())
mini = min(projected_data.flatten())

figs = plt.figure(figsize=(8, 8))
pltx = fig.add_subplot(111, projection='3d')
pltx.scatter(projected_data[:, 0], projected_data[:, 1],
projected_data[:, 2], c=klabels)
pltx.set_xlim(mini, Maxi)
pltx.set_ylim(mini, Maxi)
pltx.set_zlim(mini, Maxi)
pltx.set_title("After normalization")
```

The plot looks like this:

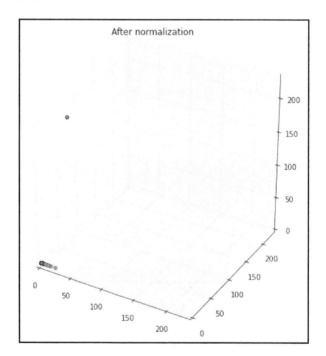

Before we move on to complete our model, we need to add one final thing, which is changing categorical variables to numerical ones. We do this by using **one-hot encoding**. One-hot encoding is the process of transforming categorical variables to forms that can be processed for statistical analysis:

```
col1 = raw_data.map(lambda line: line.split(",")[1]).distinct().collect()
col2 = raw_data.map(lambda line: line.split(",")[2]).distinct().collect()
col2 = raw_data.map(lambda line: line.split(",")[3]).distinct().collect()

def parseWithOneHotEncoding(line):
 column = line.split(',')
 thelabel = column[-1]
 thevector = column[0:-1]

 col1 = [0]*len(featureCol1)
 col1[col1.index(vector[1])] = 1
 col2 = [0]*len(col2)
 col2[featureCol1.index(vector[2])] = 1
 col2 = [0]*len(featureCol3)
 col2[featureCol1.index(vector[3])] = 1

 thevector = ([thevector[0]] + col1 + col2 + col3 + thevector[4:])

 thevector = np.array(thevector, dtype=np.float)

return (thelabel, thevector)
labelsAndData = raw_data.map(parseLineWithHotEncoding)

thedata = labelsAndData.values().cache()

normalized = normalize(thedata).cache()
```

The output is the following:

```
[ 0.00000000e+00 2.48680000e+04 3.50832000e+05 0.00000000e+00
  0.00000000e+00 0.00000000e+00 1.00000000e+00 0.00000000e+00
  1.01000000e+02 0.00000000e+00 0.00000000e+00 0.00000000e+00
  0.00000000e+00 0.00000000e+00 0.00000000e+00 0.00000000e+00
  0.00000000e+00 0.00000000e+00 0.00000000e+00 7.79000000e+02
  1.03300000e+03 0.00000000e+00 0.00000000e+00 0.00000000e+00
  0.00000000e+00 1.01000000e+02 0.00000000e+00 5.51000000e+00
  7.78300000e+03 2.26050000e+04 1.01000000e+02 0.00000000e+00
  9.05000000e+00 3.15000000e+00 0.00000000e+00 0.00000000e+00
  0.00000000e+00 0.00000000e+00]
```

Finally, to normalize the data, we have an optimal value for k, and the categorical variables have been taken care of. We perform k-means again as shown:

```
kclusters = KMeans.train(data, 100, maxIterations=10, runs=10,
initializationMode="random")

anomaly = normalized.map(lambda point: (point, error(clusters,
point))).takeOrdered(100, lambda key: key[1])
plt.plot([ano[1] for ano in anomaly])
```

The output plot consists of several steps, each of which depicts a threshold:

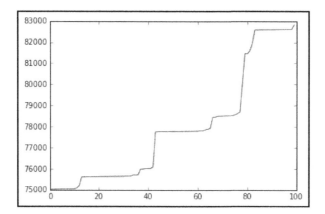

The number of anomalies per threshold will be as follows:

Threshold	# of anomalies
75200	10
75900	35
78200	65
78800	78
82800	95

Manual verification

The ideal next step after we get the anomalies listed is to take each one and get them manually verified by a **System and Organization Controls (SOC)** team who can look at them individually.

Summary

In this chapter, we have learned about the different stages of a network attack including the different phases and dealing with lateral movement in the network. We also learned about Windows event logs to detect network anomalies. We studied about ingesting AD data along with anomaly detection in a network with k-means.

This chapter concluded with choosing k for k-means, along with normalizing features and manual verification. In the next chapter, we will study decision trees and context-based malicious event detection.

7

Decision Tree and Context-Based Malicious Event Detection

Malware destructs computer exploits that are responsible for increased CPU usage, slower computer speeds, and much more. It reduces network speeds, freezes or crashes systems, and modifies or deletes files. Malware often messes with default computer configurations and performs strange computer activities with or without the knowledge of a user.

Malicious software is used to steal data, bypass firewalls, and handicap access controls. Malware, at the end of the day, hosts some sort of malicious code and can be categorized into multiple types based on the type of malicious activity it performs.

Next, we will discuss a list of such malware and the injections that it performs:

- Types of malware
- Malicious data injection in databases
- Malicious data injection in wireless networks
- Intrusion detection with decision tree
- Malicious URL detection with decision tree

Adware

Commonly known as **pop-up ads**, adware delivers unauthorized adware or short advertising software. They are often bundled in with a software package. Adware is sponsored by advertisers to generate revenue. Commonly, adware does not steal information, but sometimes it may be disguised spyware.

Bots

Bots are programs that are capable of performing automative tasks. Bots might not be malicious, but in recent times they have been primarily used for malicious purposes only. A computer acting as a bot when aggregated with several other such computers is called a **botnet**, and primarily called a **spam botnet**. Spam botnets are used to spread spam emails and initiate DDoS attacks on servers; they may or may not have web scrapers spidering that automatically gather data.

Bugs

Bugs are software flaws and are caused by human errors while building a software. They are source code defects that have gone undetected during compilation of the code; hence, they effect code execution capabilities. Bugs can lead to freezing or crashing of software. They can also allow potential software attacks because the malicious attackers use these flaws to accelerate privilege, bypass filters, and steal data.

Ransomware

This is malware that hijacks computers and blocks access to all files and does not release access to the system until a ransom amount is paid. It encrypts system files and renders it impossible for anyone to access the file system. It replicates like regular computer works by exercising control over system vulnerabilities.

Rootkit

Rootkits, like botnets, remotely access computers and do not get detected by the systems. Rootkits are enabled in such a fashion that the malware can be remotely executed by the malicious personnel. Roots access, modify, and delete files. They are used to steal information by staying concealed. Since rootkits are stealthy, they are extremely difficult to detect. Regular system updates are patches which are the only means to keep away from rootkits.

Spyware

This is malware that is primarily involved in reconnaissance. Reconnaissance includes keystroke collectors; harvesting of data points, especially those related to **Personally Identifiable Information (PII)** such as banking information; log-in credentials such as user IDs and passwords; and confidential data. They are also responsible for port sniffing and interfering network connections. Much like rootkits, spyware also exploits loose ends of the network software system.

Trojan horses

Trojan or Trojan horses are malware that exploit vulnerable users and lure them to download unsolicited software. Once downloaded, similar to bots, these too grant remote access to the computer. Such remote access is followed by credential compromise, data stealing, screen watching, and anonymous user activity from the infected person's computer.

Viruses

Viruses are malware that infect computers and then vigorously multiply. They usually spread disguised as file systems, cross-site scripts, web app leakages, and so on. Viruses are also responsible for setting botnets and releasing ransomware and adware.

Worms

Worms are also a specialized form of malware that vigorously spread across multiple computer systems. Worms typically cause hindrances to the computer system and eat up bandwidth with payload that may even damage the system. Worms, unlike viruses, do not require any human intervention to multiply or replicate. They have the capability of self replication.

In the previous chapters, we have already established the fact that the most popular attacks are malware, phishing, or cross-site scripting. Other ways of malware spreading within the network systems are through malware injections.

Malicious data injection within databases

Better know as SQL injections, these attacks manipulate SQL queries, and are hence able to manage data sources residing in different databases. SQL injections basically trick databases to produce an undesired output. These could include privilege escalation by granting all access rights, deleting or dropping entire tables with potential PII data, enabling data ex-filtration by running `select *` queries, and then dumping entire data in external devices.

Malicious injections in wireless sensors

Physical devices and sensors detect occurrences of events such as hazards, fires, abnormal activities, and health emergencies. However, these devices can be tampered with so that they create fake events and emergencies.

Use case

We will now discuss some of the earlier intrusions and injections that we have already discussed at the beginning of the chapter. For the purpose of our experiment, we will use the KDD Cup 1999 computer network intrusion detection dataset. The goal of this experiment is to distinguish between the good and bad network connections.

The dataset

The data sources are primarily sourced from the 1998 DARPA Intrusion Detection Evaluation Program by MIT Lincoln Labs. This dataset contains a variety of network events that have been simulated in the military network environment. The data is a TCP dump that has been accumulated from the local area network of an Air Force environment. The data is peppered with multiple attacks.

In general, a typical TCP dump looks as follows:

```
13:08:05.737768 ppp0 > slip139-92-26-177.ist.tr.ibm.net.1221 > dsl-usw-cust-110.inetarena.com.www: . 342:342(0) ack 1449 win 31856 <nop
,nop,timestamp 1247771 114849487> (DF)
13:08:07.467571 ppp0 < dsl-usw-cust-110.inetarena.com.www > slip139-92-26-177.ist.tr.ibm.net.1221: . 1449:2897(1448) ack 342 win 31856
<nop,nop,timestamp 114849637 1247771> (DF)
13:08:07.707634 ppp0 < dsl-usw-cust-110.inetarena.com.www > slip139-92-26-177.ist.tr.ibm.net.1221: . 2897:4345(1448) ack 342 win 31856
<nop,nop,timestamp 114849637 1247771> (DF)
13:08:07.707922 ppp0 > slip139-92-26-177.ist.tr.ibm.net.1221 > dsl-usw-cust-110.inetarena.com.www: . 342:342(0) ack 4345 win 31856 <nop
,nop,timestamp 1247968 114849813> (DF)
13:08:08.057841 ppp0 > slip139-92-26-177.ist.tr.ibm.net.1045 > ns.de.ibm.net.domain: 8928+ PTR? 110.107.102.209.in-addr.arpa. (46)
13:08:08.747598 ppp0 < dsl-usw-cust-110.inetarena.com.www > slip139-92-26-177.ist.tr.ibm.net.1221: P 4345:5793(1448) ack 342 win 31856
<nop,nop,timestamp 114849813 1247968> (DF)
13:08:08.847870 ppp0 < dsl-usw-cust-110.inetarena.com.www > slip139-92-26-177.ist.tr.ibm.net.1221: FP 5793:6297(504) ack 342 win 31856
<nop,nop,timestamp 114849813 1247968> (DF)
13:08:08.848063 ppp0 > slip139-92-26-177.ist.tr.ibm.net.1221 > dsl-usw-cust-110.inetarena.com.www: . 342:342(0) ack 6298 win 31856 <nop
,nop,timestamp 1247968 114849813> (DF)
13:08:08.907566 ppp0 < ns.de.ibm.net.domain > slip139-92-26-177.ist.tr.ibm.net.1045: 8928* 3/1/1 PTR dsl-usw-cust-110.inetarena.com., P
TR fingerless.or (199)
13:08:09.151742 ppp0 > slip139-92-26-177.ist.tr.ibm.net.1221 > dsl-usw-cust-110.inetarena.com.www: F 342:342(0) ack 6298 win 31856 <nop
,nop,timestamp 1248112 114849813> (DF)
13:08:10.137603 ppp0 < dsl-usw-cust-110.inetarena.com.www > slip139-92-26-177.ist.tr.ibm.net.1221: . 6298:6298(0) ack 343 win 31856 <no
p,nop,timestamp 114849967 1248112> (DF)
13:09:01.984210 ppp0 > slip139-92-26-177.ist.tr.ibm.net.1222 > dsl-usw-cust-110.inetarena.com.www: S 920197285:920197285(0) win 32120 <
mss 1460,sackOK,timestamp 1253395 0,nop,wscale 0> (DF)
13:09:03.097569 ppp0 < dsl-usw-cust-110.inetarena.com.www > slip139-92-26-177.ist.tr.ibm.net.1222: S 1222277738:1222277738(0) ack 92019
7286 win 32120 <mss 1460,sackOK,timestamp 114855252 1253395,nop,wscale 0> (DF)
13:09:03.098197 ppp0 > slip139-92-26-177.ist.tr.ibm.net.1222 > dsl-usw-cust-110.inetarena.com.www: . 1:1(0) ack 1 win 32120 <nop,nop,ti
mestamp 1253507 114855252> (DF)
13:09:03.102171 ppp0 > slip139-92-26-177.ist.tr.ibm.net.1222 > dsl-usw-cust-110.inetarena.com.www: P 1:322(321) ack 1 win 32120 <nop,no
p,timestamp 1253507 114855252> (DF)
13:09:04.147613 ppp0 < dsl-usw-cust-110.inetarena.com.www > slip139-92-26-177.ist.tr.ibm.net.1222: . 1:1(0) ack 322 win 31856 <nop,nop,
timestamp 114855369 1253507> (DF)
13:09:04.507608 ppp0 < dsl-usw-cust-110.inetarena.com.www > slip139-92-26-177.ist.tr.ibm.net.1222: . 1:1449(1448) ack 322 win 31856 <no
p,nop,timestamp 114855369 1253507> (DF)
13:09:04.507934 ppp0 > slip139-92-26-177.ist.tr.ibm.net.1222 > dsl-usw-cust-110.inetarena.com.www: . 322:322(0) ack 1449 win 31856 <nop
,nop,timestamp 1253648 114855369> (DF)
13:09:05.627604 ppp0 < dsl-usw-cust-110.inetarena.com.www > slip139-92-26-177.ist.tr.ibm.net.1222: . 1449:2897(1448) ack 322 win 31856
<nop,nop,timestamp 114855491 1253648> (DF)
13:09:05.857649 ppp0 < dsl-usw-cust-110.inetarena.com.www > slip139-92-26-177.ist.tr.ibm.net.1222: . 2897:4345(1448) ack 322 win 31856
<nop,nop,timestamp 114855491 1253648> (DF)
13:09:05.857918 ppp0 > slip139-92-26-177.ist.tr.ibm.net.1222 > dsl-usw-cust-110.inetarena.com.www: . 322:322(0) ack 4345 win 31856 <nop
,nop,timestamp 1253783 114855491> (DF)
13:09:06.907557 ppp0 < dsl-usw-cust-110.inetarena.com.www > slip139-92-26-177.ist.tr.ibm.net.1222: FP 4345:5792(1447) ack 322 win 31856
 <nop,nop,timestamp 114855627 1253783> (DF)
13:09:06.907887 ppp0 > slip139-92-26-177.ist.tr.ibm.net.1222 > dsl-usw-cust-110.inetarena.com.www: . 322:322(0) ack 5793 win 31856 <nop
,nop,timestamp 1253888 114855627> (DF)
13:09:07.401205 ppp0 > slip139-92-26-177.ist.tr.ibm.net.1222 > dsl-usw-cust-110.inetarena.com.www: F 322:322(0) ack 5793 win 31856 <nop
,nop,timestamp 1253937 114855627> (DF)
13:09:08.317623 ppp0 < dsl-usw-cust-110.inetarena.com.www > slip139-92-26-177.ist.tr.ibm.net.1222: . 5793:5793(0) ack 323 win 31856 <no
p,nop,timestamp 114855780 1253937> (DF)
```

The training data set is about four gigabytes in size and consists of a compressed transmission control protocol dump distributed across seven weeks. This dataset consists of about five million network connections. We also collected two weeks of test data of the same type as the training data, and the total test data set size consists of approximately two million connections.

The preceding attacks in the data can be distinguished into the following categories:

- **Denial-Of-Service (DOS)** attacks: A more advanced form of this attack is called the **Distributed Denial-Of-Service (DDoS)** attack
- **Password-guessing attacks**: These are unauthorized access from a remote machine

- **Buffer overflow attacks**: These are unauthorized access to local superuser (root) privileges
- **Reconnaissance attacks**: These deal with probing surveillance and port scanning

Importing packages

We use the machine learning/data science packages such as numpy, sklearn, pandas, and matplotlib for visualization:

```
from time import time
import numpy as np
import matplotlib.pyplot as plt
import pandas as pd
from sklearn.model_selection import cross_val_score
```

To implement the isolation forest, we use the sklearn.ensemble package:

```
from sklearn.ensemble import IsolationForest
```

To measure the performance, we use the ROC and AUC, and we will discuss these in details in a later part of this chapter.

The following code imports the relevant packages and loads the KDD data:

```
from sklearn.metrics import roc_curve, auc
from sklearn.datasets import fetch_kddcup99
%matplotlib inline

dataset = fetch_kddcup99(subset=None, shuffle=True, percent10=True)
# http://www.kdd.org/kdd-cup/view/kdd-cup-1999/Tasks
X = dataset.data
y = dataset.target
```

Features of the data

The KDD data that we use for this example has the following features that are listed as follows.

The following table shows the basic features of individual TCP connections:

Feature name	Description	Type
duration	Length (number of seconds) of the connection	continuous
protocol_type	Type of the protocol, for example, tcp, udp, and so on	discrete

service	Network service on the destination, for example, http, telnet, and so on	discrete
src_bytes	Number of data bytes from source to destination	continuous
dst_bytes	Number of data bytes from destination to source	continuous
flag	Normal or error status of the connection	discrete
land	1 if connection is from/to the same host/port; 0 otherwise	discrete
wrong_fragment	Number of wrong fragments	continuous
urgent	Number of urgent packets	continuous

The preceding table also shows the content features within a connection suggested by domain knowledge. The following table shows the traffic features computed using a two-second time window:

Feature name	Description	Type
count	Number of connections to the same host as the current connection in the past two seconds	continuous

The following features refer to these same-host connections:

Feature name	Description	Type
serror_rate	% of connections that have SYN errors	continuous
rerror_rate	% of connections that have REJ errors	continuous
same_srv_rate	% of connections to the same service	continuous
diff_srv_rate	% of connections to different services	continuous

The following features refer to these same-service connections:

Feature name	Description	Type
srv_count	Number of connections to the same service as the current connection in the past two seconds	continuous
srv_serror_rate	% of connections that have SYN errors	continuous
srv_rerror_rate	% of connections that have REJ errors	continuous
srv_diff_host_rate	% of connections to different hosts	continuous

Now let us print the few values from the table:

```
feature_cols = ['duration', 'protocol_type', 'service', 'flag',
'src_bytes', 'dst_bytes', 'land', 'wrong_fragment', 'urgent', 'hot',
'num_failed_logins', 'logged_in', 'num_compromised', 'root_shell',
'su_attempted', 'num_root', 'num_file_creations', 'num_shells',
'num_access_files', 'num_outbound_cmds', 'is_host_login', 'is_guest_login',
'count', 'srv_count', 'serror_rate', 'srv_serrer_rate', 'rerror_rate',
'srv_rerror_rate', 'same_srv_rate', 'diff_srv_rate', 'srv_diff_host_rate',
```

```
'dst_host_count', 'dst_host_srv_count', 'dst_host_same_srv_rate',
'dst_host_diff_srv_rate', 'dst_host_same_src_port_rate',
'dst_host_srv_diff_host_rate', 'dst_host_serror_rate',
'dst_host_srv_serror_rate', 'dst_host_rerror_rate',
'dst_host_srv_rerror_rate']
 X = pd.DataFrame(X, columns = feature_cols)

 y = pd.Series(y)
 X.head()
```

Previous code will display first few row of the table with all the column names. Then we convert the columns into floats for efficient processing:

```
for col in X.columns:
    try:
        X[col] = X[col].astype(float)
    except ValueError:
        pass
```

We convert the categorical into dummy or indicator variables:

```
X = pd.get_dummies(X, prefix=['protocol_type_', 'service_', 'flag_'],
drop_first=True)
X.head()
```

Now we will generate the counts.

On executing, the previous code displays around 5 rows × 115 columns:

```
y.value_counts()

Out:
smurf.            280790
neptune.          107201
normal.            97278
back.               2203
satan.              1589
ipsweep.            1247
portsweep.          1040
warezclient.        1020
teardrop.            979
pod.                 264
nmap.                231
guess_passwd.         53
buffer_overflow.      30
land.                 21
warezmaster.          20
imap.                 12
```

```
rootkit.               10
loadmodule.             9
ftp_write.              8
multihop.               7
phf.                    4
perl.                   3
spy.                    2
dtype: int64
```

We fit a classification tree with `max_depth=7` on all data as follows:

```
from sklearn.tree import DecisionTreeClassifier, export_graphviz

treeclf = DecisionTreeClassifier(max_depth=7)

scores = cross_val_score(treeclf, X, y, scoring='accuracy', cv=5)

print np.mean(scores)

treeclf.fit(X, y)
```

The output of the preceding model fit is as follows:

```
0.9955204407492013
```

Model

We use decision trees to classify the data into malicious and non malicious categories. Before we dive deep into the decision tree function, we will deal with the theory behind decision trees.

Decision tree

Decision trees are supervised approaches that are mostly used to classify problems. They deal with categorical and non categorical variables where the differentiator divides the variable into multiple homogeneous subsets.

Decision trees are based on linear decision rules where outcome is the content of a leaf node:

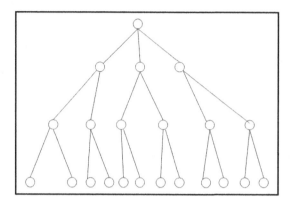

Types of decision trees

Based on the types of target, variables present a decision tree can be divided into two major categories.

Categorical variable decision tree

A decision tree variable can be categorical, that is, the answer is yes or no. A typical example will be: *A candidate will pass the exam, YES or NO.*

Continuous variable decision tree

Decision trees where the target variable is continuous is called a **continuous variable decision tree**. A continuous variable is a variable where the value has infinite speed. An example would be: *Time to finish a computer job is 1.333333333333333.*

Gini coeffiecient

The following code shows the `gini` coefficient:

```
DecisionTreeClassifier(class_weight=None, criterion='gini', max_depth=7,
        max_features=None, max_leaf_nodes=None,
        min_impurity_decrease=0.0, min_impurity_split=None,
        min_samples_leaf=1, min_samples_split=2,
        min_weight_fraction_leaf=0.0, presort=False, random_state=None,
        splitter='best')
```

To visualize the results of the decision with a graph, use the `graphviz` function:

```
export_graphviz(treeclf, out_file='tree_kdd.dot', feature_names=X.columns)
```

At the command line, we run this into convert to PNG:

```
# dot -Tpng tree_kdd.dot -o tree_kdd.png
```

We then extract the feature importance:

```
pd.DataFrame({'feature':X.columns,
'importance':treeclf.feature_importances_}).sort_values('importance',
ascending=False).head(10)
```

The output can be seen as follows:

Feature	Importance	
20	srv_count	0.633722
25	same_srv_rate	0.341769
9	num_compromised	0.013613
31	dst_host_diff_srv_rate	0.010738
1	src_bytes	0.000158
85	service__red_i	0.000000
84	service__private	0.000000
83	service__printer	0.000000
82	service__pop_3	0.000000
75	service__netstat	0.000000

Random forest

Random forests are ensemble learning methods that are used for either classification or regression purposes. Random forests are composed of several decision trees that are combined together to make a unanimous decision or classification. Random forest are better than just regular decision trees because they do not cause overfitting of the data:

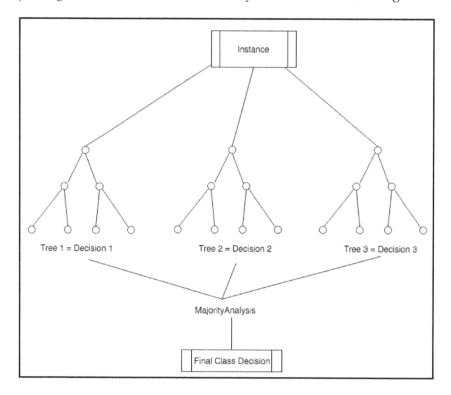

We would then try to use the random forest classifier:

```
from sklearn.ensemble import RandomForestClassifier
 rf = RandomForestClassifier()
scores = cross_val_score(rf, X, y, scoring='accuracy', cv=5)
print np.mean(scores)
# nicer
rf.fit(X, y)
```

The output can be seen as follows:

```
Out[39]:
0.9997307783262454
```

With random forest, we are able to get more best term to use than a single decision tree:

```
RandomForestClassifier(bootstrap=True, class_weight=None, criterion='gini',
            max_depth=None, max_features='auto', max_leaf_nodes=None,
            min_impurity_decrease=0.0, min_impurity_split=None,
            min_samples_leaf=1, min_samples_split=2,
            min_weight_fraction_leaf=0.0, n_estimators=10, n_jobs=1,
            oob_score=False, random_state=None, verbose=0,
            warm_start=False)
  pd.DataFrame({'feature':X.columns,
  'importance':rf.feature_importances_}).sort_values('importance',
ascending=False).head(10)
```

The features importance can be seen here:

	Feature	Importance
53	service__ecr_i	0.278599
25	same_srv_rate	0.129464
20	srv_count	0.108782
1	src_bytes	0.101766
113	flag__SF	0.073368
109	flag__S0	0.058412
19	count	0.055665
29	dst_host_srv_count	0.038069
38	protocol_type__tcp	0.036816
30	dst_host_same_srv_rate	0.026287

Anomaly detection

An outlier is an observation in a dataset that appears to be inconsistent with the remainder of that set of data. Anomaly detection can be defined as a process that will detect such outliers. Anomaly detection can be categorized into the following types based on the percentage of labelled data:

- Supervised anomaly detection is characterized by the following:
  - Labels available for both normal data and anomalies
  - Similar to rare class mining/imbalanced classification

- Unsupervised anomaly detection (outlier detection):
    - No labels; *training set = normal + abnormal data,*
  - Assumption: anomalies are very rare
- Semi-supervised anomaly detection (novelty detection):
    - Only normal data available to train
    - The algorithm learns on normal data only

Isolation forest

The **isolation forest** isolates observations by randomly selecting a feature and then randomly selecting a split value between the maximum and minimum values of the selected feature.

Since recursive partitioning can be represented by a tree structure, the number of splittings required to isolate a sample is equivalent to the path length from the root node to the terminating node.

This path length, averaged over a forest of such random trees, is a measure of normality and our decision function.

Random partitioning produces noticeably shorter paths for anomalies. Hence, when a forest of random trees collectively produces shorter path lengths for particular samples, they are highly likely to be anomalies.

Supervised and outlier detection with Knowledge Discovery Databases (KDD)

In this example, we will want to use binary data where 1 will represent a *not-normal* attack:

```
from sklearn.model_selection import train_test_split
y_binary = y != 'normal.'
y_binary.head()
```

The output can be seen as follows:

```
Out[43]:

0    True
 1     True
 2     True
 3     True
 4     True
dtype: bool
```

We divide the data into train and test sets and perform the following actions:

```
X_train, X_test, y_train, y_test = train_test_split(X, y_binary)

y_test.value_counts(normalize=True) # check our null accuracy
```

The output looks as follows:

```
True        0.803524
 False       0.196476
 dtype: float64
```

On using the isolation forest model, we get this:

```
model = IsolationForest()
 model.fit(X_train)   # notice that there is no y in the .fit
```

We can see the output here:

```
Out[61]:

IsolationForest(bootstrap=False, contamination=0.1, max_features=1.0,
max_samples='auto', n_estimators=100, n_jobs=1, random_state=None,
        verbose=0)
```

We make a prediction as follows:

```
y_predicted = model.predict(X_test)
pd.Series(y_predicted).value_counts()
Out[62]:
1     111221
 -1     12285
 dtype: int64
```

The input data is given as follows:

```
In [63]:
y_predicted = np.where(y_predicted==1, 1, 0)   # turn into 0s and 1s
pd.Series(y_predicted).value_counts()   # that's better

Out[63]:
1     111221
 0      12285
 dtype: int64

scores = model.decision_function(X_test)
scores   # the smaller, the more anomolous
```

```
Out[64]:
array([-0.06897078,  0.02709447, 0.16750811, ..., -0.02889957,
        -0.0291526,  0.09928597])
```

This is how we plot the series:

```
pd.Series(scores).hist()
```

The graph can be seen as follows:

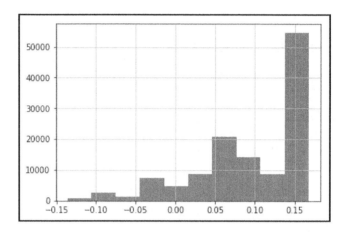

We get the output as seen in the following snippet:

```
from sklearn.metrics import accuracy_score
preds = np.where(scores < 0, 0, 1)  # customize threshold
accuracy_score(preds, y_test)
```

```
0.790868459831911
```

```
for t in (-2, -.15, -.1, -.05, 0, .05):
    preds = np.where(scores < t, 0, 1)  # customize threshold
    print t, accuracy_score(preds, y_test)
```

```
-2 0.8035237154470228
 -0.15 0.8035237154470228
 -0.1 0.8032889090408564
 -0.05 0.8189480673003741
 0 0.790868459831911
 0.05 0.7729260116917397
```

`-0.05 0.816988648325` gives us better than null accuracy, without ever needing the testing set. This shows how we can can achieve predictive results without labelled data.

This is an interesting use case of novelty detection, because generally when given labels, we do not use such tactics.

Revisiting malicious URL detection with decision trees

We will revisit a problem that is detecting malicious URLs, and we will find a way to solve the same with decision trees. We start by loading the data:

```
from urlparse import urlparse
import pandas as pd
urls = pd.read_json("../data/urls.json")
print urls.shape
urls['string'] = "http://" + urls['string']
```

```
(5000, 3)
```

On printing the head of the `urls`:

```
urls.head(10)
```

The output looks as follows:

	pred	string	truth
0	1.574204e-05	http://startbuyingstocks.com/	0
1	1.840909e-05	http://qqcvk.com/	0
2	1.842080e-05	http://432parkavenue.com/	0
3	7.954729e-07	http://gamefoliant.ru/	0
4	3.239338e-06	http://orka.cn/	0
5	3.043137e-04	http://media2.mercola.com/	0
6	4.107331e-37	http://ping.chartbeat.net/ping?h=sltrib.comp=...	0
7	1.664497e-07	http://stephensteels.com/	0
8	1.400715e-05	http://kbd-eko.pl/	0
9	2.273991e-05	http://ceskaposta.cz/	0

Following code is used to produce the output in formats of truth and string from the dataset:

```
X, y = urls['truth'], urls['string']
X.head()  # look at X
```

On executing previous code you will have the following output:

```
0       http://startbuyingstocks.com/
1                   http://qqcvk.com/
2           http://432parkavenue.com/
3            http://gamefoliant.ru/
4                   http://orka.cn/
Name: string, dtype: object
```

We get our null accuracy because we are interested in prediction where 0 is not malicious:

```
y.value_counts(normalize=True)
```

```
0    0.9694
1    0.0306
Name: truth, dtype: float64
```

We create a function called `custom_tokenizer` that takes in a string and outputs a list of tokens of the string:

```
from sklearn.feature_extraction.text import CountVectorizer
import re

def custom_tokenizer(string):
    final = []
    tokens = [a for a in list(urlparse(string)) if a]
    for t in tokens:
        final.extend(re.compile("[.-]").split(t))
    return final

print custom_tokenizer('google.com')

 print
custom_tokenizer('https://google-so-not-fake.com?fake=False&seriously=True'
)

['google', 'com']
['https', 'google', 'so', 'not', 'fake', 'com',
'fake=False&seriously=True']
```

We first use logistic regression . The relevant packages are imported as follows:

```
from sklearn.pipeline import Pipeline
 from sklearn.linear_model import LogisticRegression
vect = CountVectorizer(tokenizer=custom_tokenizer)
 lr = LogisticRegression()
 lr_pipe = Pipeline([('vect', vect), ('model', lr)])

from sklearn.model_selection import cross_val_score, GridSearchCV,
train_test_split
scores = cross_val_score(lr_pipe, X, y, cv=5)
scores.mean()   # not good enough!!
```

The output can be seen as follows:

```
0.980002384002384
```

We will be using random forest to detect malicious `urls`. The theory of random forest will be discussed in the next chapter on decision trees. To import the pipeline, we get the following:

```
from sklearn.pipeline import Pipeline
 from sklearn.ensemble import RandomForestClassifier

 rf_pipe = Pipeline([('vect', vect), ('model',
RandomForestClassifier(n_estimators=500))])
 scores = cross_val_score(rf_pipe, X, y, cv=5)

 scores.mean()   # not as good
```

The output can be seen as follows:

```
0.981002585002585
```

We will be creating the test and train datasets and then creating the confusion matrix for this as follows:

```
X_train, X_test, y_train, y_test = train_test_split(X, y)
from sklearn.metrics import confusion_matrix
rf_pipe.fit(X_train, y_train)
preds = rf_pipe.predict(X_test)
 print confusion_matrix(y_test, preds)   # hmmmm
```

```
[[1205    0]
 [  27 18]]
```

We get the predicted probabilities of malicious data:

```
probs = rf_pipe.predict_proba(X_test)[:,1]
```

We play with the threshold to alter the false positive/negative rate:

```
import numpy as np
 for thresh in [.1, .2, .3, .4, .5, .6, .7, .8, .9]:
    preds = np.where(probs >= thresh, 1, 0)
    print thresh
    print confusion_matrix(y_test, preds)
    print
```

The output looks as follows:

```
0.1
[[1190   15]
 [  15 30]]

0.2
[[1201    4]
 [  17 28]]

0.3
[[1204    1]
 [  22 23]]

0.4
[[1205    0]
 [  25 20]]

0.5
[[1205    0]
 [  27 18]]

0.6
[[1205    0]
 [  28 17]]

0.7
[[1205    0]
 [  29 16]]

0.8
[[1205    0]
 [  29 16]]
```

```
0.9
[[1205    0]
 [  30 15]]
```

We dump the importance metric to detect the importance of each of the `urls`:

```
pd.DataFrame({'feature':rf_pipe.steps[0][1].get_feature_names(),
'importance':rf_pipe.steps[-1][1].feature_importances_}).sort_values('impor
tance', ascending=False).head(10)
```

The following table shows the importance of each feature.

	Feature	Importance
4439	decolider	0.051752
4345	cyde6743276hdjheuhde/dispatch/webs	0.045464
789	/system/database/konto	0.045051
8547	verifiziren	0.044641
6968	php/	0.019684
6956	php	0.015053
5645	instantgrocer	0.014205
381	/errors/report	0.013818
4813	exe	0.009287
92	/	0.009121

We will use the decision tree classifier as follows:

```
treeclf = DecisionTreeClassifier(max_depth=7)

tree_pipe = Pipeline([('vect', vect), ('model', treeclf)])

vect = CountVectorizer(tokenizer=custom_tokenizer)

scores = cross_val_score(tree_pipe, X, y, scoring='accuracy', cv=5)

print np.mean(scores)

tree_pipe.fit(X, y)

export_graphviz(tree_pipe.steps[1][1], out_file='tree_urls.dot',
feature_names=tree_pipe.steps[0][1].get_feature_names())
```

The level of accuracy is `0.98`:

```
0.9822017858017859
```

The tree diagram below shows how the decision logic for maliciousness detection works.

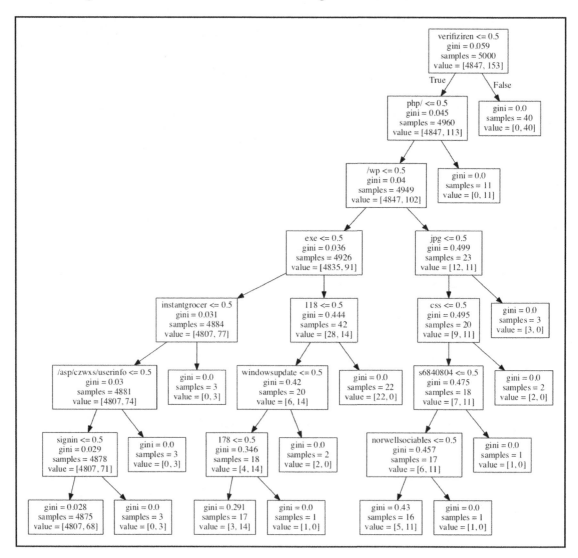

Summary

In this chapter, we studied different malicious data types along with malicious injections in wireless sensors. We also covered the different types of decision trees, which included categorical and continuous variable decision trees. This chapter then concluded by revisiting malicious URL detection with decision trees.

In the next chapter, we will learn about how can we catch impersonators and hackers red-handed.

Catching Impersonators and Hackers Red Handed

8

Impersonation attacks are the form of cyber attack that has evolved the most in recent years. Impersonation in its most basic form is the act of pretexting as another person. Pretexting is the basic form of social engineering, where a person mimics another person to obtain data or resources that have been assigned to the privileged person only.

To understand impersonation attacks better, and to detect the different attacks and see how machine learning can solve them, we will go through the following topics:

- Understanding impersonation
- Different types of impersonation fraud
- Understanding Levenshtein distance
- Use case on finding malicious domain similarity
- Use case to detect authorship attribution

Understanding impersonation

In the USA, the top two people to impersonate are the following:

- **Someone impersonating a USPS agent**: Here, someone dressed in a USPS costume to get access to a secure location on the pretext of delivering packages, and will be able to get access to unauthorized areas.

- **Someone impersonating a tech support guy**: If it's tech support, we are comfortable sharing our credentials, such as login passwords. Tech support impersonators not only steal personally identifiable information, but also have physical access to the servers. A tech support guy can potentially steal a lot with a single pen drive. Tech support guys can not only attack individuals, but also have the capacity to crash entire networks. Just by downloading unauthorized software on the pretext of downloading antiviruses and patches, they can create gateways to access the computer as a background process.

Other popular people to impersonate include the following:

- Law enforcement personnel
- A delivery man

Different types of impersonation fraud

According to a recent report, at least 75 percent of companies are the target of impersonation attempts each year. There are several variations of impersonation; the most popular ones are the following:

- **Executive impersonation**: These are cases where the impersonator either takes over an executive account, such as a CEO or CFO of the company. The impersonator may also try to spook emails from the executive by putting minute variations in the email IDs, such as `janedoe@xyz.com` being changed to `jandoe@xyz.com`. The content of these emails will deal with sensitive issues needing immediate action, such as a wire transfer that needs to be mailed urgently. Employees usually ignore the falsification of the email ID and carry out the activity.
- **Vendor impersonation**: This is another type of fraud, where the impersonator spooks email IDs of legitimate vendors and sends out emails about changes in payment information. The emails will have a new banking address where future emails need to be sent.
- **Customer impersonation**: Some impersonators spoof the customer's account just to collect confidential or valuable information that can be used in future fraud.
- **Identity theft**: This is a popular form of impersonation, done at times for financial advantage, and sometimes to facilitate a criminal activity, such as for identity cloning and medical identity theft. Identity theft helps in facilitating other crimes such as immigration fraud, attacking payment systems for terrorism, phishing, and espionage.

- **Industrial espionage**: Industrial espionage is known to happen in industrial companies, software and automobiles, where planned acts of sabotage are carried out by competitors or by the government to gather information and competitive intelligence. Industrial espionage is facilitated by impersonators gathering information from dissatisfied employees, via the use of malware, or by performing a distributed denial of service:

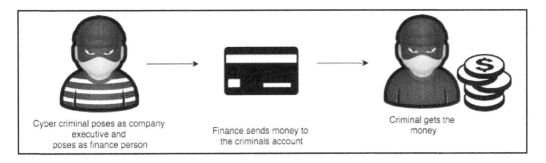

Cyber criminal poses as company executive and poses as finance person — Finance sends money to the criminals account — Criminal gets the money

Impersonators gathering information

Usually, impersonators gather information by social engineering and then patiently wait to put pieces of information together and then stitch them. Thus, even a small piece of information serves as a connecting part of the puzzle.

Common social engineering methods include the following:

- Stalking
- Crawling compromised sites
- Sending phishing emails
- Dumpster diving
- Eavesdropping
- Tailgating
- Shoulder surfing
- The use of USB devices loaded with malware and many more

How an impersonation attack is constructed

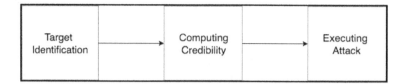

In the software industry, the most popular methods of impersonation are the following:

- Registering domains in bulk and the ones that are lookalikes for a legitimate domain. Let's assume that `abclegit.com` is a legitimate site. An impersonator will register clones like these:

  `abcleg1t.com abdlegit.com abcl3git.com abclegil.com`

- Mimicking the display name: Another way to perform impersonation fraud is to change the display name of the victim. Here again, the changed name lies in very close proximity to the actual name. If an email is sent using the victim's display name with minor changes, users can be lured into believing that its a legitimate email ID. Taking the previous example, `janedoe@example.com` is morphed to `jamedoe@example.com`.

Using data science to detect domains that are impersonations

For both the preceding examples, we can use certain machine learning algorithms that detect any changes that exist between the two strings.

Levenshtein distance

Levenshtein distance is an editing distance-based metric that helps to detect the distance between two alphanumeric string sequences. It computes the number of edits (replacements or insertions) required to traverse from the first character sequence to the second character sequence.

The Levenshtein distance between two alphanumeric sequences a and b can be computed as follows:

$$\text{lev}_{a,b}(i,j) = \begin{cases} \max(i,j) & \text{if } \min(i,j) = 0, \\ \min \begin{cases} \text{lev}_{a,b}(i-1,j)+1 \\ \text{lev}_{a,b}(i,j-1)+1 \\ \text{lev}_{a,b}(i-1,j-1)+1_{(a_i \neq b_j)} \end{cases} & \text{otherwise.} \end{cases}$$

Where $1(a_i \neq b_i)$ is the indicator function equal to 0 when $a_i = b_i$, and equal to 1 otherwise.

We will now see examples based on Levenshtein distance.

Finding domain similarity between malicious URLs

The following code is a Python-based implementation of the iterative Levenshtein distance:

```
def iterative_levenshtein(a, b):
    rows = len(a)+1    cols = len(b)+1
    dist = [[0 for x in range(cols)]
for x in range(rows)]
```

The preceding `dist[i,j]` function contains the Levenshtein distance between the `i` and `j` characters of the sequences `a` and `b`:

```
#edit distance by deleting character
for i in range(1, rows):
    dist[i][0] = i
# edit distance by inserting the characters
for i in range(1, cols):       dist[0][i] = i
```

The edit distances are computed either by deleting or by inserting characters from/into the string sequences:

```
for col in range(1, cols):
for row in range(1, rows):
    if s[row-1] == t[col-1]:
        cost = 0
    else:
        cost = 1
dist[row][col] = min(dist[row-1][col] + 1,
# by deletes
```

```
dist[row][col-1] + 1, # by inserts
dist[row-1][col-1] + cost) # by substitutes
```

Finally, we print the distance between `abclegit.com` and `abcleg1t.com`, as shown in the following code:

```
    for r in range(rows):
print(dist[r])
return
dist[row][col]print(iterative_levenshtein("abclegit", "abcleg1t"))
```

Authorship attribution

Authorship is a behavioural aspect of an author. Their sentential structure is distinctive and can be used to identify authors. **Natural language processing (NLP)** and semantic methods can be used to detect attribution. **Authorship attribution (AA)** has gained interest in various fields, including technology, education, and criminal forensics, because it is, in a way, a digital fingerprint that can be detected statistically. AA plays a vital role in information extraction and question answering systems. It is a non-topic classification problem.

AA detection for tweets

We will use the Python package `tweepy` to access the Twitter API. If you do not have it installed, please follow these steps:

1. Install it from PyPI:

   ```
   easy_install tweepy
   ```

   Install it from source:

   ```
   git clone git://github.com/tweepy/tweepy.git
   cd tweepy
   python setup.py install
   ```

2. Once installed, we begin with importing `tweepy`:

   ```
   import tweepy
   ```

3. We import the consumer keys and access tokens used for authentication (OAuth):

```
api_key = 'q5uPIpw80nULQI1gfklv2zrh4'api_secret =
'cOWvNWxYvPmEZ0ArZVeeVVvJu41QYHdUS2GpqIKtSQ1isd5PJy'access_token =
'49722956-TWl8J0aAS6KTdcbz3ppZ7NfqZEmrwmbsb9cYPNELG'access_secret =
'3eqrVssF3ppv23qyflyAto8wLEiYRA8sXEPSghuOJWTub
```

4. We complete the OAuth process, using the keys and tokens that we imported in *step 4*:

```
auth = tweepy.OAuthHandler(api_key,
api_secret)auth.set_access_token(access_token, access_secret)
```

5. We create the actual interface, using authentication in this step:

```
api = tweepy.API(auth)my_tweets, other_tweets = [], []
```

6. We get 500 unique tweets through the Twitter API. We do not consider retweets as these are not the original authorship. The idea is to compare our own tweets with other tweets on Twitter:

```
to_get = 500for status in tweepy.Cursor(api.user_timeline,
screen_name='@prof_oz').items():  text = status._json['text']  if
text[:3] != 'RT ': # we don't want retweets because they didn't
author those!   my_tweets.append(text)  else:
other_tweets.append(text)  to_get -= 1  if to_get <=0:       break
```

7. We count the number of real tweets and the number of other tweets. Note that all other tweets are not to be considered as impersonated tweets:

```
In [67]:len(real_tweets), len(other_tweets)
```

The output can be seen as follows:

```
Out[67]:(131, 151)
```

8. We view the headers of each of the two types of gathered tweets:

```
real_tweets[0], other_tweets[0]
```

The output can be seen as follows:

```
(u'@stanleyyork Definitely check out the Grand Bazaar as well as a
tour around the Mosques and surrounding caf\xe9s / sho\u2026
https://t.co/ETREtznTgr',u'RT @SThornewillvE: This weeks
@superdatasci podcast has a lot of really interesting talk about
#feature engineering, with @Prof_OZ, the auth\u2026')
```

We put the data in a data frame using pandas, and we also add an extra column, `is_mine`. The value of the `is_mine` column is set to `True` for all tweets that are real tweets; it is set to `False` for all other tweets:

```
import pandasdf = pandas.DataFrame({'text': my_tweets+other_tweets,
'is_mine': [True]*len(my_tweets)+[False]*len(other_tweets)})
```

Viewing the shape that is the dimension of the dataframe, we use the following:

```
df.shape
(386, 2)Hello
```

Let's view first few rows of the table:

```
df.head(2)
```

The output will look like the following table:

	is_mine	text
0	True	@stanleyyork Definitely check out the Grand Ba...
1	True	12 Exciting Ways You Can Use Voice-Activated T...

Let's view last few rows of the table:

```
df.tail(2)
```

The output of the preceding code will give the following table:

	is_mine	text
384	False	RT @Variety: BREAKING: #TheInterview will be s...
385	False	RT @ProfLiew: Let's all congratulate Elizabeth...

We extract a portion of the dataset for validation purposes:

```
import numpy as np
np.random.seed(10)

remove_n = int(.1 * df.shape[0])   # remove 10% of rows for validation set

drop_indices = np.random.choice(df.index, remove_n, replace=False)
validation_set = df.iloc[drop_indices]
training_set = df.drop(drop_indices)
```

Difference between test and validation datasets

The validation dataset is a part of the data that is kept aside and not used to train the model. This data is later used to tune hyperparameters and estimate model efficiency.

The validation dataset is not the same as the test dataset (other data that is also kept aside during the training phase). The difference between the test and validation datasets is that the test dataset will be used for model selection after it has been completely tuned.

However, there are cases where the validation dataset is not enough to tune the hyperparameters. In such cases, k-fold cross validation is performed on the model.

The input can be seen as follows:

```
validation_set.shape, training_set.shape
```

We get the following output:

```
((38, 2), (348, 2))

X, y = training_set['text'], training_set['is_mine']
```

Once we have sorted the data into different sets, we import the modules that will be used to perform the modeling of the data. We will be using sklearn to model this. If you do not have `sklearn` installed by now, use `pip` to install it:

```
from sklearn.feature_extraction.text import CountVectorizer

class sklearn.feature_extraction.text.CountVectorizer(input='content',
encoding='utf-8', decode_error='strict', strip_accents=None,
lowercase=True, preprocessor=None, tokenizer=None, stop_words=None,
token_pattern='(?u)\b\w\w+\b', ngram_range=(1, 1), analyzer='word',
max_df=1.0, min_df=1, max_features=None, vocabulary=None, binary=False,
dtype=<class 'numpy.int64'>)
```

`CountVectorizor` is a function that is widely used to convert a collection of text documents to vectors or matrices with respective token counts. `CountVectorizor` has the ability to transform uppercase to lowercase and can be used to get rid of punctuation marks. However, `CountVectorizor` cannot be used to stem strings. Stemming here refers to cutting either the beginning or the end of the word to account for prefixes and suffixes.

Basically, the idea of stemming is to remove derived words from the corresponding stem word.

Here is an example:

Stemword	Before stemming
Hack	Hackes
Hack	Hacking
Cat	Catty
Cat	Catlike

Similar to stimming, `CountVectorizor` can perform lemmatization of the source text as well. Lemmatization refers to the morphological analysis of the words. It thus removes all inflectional words and prints the root work, which is often said to be the lemma. Thus, in a way, lemmatization and stemming are closely related to each other:

Rootword	Un-lemmatized word
good	better
good	best

`CountVectorizer` can create features such as a bag of words with the n-gram range set to 1. Depending on the value we provide to the n-gram, we can generate bigrams, trigrams, and so on. The `CountVectorizor` has:

```
from sklearn.pipeline import Pipeline, FeatureUnion, make_pipeline
```

Sklearn pipeline

While coding for a machine learning model, there are certain steps/actions that need to be repeatedly performed. A pipeline is the way forward in such cases where routine processes can be streamlined within encapsulations containing small bits of logic; this helps avoid writing a bunch of code.

A pipeline helps to prevent/identify data leakages. They perform the following tasks:

- Fit
- Transform
- Predict

There are functions to transform/fit the training and test data. If we end up creating multiple pipelines to generate features in our Python code, we can run the feature union function to join them in a sequence one after the other. Thus, a pipeline enables us to perform all three transformations with a resulting estimator:

```
from sklearn.naive_bayes import MultinomialNB
```

Naive Bayes classifier for multinomial models

The multinomial Naive Bayes classifier is suitable for classification with discrete features (for example, word counts for text classification). The multinomial distribution normally requires integer feature counts. However, in practice, fractional counts such as TF-IDF may also work:

```
pipeline_parts = [
    ('vectorizer', CountVectorizer()),
    ('classifier', MultinomialNB())
]
simple_pipeline = Pipeline(pipeline_parts)
```

A simple pipeline with Naive Bayes and the `CountVectorizer` is created as shown previously.

Import `GridSearchCV` as shown here:

```
from sklearn.model_selection import GridSearchCV
```

`GridSearch` performs an exhaustive search over specified parameter values for an estimator, and is thus helpful for hyperparameter tuning. `GridSearch` consists of the members fit and predict.

`GridSearchCV` implements a `fit` and a `score` method. It also implements `predict`, `predict_proba`, `decision_function`, `transform`, and `inverse_transform` if they are implemented in the estimator used.

The parameters of the estimator used to apply these methods are optimized by a cross-validated grid search over a parameter grid as follows:

```
simple_grid_search_params = {    "vectorizer__ngram_range": [(1, 1), (1,
3), (1, 5)],    "vectorizer__analyzer": ["word", "char",
"char_wb"],}grid_search = GridSearchCV(simple_pipeline,
simple_grid_search_params)grid_search.fit(X, y)
```

We set the grid search parameters and fit them. The output is shown as follows:

```
Out[97]: GridSearchCV(cv=None, error_score='raise',
        estimator=Pipeline(memory=None,
      steps=[('vectorizer', CountVectorizer(analyzer=u'word', binary=False,
decode_error=u'strict',
          dtype=<type 'numpy.int64'>, encoding=u'utf-8', input=u'content',
          lowercase=True, max_df=1.0, max_features=None, min_df=1,
          ngram_range=(1, 1), pre...one, vocabulary=None)), ('classifier',
MultinomialNB(alpha=1.0, class_prior=None, fit_prior=True))]),
        fit_params=None, iid=True, n_jobs=1,
        param_grid={'vectorizer__ngram_range': [(1, 1), (1, 3), (1, 5)],
'vectorizer__analyzer': ['word', 'char', 'char_wb']},
        pre_dispatch='2*n_jobs', refit=True, return_train_score='warn',
        scoring=None, verbose=0)
```

We obtain the best cross validated accuracy as follows:

```
grid_search.best_score_  # best cross validated accuracy

0.896551724137931

model = grid_search.best_estimator_

# % False, % True
model.predict_proba([my_tweets[0]])

array([[2.56519064e-07, 9.99999743e-01]])
```

Finally, we test the accuracy of the model using the accuracy score sub-package that is available in the `sklearn.metrics` package:

```
from sklearn.metrics import
accuracy_scoreaccuracy_score(model.predict(validation_set['text']),
validation_set['is_mine']) # accuracy on validation set. Very good!
```

The model is able to give an accuracy of more than 90%:

```
0.9210526315789473
```

This model can now be used to monitor timelines to spot whether an author's style has changed or they are being hacked.

Identifying impersonation as a means of intrusion detection

We will use AWID data for identifying impersonation. AWID is a family of datasets focused on intrusion detection. AWID datasets consist of packets of data, both large and small. These datasets are not inclusive of one another.

See `http://icsdweb.aegean.gr/awid` for more information.

Each version has a training set (denoted as **Trn**) and a test set (denoted as **Tst**). The test version has not been produced from the corresponding training set.

Finally, a version is provided where labels that correspond to different attacks (ATK), as well as a version where the attack labels are organized into three major classes (CLS). In that case the datasets only differ in the label:

Name	Classes	Size	Type	Records	Hours
AWID-ATK-F-Trn	10	Full	Train	162,375,247	96
AWID-ATK-F-Tst	17	Full	Test	48,524,866	12
AWID-CLS-F-Trn	4	Full	Train	162,375,247	96
AWID-CLS-F-Tst	4	Full	Test	48,524,866	12
AWID-ATK-R-Trn	10	Reduced	Train	1,795,575	1
AWID-ATK-R-Tst	15	Reduced	Test	575,643	1/3
AWID-CLS-R-Trn	4	Reduced	Train	1,795,575	1
AWID-CLS-R-Tst	4	Reduced	Test	530,643	1/3

This dataset has 155 attributes.

A detailed description is available at this link: `http://icsdweb.aegean.gr/awid/features.html`.

FIELD NAME	DESCRIPTION	TYPE	VERSIONS
comment	Comment	Character string	1.8.0 to 1.8.15
frame.cap_len	Frame length stored into the capture file	Unsigned integer, 4 bytes	1.0.0 to 2.6.4

`frame.coloring_rule.name`	Coloring Rule Name	Character string	1.0.0 to 2.6.4
`frame.coloring_rule.string`	Coloring Rule String	Character string	1.0.0 to 2.6.4
`frame.comment`	Comment	Character string	1.10.0 to 2.6.4
`frame.comment.expert`	Formatted comment	Label	1.12.0 to 2.6.4
`frame.dlt`	WTAP_ENCAP	Signed integer, 2 bytes	1.8.0 to 1.8.15
`frame.encap_type`	Encapsulation type	Signed integer, 2 bytes	1.10.0 to 2.6.4
`frame.file_off`	File Offset	Signed integer, 8 bytes	1.0.0 to 2.6.4
`frame.ignored`	Frame is ignored	Boolean	1.4.0 to 2.6.4
`frame.incomplete`	Incomplete dissector	Label	2.0.0 to 2.6.4
`frame.interface_description`	Interface description	Character string	2.4.0 to 2.6.4
`frame.interface_id`	Interface id	Unsigned integer, 4 bytes	1.8.0 to 2.6.4
`frame.interface_name`	Interface name	Character string	2.4.0 to 2.6.4
`frame.len`	Frame length on the wire	Unsigned integer, 4 bytes	1.0.0 to 2.6.4
`frame.link_nr`	Link Number	Unsigned integer, 2 bytes	1.0.0 to 2.6.4
`frame.marked`	Frame is marked	Boolean	1.0.0 to 2.6.4
`frame.md5_hash`	Frame MD5 Hash	Character string	1.2.0 to 2.6.4
`frame.number`	Frame Number	Unsigned integer, 4 bytes	1.0.0 to 2.6.4

`frame.offset_shift`	Time shift for this packet	Time offset	1.8.0 to 2.6.4
`frame.p2p_dir`	Point-to-Point Direction	Signed integer, 1 byte	1.0.0 to 2.6.4
`frame.p_prot_data`	Number of per-protocol-data	Unsigned integer, 4 bytes	1.10.0 to 1.12.13
`frame.packet_flags`	Packet flags	Unsigned integer, 4 bytes	1.10.0 to 2.6.4
`frame.packet_flags_crc_error`	CRC error	Boolean	1.10.0 to 2.6.4
`frame.packet_flags_direction`	Direction	Unsigned integer, 4 bytes	1.10.0 to 2.6.4
`frame.packet_flags_fcs_length`	FCS length	Unsigned integer, 4 bytes	1.10.0 to 2.6.4
`frame.packet_flags_packet_too_error`	Packet too long error	Boolean	1.10.0 to 2.6.4
`frame.packet_flags_packet_too_short_error`	Packet too short error	Boolean	1.10.0 to 2.6.4
`frame.packet_flags_preamble_error`	Preamble error	Boolean	1.10.0 to 2.6.4
`frame.packet_flags_reception_type`	Reception type	Unsigned integer, 4 bytes	1.10.0 to 2.6.4
`frame.packet_flags_reserved`	Reserved	Unsigned integer, 4 bytes	1.10.0 to 2.6.4
`frame.packet_flags_start_frame_delimiter_error`	Start frame delimiter error	Boolean	1.10.0 to 2.6.4
`frame.packet_flags_symbol_error`	Symbol error	Boolean	1.10.0 to 2.6.4
`frame.packet_flags_unaligned_frame_error`	Unaligned frame error	Boolean	1.10.0 to 2.6.4
`frame.packet_flags_wrong_inter_frame_gap_error`	Wrong interframe gap error	Boolean	1.10.0 to 2.6.4

`frame.pkt_len`	Frame length on the wire	Unsigned integer, 4 bytes	1.0.0 to 1.0.16
`frame.protocols`	Protocols in frame	Character string	1.0.0 to 2.6.4
`frame.ref_time`	This is a Time Reference frame	Label	1.0.0 to 2.6.4
`frame.time`	Arrival Time	Date and time	1.0.0 to 2.6.4
`frame.time_delta`	Time delta from previous captured frame	Time offset	1.0.0 to 2.6.4
`frame.time_delta_displayed`	Time delta from previous displayed frame	Time offset	1.0.0 to 2.6.4
`frame.time_epoch`	Epoch Time	Time offset	1.4.0 to 2.6.4
`frame.time_invalid`	Arrival Time: Fractional second out of range (0-1000000000)	Label	1.0.0 to 2.6.4
`frame.time_relative`	Time since reference or first frame	Time offset	1.0.0 to 2.6.4

The sample dataset is available in the GitHub library. The intrusion data is converted into a `DataFrame` using the Python `pandas` library:

```
import pandas as pd
```

The feature discussed earlier is imported into the `DataFrame`:

```
# get the names of the features    features = ['frame.interface_id',
'frame.dlt', 'frame.offset_shift', 'frame.time_epoch', 'frame.time_delta',
'frame.time_delta_displayed', 'frame.time_relative', 'frame.len',
'frame.cap_len', 'frame.marked', 'frame.ignored', 'radiotap.version',
'radiotap.pad', 'radiotap.length', 'radiotap.present.tsft',
'radiotap.present.flags', 'radiotap.present.rate',
'radiotap.present.channel', 'radiotap.present.fhss',
'radiotap.present.dbm_antsignal', 'radiotap.present.dbm_antnoise',
'radiotap.present.lock_quality', 'radiotap.present.tx_attenuation',
'radiotap.present.db_tx_attenuation', 'radiotap.present.dbm_tx_power',
'radiotap.present.antenna', 'radiotap.present.db_antsignal',
'radiotap.present.db_antnoise',........ 'wlan.qos.amsdupresent',
'wlan.qos.buf_state_indicated', 'wlan.qos.bit4', 'wlan.qos.txop_dur_req',
```

```
'wlan.qos.buf_state_indicated', 'data.len', 'class']
```

Next, we import the training dataset and count the number of rows and columns available in the dataset:

```
# import a training setawid = pd.read_csv("../data/AWID-CLS-R-Trn.csv",
header=None, names=features)# see the number of rows/columnsawid.shape
```

The output can be seen as follows:

```
Out[4]:(1795575, 155)
```

The dataset uses ? as a null attribute. We will eventually have to replace them with None values:

```
awid.head()
```

The following code will display values around 5 rows × 155 columns from the table. Now we will see the distribution of response variables:

```
awid['class'].value_counts(normalize=True)

normal 0.909564injection 0.036411impersonation 0.027023flooding
0.027002Name: class, dtype: float64
```

We revisit the claims there are no null values because of the ? instances:

```
awid.isna().sum()

frame.interface_id 0frame.dlt 0frame.offset_shift 0frame.time_epoch
0frame.time_delta 0frame.time_delta_displayed 0frame.time_relative
0frame.len 0frame.cap_len 0frame.marked 0frame.ignored 0radiotap.version
0radiotap.pad 0radiotap.length 0radiotap.present.tsft
0radiotap.present.flags 0radiotap.present.rate 0radiotap.present.channel
0radiotap.present.fhss 0radiotap.present.dbm_antsignal
0radiotap.present.dbm_antnoise 0radiotap.present.lock_quality
0radiotap.present.tx_attenuation 0radiotap.present.db_tx_attenuation
0radiotap.present.dbm_tx_power 0radiotap.present.antenna
0radiotap.present.db_antsignal 0radiotap.present.db_antnoise
0radiotap.present.rxflags 0radiotap.present.xchannel 0
..wlan_mgt.rsn.version 0wlan_mgt.rsn.gcs.type 0wlan_mgt.rsn.pcs.count
0wlan_mgt.rsn.akms.count 0wlan_mgt.rsn.akms.type
0wlan_mgt.rsn.capabilities.preauth 0wlan_mgt.rsn.capabilities.no_pairwise
0wlan_mgt.rsn.capabilities.ptksa_replay_counter
0wlan_mgt.rsn.capabilities.gtksa_replay_counter
0wlan_mgt.rsn.capabilities.mfpr 0wlan_mgt.rsn.capabilities.mfpc
0wlan_mgt.rsn.capabilities.peerkey 0wlan_mgt.tcprep.trsmt_pow
0wlan_mgt.tcprep.link_mrg 0wlan.wep.iv 0wlan.wep.key 0wlan.wep.icv
0wlan.tkip.extiv 0wlan.ccmp.extiv 0wlan.qos.tid 0wlan.qos.priority
```

```
0wlan.qos.eosp 0wlan.qos.ack 0wlan.qos.amsdupresent
0wlan.qos.buf_state_indicated 0wlan.qos.bit4 0wlan.qos.txop_dur_req
0wlan.qos.buf_state_indicated.1 0data.len 0class 0Length: 155, dtype: int64
```

We replace the ? marks with `None`:

```
awid.replace({"?": None}, inplace=True
```

We count how many missing pieces of data are shown:

```
awid.isna().sum()
```

The output will be as follows:

```
frame.interface_id                         0
frame.dlt                            1795575
frame.offset_shift                         0
frame.time_epoch                           0
frame.time_delta                           0
frame.time_delta_displayed                 0
frame.time_relative                        0
frame.len                                  0
frame.cap_len                              0
frame.marked                               0
frame.ignored                              0
radiotap.version                           0
radiotap.pad                               0
radiotap.length                            0
radiotap.present.tsft                      0
radiotap.present.flags                     0
radiotap.present.rate                      0
radiotap.present.channel                   0
radiotap.present.fhss                      0
radiotap.present.dbm_antsignal             0
radiotap.present.dbm_antnoise              0
radiotap.present.lock_quality              0
radiotap.present.tx_attenuation            0
radiotap.present.db_tx_attenuation         0
radiotap.present.dbm_tx_power              0
radiotap.present.antenna                   0
radiotap.present.db_antsignal              0
radiotap.present.db_antnoise               0
radiotap.present.rxflags                   0
radiotap.present.xchannel                  0
                                         ...
wlan_mgt.rsn.version                 1718631
wlan_mgt.rsn.gcs.type                1718631
wlan_mgt.rsn.pcs.count               1718631
```

```
wlan_mgt.rsn.akms.count                              1718633
wlan_mgt.rsn.akms.type                               1718651
wlan_mgt.rsn.capabilities.preauth                    1718633
wlan_mgt.rsn.capabilities.no_pairwise                1718633
wlan_mgt.rsn.capabilities.ptksa_replay_counter       1718633
wlan_mgt.rsn.capabilities.gtksa_replay_counter       1718633
wlan_mgt.rsn.capabilities.mfpr                       1718633
wlan_mgt.rsn.capabilities.mfpc                       1718633
wlan_mgt.rsn.capabilities.peerkey                    1718633
wlan_mgt.tcprep.trsmt_pow                            1795536
wlan_mgt.tcprep.link_mrg                            1795536
wlan.wep.iv                                           944820
wlan.wep.key                                          909831
wlan.wep.icv                                          944820
wlan.tkip.extiv                                     1763655
wlan.ccmp.extiv                                     1792506
wlan.qos.tid                                        1133234
wlan.qos.priority                                   1133234
wlan.qos.eosp                                       1279874
wlan.qos.ack                                        1133234
wlan.qos.amsdupresent                               1134226
wlan.qos.buf_state_indicated                        1795575
wlan.qos.bit4                                       1648935
wlan.qos.txop_dur_req                               1648935
wlan.qos.buf_state_indicated.1                      1279874
data.len                                             903021
class                                                      0
Length: 155, dtype: int64
```

The goal here is to remove columns that have over 50% of their data missing:

```
columns_with_mostly_null_data = awid.columns[awid.isnull().mean() >= 0.5]
```

We see 72 columns are going to be affected:

```
columns_with_mostly_null_data.shape
```

The output is as follows:

```
(72,)
```

We drop the columns with over half of their data missing:

```
awid.drop(columns_with_mostly_null_data, axis=1, inplace=True)awid.shape
```

The preceding code gives the following output:

```
(1795575, 83)
```

Drop the rows that have missing values:

```
awid.dropna(inplace=True) # drop rows with null data
```

We lose 456,169 rows:

```
awid.shape
```

The following is the output of the preceding code:

```
(1339406, 83)
```

However, dropping doesn't affect our distribution too much:

```
# 0.878763 is our null accuracy. Our model must be better than this number
to be a contenderawid['class'].value_counts(normalize=True)
```

The output can be seen as follows:

```
normal 0.878763injection 0.048812impersonation 0.036227flooding
0.036198Name: class, dtype: float64
```

Now we execute the following code:

```
# only select numeric columns for our ML algorithms, there should be more..
awid.select_dtypes(['number']).shape.
```

```
(1339406, 45)
```

```
# transform all columns into numerical dtypesfor col in awid.columns:
awid[col] = pd.to_numeric(awid[col], errors='ignore')# that makes more
senseawid.select_dtypes(['number']).shape
```

The preceding code gives the following output:

```
(1339406, 74)
```

Now execute the `awid.describe()` code as shown in the following snippet:

```
# basic descroptive statistics
awid.describe()
```

The output will display a table of 8 rows × 74 columns.

```
X, y = awid.select_dtypes(['number']), awid['class']

# do a basic naive bayes fitting
from sklearn.naive_bayes import GaussianNB

nb = GaussianNB()

# fit our model to the data
nb.fit(X, y)

GaussianNB(priors=None)
```

We read in the test data and do the same transformations to it, to match the training data:

```
awid_test = pd.read_csv("../data/AWID-CLS-R-Tst.csv", header=None,
names=features)
# drop the problematic columns
awid_test.drop(columns_with_mostly_null_data, axis=1, inplace=True)
# replace ? with None
awid_test.replace({"?": None}, inplace=True)
# drop the rows with null data
awid_test.dropna(inplace=True)  # drop rows with null data
# convert columns to numerical values
for col in awid_test.columns:
    awid_test[col] = pd.to_numeric(awid_test[col], errors='ignore')
awid_test.shape
```

The output can be seen as follows:

```
Out[45]:(389185, 83)
```

To check basic metric, accuracy of the code:

```
from sklearn.metrics import accuracy_score

X_test = awid_test.select_dtypes(['number'])
y_test = awid_test['class']

# simple function to test the accuracy of a model fitted on training data
on our testing data
def get_test_accuracy_of(model):
    y_preds = model.predict(X_test)
    return accuracy_score(y_preds, y_test)
```

```
# naive abyes does very poorly on its own!
get_test_accuracy_of(nb)
```

The output is seen as follows:

```
0.26535452291326744
```

We will be using logistic regression for the following problem:

```
from sklearn.linear_model import LogisticRegression

lr = LogisticRegression()

lr.fit(X, y)

# Logistic Regressions does even worse
get_test_accuracy_of(lr)
```

The following is the output:

```
0.015773989233911892
```

Importing a decision tree classifier, we get the following:

```
from sklearn.tree import DecisionTreeClassifier

tree = DecisionTreeClassifier()

tree.fit(X, y)

# Tree does very well!
get_test_accuracy_of(tree)
```

The output looks like this:

```
0.9336639387437851
```

We see the Gini scores of the decision tree's features:

```
pd.DataFrame({'feature':awid.select_dtypes(['number']).columns,
'importance':tree.feature_importances_}).sort_values('importance',
ascending=False).head(10)
```

We will get output like this:

feature	importance	
6	`frame.len`	0.230466
3	`frame.time_delta`	0.221151
68	`wlan.fc.protected`	0.145760
70	`wlan.duration`	0.127612
5	`frame.time_relative`	0.079571
7	`frame.cap_len`	0.059702
62	`wlan.fc.type`	0.040192
72	`wlan.seq`	0.026807
65	`wlan.fc.retry`	0.019807
58	`radiotap.dbm_antsignal`	0.014195

```
from sklearn.ensemble import RandomForestClassifier

forest = RandomForestClassifier()

forest.fit(X, y)

# Random Forest does slightly worse
get_test_accuracy_of(forest)
```

The output can be seen as follows:

```
0.9297326464277914
```

Create a pipeline that will scale the numerical data and then feed the resulting data into a decision tree:

```
from sklearn.pipeline import Pipeline
from sklearn.preprocessing import StandardScaler
from sklearn.model_selection import GridSearchCV

preprocessing = Pipeline([
    ("scale", StandardScaler()),
])

pipeline = Pipeline([
    ("preprocessing", preprocessing),
    ("classifier", DecisionTreeClassifier())
])

# try varying levels of depth
```

```
params = {
    "classifier__max_depth": [None, 3, 5, 10],
        }

# instantiate a gridsearch module
grid = GridSearchCV(pipeline, params)
# fit the module
grid.fit(X, y)

# test the best model
get_test_accuracy_of(grid.best_estimator_)
```

The following shows the output:

```
0.9254930174595629
```

We try the same thing with a random forest:

```
preprocessing = Pipeline([
    ("scale", StandardScaler()),
])

pipeline = Pipeline([
    ("preprocessing", preprocessing),
    ("classifier", RandomForestClassifier())
])

# try varying levels of depth
params = {
    "classifier__max_depth": [None, 3, 5, 10],
        }

grid = GridSearchCV(pipeline, params)
grid.fit(X, y)
# best accuracy so far!
get_test_accuracy_of(grid.best_estimator_)
```

The final accuracy is as follows:

```
0.9348176317175636
```

Summary

In this chapter, we looked at understanding different types of impersonation and how the impersonators gather information. We learned about how the impersonation attack is constructed and how data science helps to detect domains that are impersonating someone. This chapter explained Levenshtein distance, along with finding domain similarity between malicious URLs and authorship attribution.

In the next chapter, we will look at changing the game with TensorFlow.

Changing the Game with TensorFlow

9

TensorFlow is an open source software library developed by the Google Brain team to do high-performance numerical computations. The TensorFlow library helps in programming across a range of numerical tasks.

In this chapter, we will look at some of the older use cases for using TensorFlow. Some of the major topics covered in the chapter are as follows:

- Introduction to TensorFlow
- Installation of TensorFlow
- TensorFlow for Windows users
- Hello world in TensorFlow
- Importing the MNIST dataset
- Computation graphs
- Tensor processing unit
- Using TensorFlow for intrusion detection
- Hands-on Tensor flow coding

Introduction to TensorFlow

TensorFlow is written in C++ and comprises two languages in the frontend. They are C++ and Python. Since most developers code in Python, the Python frontend is more developed than the C++ one. However, the C++ frontend's low-level API is good for running embedded systems.

TensorFlow was designed for probabilistic systems and gives flexibility to users to run models with ease, and across a variety of platforms. With TensorFlow, it is extremely easy to optimize various machine learning algorithms without having to set gradients at the beginning of the code, which is quite difficult. TensorFlow comes packed with TensorBoard, which helps visualize the flow with graphs and loss functions. The following screenshot shows the TensorFlow website:

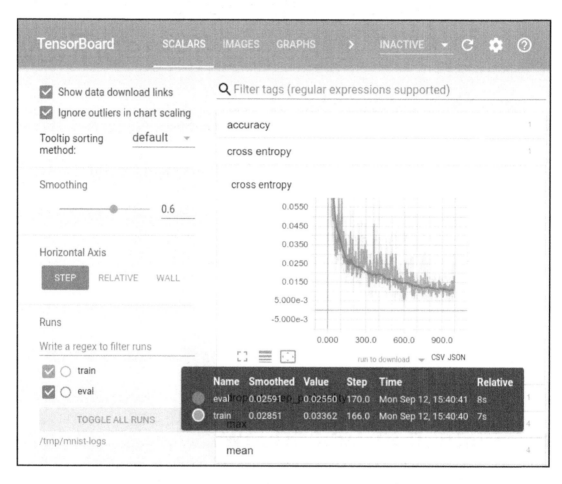

TensorFlow, with all these capabilities, makes it super easy to deploy and build for industry use cases that solve real-life artificial intelligence problems. Since it allows distributed computing, it is usually used to handle massive amounts of data. Unlike other packages, TensorFlow allows us to port the same code for both distributed and localized use, without compromising scalability. Deployment to Google Cloud Platform or Amazon Web Services is achieved with ease.

TensorFlow is packed with primitives that define functions on tensors and implicitly compute derivatives. Tensors here are multilinear maps that connect vector spaces to real numbers. Thus, we can call them multidimensional arrays of numbers, making scalars, vectors, and matrices all tensors. TensorFlow is therefore in many ways similar to NumPy packages providing N-d Libraries. They are dissimilar, however, because NumPy does not have tensors and does not provide GPU capabilities.

There are several other lesser-known packages that perform almost the same in terms to capabilities as TensorFlow. They are as follows:

- Torch
- Caffe
- Theano (Keras and Lasagne)
- CuDNN
- Mxnet

Installation of TensorFlow

By performing a simple and clean TensorFlow installation, the installation becomes very easy, and a simple `pip` statement will be fine. So if your are installing TensorFlow just to learn its capabilities, you can run the following code:

```
$ pip install tensorflow
```

To install TensorFlow in a `conda` environment, run the following:

```
conda install -n tensorflow spyder
```

TensorFlow, however, overrides existing installations of Python. So if Python is being used for other processes, the previous installation may break the existing versions. In such a case, it is recommended that you either check the respective dependencies or get hold of a virtual environment where you can do the TensorFlow installation.

In the following section, we will set up a virtual environment where we will install TensorFlow. We start with installing `virtualenv` in the machine, as shown:

```
$ pip install virtualenv
```

The `virtualenv` functions enable us to have a virtual environment in your system. In the virtual system, we create a folder called `tf` where we install TensorFlow, as shown here:

```
$ cd ~
$ mkdir tf
$ virtualenv ~/tf/tensorflow
```

We activate the TensorFlow environment with the following command:

```
$ source ~/tf/tensorflow/bin/activate
```

We then install TensorFlow in the environment:

```
(tensorflow) $ pip install tensorflow
```

TensorFlow gets installed with the required dependencies. To exit from the TensorFlow environment, run the following command:

```
(tensorflow) $ deactivate
```

This will get you back to the regular prompt:

```
$
```

TensorFlow for Windows users

Any version of TensorFlow that is beyond 0.12 can be installed in a Windows system:

```
pip install tensorflow
```

Do this to install the GPU version (CUDA 8):

```
pip install tensorflow-gpu
```

Hello world in TensorFlow

```
#package Import
import tensorflow as tensorF

hello = tensorF.constant("Hello")

world = tensorF.constant(" World!")
```

We begin by importing the TensorFlow package and loading the string:

```
helloworld=hello+world

with tensorF.Session() as sess:
    answer = sess.run(helloworld)
print (answer)
```

The preceding code is the most basic form of TensorFlow code that we will be writing. Later in this chapter, we will be dealing with examples that we looked at in the previous chapter.

Importing the MNIST dataset

The MNSIT dataset is a database of handwritten digits, and contains 60,000 training examples and 10,000 testing examples:

```
from tensorflow.examples.tutorials.mnist import input_data

 mnist = input_data.read_data_sets("MNIST_data/", one_hot=True)
```

We will load the image database from MNIST:

```
import matplotlib.pyplot as plt

im = mnist.train.images[0,:]

label = mnist.train.labels[0,:]

im = im.reshape([28,28])
```

We can construct a fully connected feed-forward neural network that is one layer deep to complete the example.

Computation graphs

In TensorFlow, computational operations are interdependent and thus interact with one another. Computational graphs help to track these interdependencies, thus making sense of a complicated functional architecture.

What is a computation graph?

Each node in the TensorFlow graph is a symbolic representation of an operational process. When the data reaches a particular node during the flow, the corresponding operational function associated with the node is performed. The output of the process is fed to the next node as an input.

The primary benefit of graph computation is that it helps to perform optimized computations:

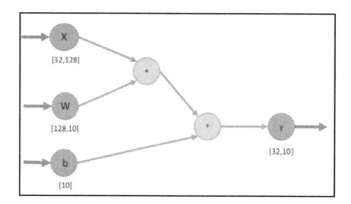

Tensor processing unit

A **Tensor processing unit** (TPU) is a hardware chip with an integrated circuit that has been specifically designed for TensorFlow to enhance its machine learning capabilities. The TPU provides accelerated artificial intelligence capabilities and has high throughput. The TPU comes from Google and has been successfully used in their data centers for some time. It is available in Google Cloud Platform Beta version.

Using TensorFlow for intrusion detection

We will use the intrusion detection problem again to detect anomalies. Initially, we will import pandas, as shown:

```
import pandas as pd
```

We get the names of the features from the dataset at this link: `http://icsdweb.aegean.gr/awid/features.html`.

We will include the features code as shown here:

```
features = ['frame.interface_id',
 'frame.dlt',
 'frame.offset_shift',
 'frame.time_epoch',
 'frame.time_delta',
 'frame.time_delta_displayed',
 'frame.time_relative',
 'frame.len',
 'frame.cap_len',
 'frame.marked',
 'frame.ignored',
 'radiotap.version',
 'radiotap.pad',
 'radiotap.length',
 'radiotap.present.tsft',
 'radiotap.present.flags',
 'radiotap.present.rate',
 'radiotap.present.channel',
 'radiotap.present.fhss',
 'radiotap.present.dbm_antsignal',
 ...
```

The preceding list contains all 155 features in the AWID dataset. We import the training set and see the number of rows and columns:

```
awid = pd.read_csv("../data/AWID-CLS-R-Trn.csv", header=None,
names=features)

# see the number of rows/columns
awid.shape
```

We can ignore the warning:

```
/Users/sinanozdemir/Desktop/cyber/env/lib/python2.7/site-
packages/IPython/core/interactiveshell.py:2714: DtypeWarning: Columns
(37,38,39,40,41,42,43,44,45,47,48,49,50,51,52,53,54,55,56,57,58,59,60,61,62
,74,88) have mixed types. Specify dtype option on import or set
low_memory=False.
  interactivity=interactivity, compiler=compiler, result=result)
```

The output of the shape is a list of all the training data in the 155-feature dataset:

```
(1795575, 155)
```

We will eventually have to replace the None values:

```
# they use ? as a null attribute.
awid.head()
```

The preceding code will produce a table of 5 rows × 155 columns as an output.

We see the distribution of response vars:

```
awid['class'].value_counts(normalize=True)

normal 0.909564
injection 0.036411
impersonation 0.027023
flooding 0.027002
Name: class, dtype: float64
```

We check for NAs:

```
# claims there are no null values because of the ?'s'
awid.isna().sum()
```

The output looks like this:

```
frame.interface_id 0
frame.dlt 1795575
frame.offset_shift 0
frame.time_epoch 0
frame.time_delta 0
frame.time_delta_displayed 0
frame.time_relative 0
frame.len 0
frame.cap_len 0
frame.marked 0
frame.ignored 0
radiotap.version 0
radiotap.pad 0
radiotap.length 0
radiotap.present.tsft 0
radiotap.present.flags 0
radiotap.present.rate 0
radiotap.present.channel 0
radiotap.present.fhss 0
radiotap.present.dbm_antsignal 0
radiotap.present.dbm_antnoise 0
```

```
radiotap.present.lock_quality 0
radiotap.present.tx_attenuation 0
radiotap.present.db_tx_attenuation 0
radiotap.present.dbm_tx_power 0
radiotap.present.antenna 0
radiotap.present.db_antsignal 0
radiotap.present.db_antnoise 0
radiotap.present.rxflags 0
radiotap.present.xchannel 0
                                                           ...

wlan_mgt.rsn.version 1718631
wlan_mgt.rsn.gcs.type 1718631
wlan_mgt.rsn.pcs.count 1718631
wlan_mgt.rsn.akms.count 1718633
wlan_mgt.rsn.akms.type 1718651
wlan_mgt.rsn.capabilities.preauth 1718633
wlan_mgt.rsn.capabilities.no_pairwise 1718633
wlan_mgt.rsn.capabilities.ptksa_replay_counter 1718633
wlan_mgt.rsn.capabilities.gtksa_replay_counter 1718633
wlan_mgt.rsn.capabilities.mfpr 1718633
wlan_mgt.rsn.capabilities.mfpc 1718633
wlan_mgt.rsn.capabilities.peerkey 1718633
wlan_mgt.tcprep.trsmt_pow 1795536
wlan_mgt.tcprep.link_mrg 1795536
wlan.wep.iv 944820
wlan.wep.key 909831
wlan.wep.icv 944820
wlan.tkip.extiv 1763655
wlan.ccmp.extiv 1792506
wlan.qos.tid 1133234
wlan.qos.priority 1133234
wlan.qos.eosp 1279874
wlan.qos.ack 1133234
wlan.qos.amsdupresent 1134226
wlan.qos.buf_state_indicated 1795575
wlan.qos.bit4 1648935
wlan.qos.txop_dur_req 1648935
wlan.qos.buf_state_indicated.1 1279874
data.len 903021
class 0
Length: 155, dtype: int64
```

We replace all ? marks with None:

```
# replace the ? marks with None
awid.replace({"?": None}, inplace=True)
```

The sum shows a large amount of missing data:

```
# Many missing pieces of data!
awid.isna().sum()
```

Here is what the output looks like:

```
frame.interface_id 0
frame.dlt 1795575
frame.offset_shift 0
frame.time_epoch 0
frame.time_delta 0
frame.time_delta_displayed 0
frame.time_relative 0
frame.len 0
frame.cap_len 0
frame.marked 0
frame.ignored 0
radiotap.version 0
radiotap.pad 0
radiotap.length 0
radiotap.present.tsft 0
radiotap.present.flags 0
radiotap.present.rate 0
radiotap.present.channel 0
radiotap.present.fhss 0
radiotap.present.dbm_antsignal 0
radiotap.present.dbm_antnoise 0
radiotap.present.lock_quality 0
radiotap.present.tx_attenuation 0
radiotap.present.db_tx_attenuation 0
radiotap.present.dbm_tx_power 0
radiotap.present.antenna 0
radiotap.present.db_antsignal 0
radiotap.present.db_antnoise 0
radiotap.present.rxflags 0
radiotap.present.xchannel 0

                                                    . . .
wlan_mgt.rsn.version 1718631
wlan_mgt.rsn.gcs.type 1718631
wlan_mgt.rsn.pcs.count 1718631
wlan_mgt.rsn.akms.count 1718633
wlan_mgt.rsn.akms.type 1718651
wlan_mgt.rsn.capabilities.preauth 1718633
wlan_mgt.rsn.capabilities.no_pairwise 1718633
wlan_mgt.rsn.capabilities.ptksa_replay_counter 1718633
wlan_mgt.rsn.capabilities.gtksa_replay_counter 1718633
wlan_mgt.rsn.capabilities.mfpr 1718633
```

```
wlan_mgt.rsn.capabilities.mfpc 1718633
wlan_mgt.rsn.capabilities.peerkey 1718633
wlan_mgt.tcprep.trsmt_pow 1795536
wlan_mgt.tcprep.link_mrg 1795536
wlan.wep.iv 944820
wlan.wep.key 909831
wlan.wep.icv 944820
wlan.tkip.extiv 1763655
wlan.ccmp.extiv 1792506
wlan.qos.tid 1133234
wlan.qos.priority 1133234
wlan.qos.eosp 1279874
wlan.qos.ack 1133234
wlan.qos.amsdupresent 1134226
wlan.qos.buf_state_indicated 1795575
wlan.qos.bit4 1648935
wlan.qos.txop_dur_req 1648935
wlan.qos.buf_state_indicated.1 1279874
data.len 903021
```

Here, we remove columns that have over 50% of their data missing:

```
columns_with_mostly_null_data = awid.columns[awid.isnull().mean() >= 0.5]

# 72 columns are going to be affected!
columns_with_mostly_null_data.shape

Out[11]:
(72,)
```

We drop the columns with over 50% of their data missing:

```
awid.drop(columns_with_mostly_null_data, axis=1, inplace=True)
```

The output can be seen as follows:

```
awid.shape

(1795575, 83)
```

Now, drop the rows that have missing values:

```
#
awid.dropna(inplace=True)  # drop rows with null data
```

We lost 456,169 rows:

```
awid.shape
```

```
(1339406, 83)
```

However, it doesn't affect our distribution too much:

```
# 0.878763 is our null accuracy. Our model must be better than this number
to be a contender

awid['class'].value_counts(normalize=True)
```

```
normal 0.878763
injection 0.048812
impersonation 0.036227
flooding 0.036198
Name: class, dtype: float64
```

We only select numerical columns for our ML algorithms, but there should be more:

```
awid.select_dtypes(['number']).shape
```

```
(1339406, 45)
```

We transform all columns into numerical `dtypes`:

```
for col in awid.columns:
    awid[col] = pd.to_numeric(awid[col], errors='ignore')

# that makes more sense
awid.select_dtypes(['number']).shape
```

The output can be seen here:

```
Out[19]:
```

```
(1339406, 74)
```

We derive basic descriptive statistics:

```
awid.describe()
```

By executing the preceding code will get a table of 8 rows × 74 columns.

```
X, y = awid.select_dtypes(['number']), awid['class']
```

We do a basic Naive Bayes fitting. We fit our model to the data:

```
from sklearn.naive_bayes import GaussianNB

nb = GaussianNB()

nb.fit(X, y)
```

Gaussian Naive Bayes is performed as follows:

```
GaussianNB(priors=None, var_smoothing=1e-09)
```

We read in the test data and do the same transformations to it, to match the training data:

```
awid_test = pd.read_csv("../data/AWID-CLS-R-Tst.csv", header=None,
names=features)

# drop the problematic columns
awid_test.drop(columns_with_mostly_null_data, axis=1, inplace=True)

# replace ? with None
awid_test.replace({"?": None}, inplace=True)

# drop the rows with null data
awid_test.dropna(inplace=True) # drop rows with null data

# convert columns to numerical values
for col in awid_test.columns:
    awid_test[col] = pd.to_numeric(awid_test[col], errors='ignore')
awid_test.shape
```

The output is as follows:

```
Out[23]:

(389185, 83)
```

We compute the basic metric, accuracy:

```
from sklearn.metrics import accuracy_score
```

We define a simple function to test the accuracy of a model fitted on training data by using our testing data:

```
X_test = awid_test.select_dtypes(['number'])
y_test = awid_test['class']

def get_test_accuracy_of(model):
    y_preds = model.predict(X_test)
```

```
    return accuracy_score(y_preds, y_test)
# naive bayes does very poorly on its own!
get_test_accuracy_of(nb)
```

The output can be seen here:

```
Out[25]:

0.26535452291326744
```

We perform logistic regression, but it performs even worse:

```
from sklearn.linear_model import LogisticRegression

lr = LogisticRegression()

lr.fit(X, y)

# Logistic Regressions does even worse
get_test_accuracy_of(lr)
```

We can ignore this warning:

```
/Users/sinanozdemir/Desktop/cyber/env/lib/python2.7/site-
packages/sklearn/linear_model/logistic.py:432: FutureWarning: Default
solver will be changed to 'lbfgs' in 0.22. Specify a solver to silence this
warning.
   FutureWarning)
/Users/sinanozdemir/Desktop/cyber/env/lib/python2.7/site-
packages/sklearn/linear_model/logistic.py:459: FutureWarning: Default
multi_class will be changed to 'auto' in 0.22. Specify the multi_class
option to silence this warning.
   "this warning.", FutureWarning)
```

The following shows the output:

```
Out[26]:

0.015773989233911892
```

We test with DecisionTreeClassifier as shown here:

```
from sklearn.tree import DecisionTreeClassifier

tree = DecisionTreeClassifier()

tree.fit(X, y)
```

```
# Tree does very well!
get_test_accuracy_of(tree)
```

The output can be seen as follows:

```
Out[27]:

0.9280830453383352
```

We test the Gini scores of the decision tree features as follows:

```
pd.DataFrame({'feature':awid.select_dtypes(['number']).columns,
'importance':tree.feature_importances_}).sort_values('importance',
ascending=False).head(10)
```

The output of the preceding code gives the following table:

feature	importance	
7	frame.cap_len	0.222489
4	frame.time_delta_displayed	0.221133
68	wlan.fc.protected	0.146001
70	wlan.duration	0.127674
5	frame.time_relative	0.077353
6	frame.len	0.067667
62	wlan.fc.type	0.039926
72	wlan.seq	0.027947
65	wlan.fc.retry	0.019839
58	radiotap.dbm_antsignal	0.014197

We import `RandomForestClassifier` as shown here:

```
from sklearn.ensemble import RandomForestClassifier

forest = RandomForestClassifier()

forest.fit(X, y)

# Random Forest does slightly worse
get_test_accuracy_of(forest)
```

We can ignore this warning:

```
/Users/sinanozdemir/Desktop/cyber/env/lib/python2.7/site-
packages/sklearn/ensemble/forest.py:248: FutureWarning: The default value
of n_estimators will change from 10 in version 0.20 to 100 in 0.22.
  "10 in version 0.20 to 100 in 0.22.", FutureWarning)
```

The following is the output:

```
Out[29]:

0.9357349332579622
```

We create a pipeline that will scale the numerical data and then feed the resulting data into a decision tree:

```python
from sklearn.pipeline import Pipeline
from sklearn.preprocessing import StandardScaler
from sklearn.model_selection import GridSearchCV

preprocessing = Pipeline([
    ("scale", StandardScaler()),
])

pipeline = Pipeline([
    ("preprocessing", preprocessing),
    ("classifier", DecisionTreeClassifier())
])

# try varying levels of depth
params = {
    "classifier__max_depth": [None, 3, 5, 10],
        }

# instantiate a gridsearch module
grid = GridSearchCV(pipeline, params)
# fit the module
grid.fit(X, y)

# test the best model
get_test_accuracy_of(grid.best_estimator_)
```

We can ignore this warning:

```
/Users/sinanozdemir/Desktop/cyber/env/lib/python2.7/site-
packages/sklearn/model_selection/_split.py:1943: FutureWarning: You should
specify a value for 'cv' instead of relying on the default value. The
default value will change from 3 to 5 in version 0.22.
```

```
   warnings.warn(CV_WARNING, FutureWarning)
/Users/sinanozdemir/Desktop/cyber/env/lib/python2.7/site-
packages/sklearn/preprocessing/data.py:617: DataConversionWarning: Data
with input dtype int64, float64 were all converted to float64 by
StandardScaler.
   return self.partial_fit(X, y)
/Users/sinanozdemir/Desktop/cyber/env/lib/python2.7/site-
packages/sklearn/base.py:465: DataConversionWarning: Data with input dtype
int64, float64 were all converted to float64 by StandardScaler.
   return self.fit(X, y, **fit_params).transform(X)
/Users/sinanozdemir/Desktop/cyber/env/lib/python2.7/site-
packages/sklearn/pipeline.py:451: DataConversionWarning: Data with input
dtype int64, float64 were all converted to float64 by StandardScaler.
   Xt = transform.transform(Xt)
```

The output is as follows:

```
Out[30]:

0.926258720145946
```

We try the same thing with a random forest:

```
preprocessing = Pipeline([
    ("scale", StandardScaler()),
])

pipeline = Pipeline([
    ("preprocessing", preprocessing),
    ("classifier", RandomForestClassifier())
])

# try varying levels of depth
params = {
    "classifier__max_depth": [None, 3, 5, 10],
        }

grid = GridSearchCV(pipeline, params)
grid.fit(X, y)
# best accuracy so far!
get_test_accuracy_of(grid.best_estimator_)
```

The following shows the output:

```
Out[31]:

0.8893431144571348
```

We import `LabelEncoder`:

```
from sklearn.preprocessing import LabelEncoder
encoder = LabelEncoder()
encoded_y = encoder.fit_transform(y)
encoded_y.shape
```

The output is as follows:

```
Out[119]:

(1339406,)

encoded_y

Out[121]:

array([3, 3, 3, ..., 3, 3, 3])
```

We do this to import `LabelBinarizer`:

```
from sklearn.preprocessing import LabelBinarizer
binarizer = LabelBinarizer()
binarized_y = binarizer.fit_transform(encoded_y)
binarized_y.shape
```

We will get the following output:

```
(1339406, 4)
```

Now, execute the following code:

```
binarized_y[:5,]
```

And the output will be as follows:

```
array([[0, 0, 0, 1],
       [0, 0, 0, 1],
       [0, 0, 0, 1],
       [0, 0, 0, 1],
       [0, 0, 0, 1]])
```

Run the `y.head()` command:

```
y.head()
```

The output is as follows:

```
0       normal
1       normal
2       normal
3       normal
4       normal
Name: class, dtype: object
```

Now run the following code:

```
print encoder.classes_
print binarizer.classes_
```

The output can be seen as follows:

```
['flooding' 'impersonation' 'injection' 'normal']
[0 1 2 3]
```

Import the following packages:

```
from keras.models import Sequential
from keras.layers import Dense
from keras.wrappers.scikit_learn import KerasClassifier
```

We baseline the model for the neural network. We choose a hidden layer of 10 neurons. A lower number of neurons helps to eliminate the redundancies in the data and select the most important features:

```
def create_baseline_model(n, input_dim):
    # create model
    model = Sequential()
    model.add(Dense(n, input_dim=input_dim, kernel_initializer='normal',
activation='relu'))
    model.add(Dense(4, kernel_initializer='normal', activation='sigmoid'))
    # Compile model. We use the the logarithmic loss function, and the Adam
gradient optimizer.
    model.compile(loss='categorical_crossentropy', optimizer='adam',
metrics=['accuracy'])
    return model

KerasClassifier(build_fn=create_baseline_model, epochs=100, batch_size=5,
verbose=0, n=20)
```

We can see the following output:

```
<keras.wrappers.scikit_learn.KerasClassifier at 0x149c1c210>
```

Run the following code:

```
# use the KerasClassifier

preprocessing = Pipeline([
    ("scale", StandardScaler()),
])

pipeline = Pipeline([
    ("preprocessing", preprocessing),
    ("classifier", KerasClassifier(build_fn=create_baseline_model,
epochs=2, batch_size=128,
                                    verbose=1, n=10, input_dim=74))
])

cross_val_score(pipeline, X, binarized_y)
```

The Epoch length can be seen as follows:

```
Epoch 1/2
892937/892937 [==============================] - 21s 24us/step - loss:
0.1027 - acc: 0.9683
Epoch 2/2
892937/892937 [==============================] - 18s 20us/step - loss:
0.0314 - acc: 0.9910
446469/446469 [==============================] - 4s 10us/step
Epoch 1/2
892937/892937 [==============================] - 24s 27us/step - loss:
0.1089 - acc: 0.9682
Epoch 2/2
892937/892937 [==============================] - 19s 22us/step - loss:
0.0305 - acc: 0.9919 0s - loss: 0.0
446469/446469 [==============================] - 4s 9us/step
Epoch 1/2
892938/892938 [==============================] - 18s 20us/step - loss:
0.0619 - acc: 0.9815
Epoch 2/2
892938/892938 [==============================] - 17s 20us/step - loss:
0.0153 - acc: 0.9916
446468/446468 [==============================] - 4s 9us/step
```

The output for the preceding code is as follows:

```
array([0.97450887, 0.99176875, 0.74421683])

# notice the LARGE variance in scores of a neural network. This is due to
the high-variance nature of how networks fit
# using stochastic gradient descent

pipeline.fit(X, binarized_y)

Epoch 1/2
1339406/1339406 [==============================] - 29s 22us/step - loss:
0.0781 - acc: 0.9740
Epoch 2/2
1339406/1339406 [==============================] - 25s 19us/step - loss:
0.0298 - acc: 0.9856
```

We will get the following code as an output:

```
Pipeline(memory=None,
     steps=[('preprocessing', Pipeline(memory=None,
     steps=[('scale', StandardScaler(copy=True, with_mean=True,
with_std=True))])), ('classifier',
<keras.wrappers.scikit_learn.KerasClassifier object at 0x149c1c350>)])
```

Now execute the following code:

```
# remake
encoded_y_test = encoder.transform(y_test)
def get_network_test_accuracy_of(model):
    y_preds = model.predict(X_test)
    return accuracy_score(y_preds, encoded_y_test)

# not the best accuracy

get_network_test_accuracy_of(pipeline)

389185/389185 [==============================] - 3s 7us/step
```

The following is the output of the preceding input:

```
0.889327697624523
```

By fitting again, we get a different test accuracy. This also highlights the variance on the network:

```
#
pipeline.fit(X, binarized_y)
get_network_test_accuracy_of(pipeline)

Epoch 1/2
1339406/1339406 [==============================] - 29s 21us/step - loss:
0.0844 - acc: 0.9735 0s - loss: 0.085
Epoch 2/2
1339406/1339406 [==============================] - 32s 24us/step - loss:
0.0323 - acc: 0.9853 0s - loss: 0.0323 - acc: 0
389185/389185 [==============================] - 4s 11us/step
```

We will get the following code:

```
0.8742526048023433
```

We add some more epochs to learn more:

```
preprocessing = Pipeline([
    ("scale", StandardScaler()),
])

pipeline = Pipeline([
    ("preprocessing", preprocessing),
    ("classifier", KerasClassifier(build_fn=create_baseline_model,
epochs=10, batch_size=128,
                                    verbose=1, n=10, input_dim=74))
])

cross_val_score(pipeline, X, binarized_y)
```

We get output as follows:

```
Epoch 1/10
892937/892937 [==============================] - 20s 22us/step - loss:
0.0945 - acc: 0.9744
Epoch 2/10
892937/892937 [==============================] - 17s 19us/step - loss:
0.0349 - acc: 0.9906
Epoch 3/10
892937/892937 [==============================] - 16s 18us/step - loss:
0.0293 - acc: 0.9920
Epoch 4/10
892937/892937 [==============================] - 17s 20us/step - loss:
0.0261 - acc: 0.9932
Epoch 5/10
```

```
892937/892937 [==============================] - 18s 20us/step - loss:
0.0231 - acc: 0.9938 0s - loss: 0.0232 - ac
Epoch 6/10
892937/892937 [==============================] - 15s 17us/step - loss:
0.0216 - acc: 0.9941
Epoch 7/10
892937/892937 [==============================] - 21s 23us/step - loss:
0.0206 - acc: 0.9944
Epoch 8/10
892937/892937 [==============================] - 17s 20us/step - loss:
0.0199 - acc: 0.9947 0s - loss: 0.0198 - a
Epoch 9/10
892937/892937 [==============================] - 17s 19us/step - loss:
0.0194 - acc: 0.9948
Epoch 10/10
892937/892937 [==============================] - 17s 19us/step - loss:
0.0189 - acc: 0.9950
446469/446469 [==============================] - 4s 10us/step
Epoch 1/10
892937/892937 [==============================] - 19s 21us/step - loss:
0.1160 - acc: 0.9618
...

Out[174]:

array([0.97399595, 0.9939951 , 0.74381591])
```

By fitting again, we get a different test accuracy. This also highlights the variance on the
network:

```
pipeline.fit(X, binarized_y)
get_network_test_accuracy_of(pipeline)

Epoch 1/10
1339406/1339406 [==============================] - 30s 22us/step - loss:
0.0812 - acc: 0.9754
Epoch 2/10
1339406/1339406 [==============================] - 27s 20us/step - loss:
0.0280 - acc: 0.9915
Epoch 3/10
1339406/1339406 [==============================] - 28s 21us/step - loss:
0.0226 - acc: 0.9921
Epoch 4/10
1339406/1339406 [==============================] - 27s 20us/step - loss:
0.0193 - acc: 0.9940
Epoch 5/10
1339406/1339406 [==============================] - 28s 21us/step - loss:
0.0169 - acc: 0.9951
```

```
Epoch 6/10
1339406/1339406 [==============================] - 34s 25us/step - loss:
0.0155 - acc: 0.9955
Epoch 7/10
1339406/1339406 [==============================] - 38s 28us/step - loss:
0.0148 - acc: 0.9957
Epoch 8/10
1339406/1339406 [==============================] - 34s 25us/step - loss:
0.0143 - acc: 0.9958 3s -
Epoch 9/10
1339406/1339406 [==============================] - 29s 21us/step - loss:
0.0139 - acc: 0.9960
Epoch 10/10
1339406/1339406 [==============================] - 28s 21us/step - loss:
0.0134 - acc: 0.9961
389185/389185 [==============================] - 3s 8us/step
```

The output of the preceding code is as follows:

```
0.8725027943009109
```

This took much longer and still didn't increase the accuracy. We change our function to
have multiple hidden layers in our network:

```
def network_builder(hidden_dimensions, input_dim):
    # create model
    model = Sequential()
    model.add(Dense(hidden_dimensions[0], input_dim=input_dim,
kernel_initializer='normal', activation='relu'))

    # add multiple hidden layers
    for dimension in hidden_dimensions[1:]:
        model.add(Dense(dimension, kernel_initializer='normal',
activation='relu'))
    model.add(Dense(4, kernel_initializer='normal', activation='sigmoid'))

    # Compile model. We use the the logarithmic loss function, and the Adam
gradient optimizer.
    model.compile(loss='categorical_crossentropy', optimizer='adam',
metrics=['accuracy'])
    return model
```

We add some more hidden layers to learn more:

```
#
preprocessing = Pipeline([
    ("scale", StandardScaler()),
])
```

```
pipeline = Pipeline([
    ("preprocessing", preprocessing),
    ("classifier", KerasClassifier(build_fn=network_builder, epochs=10,
batch_size=128,
                                   verbose=1, hidden_dimensions=(60,30,10),
input_dim=74))
])

cross_val_score(pipeline, X, binarized_y)
```

We get the output as follows:

```
Epoch 1/10
892937/892937 [==============================] - 24s 26us/step - loss:
0.0457 - acc: 0.9860
Epoch 2/10
892937/892937 [==============================] - 21s 24us/step - loss:
0.0113 - acc: 0.9967
Epoch 3/10
892937/892937 [==============================] - 21s 23us/step - loss:
0.0079 - acc: 0.9977
Epoch 4/10
892937/892937 [==============================] - 26s 29us/step - loss:
0.0066 - acc: 0.9982
Epoch 5/10
892937/892937 [==============================] - 24s 27us/step - loss:
0.0061 - acc: 0.9983
Epoch 6/10
892937/892937 [==============================] - 25s 28us/step - loss:
0.0057 - acc: 0.9984
Epoch 7/10
892937/892937 [==============================] - 24s 27us/step - loss:
0.0051 - acc: 0.9985
Epoch 8/10
892937/892937 [==============================] - 24s 27us/step - loss:
0.0050 - acc: 0.9986
Epoch 9/10
892937/892937 [==============================] - 25s 28us/step - loss:
0.0046 - acc: 0.9986
Epoch 10/10
892937/892937 [==============================] - 23s 26us/step - loss:
0.0044 - acc: 0.9987
446469/446469 [==============================] - 6s 12us/step
Epoch 1/10
892937/892937 [==============================] - 27s 30us/step - loss:
0.0538 - acc: 0.9826
```

For `binarized_y`, we get this:

```
pipeline.fit(X, binarized_y)
get_network_test_accuracy_of(pipeline)
```

We get the epoch output as follows:

```
Epoch 1/10
1339406/1339406 [==============================] - 31s 23us/step - loss:
0.0422 - acc: 0.9865
Epoch 2/10
1339406/1339406 [==============================] - 28s 21us/step - loss:
0.0095 - acc: 0.9973
Epoch 3/10
1339406/1339406 [==============================] - 29s 22us/step - loss:
0.0068 - acc: 0.9981
Epoch 4/10
1339406/1339406 [==============================] - 28s 21us/step - loss:
0.0056 - acc: 0.9984
Epoch 5/10
1339406/1339406 [==============================] - 29s 21us/step - loss:
0.0051 - acc: 0.9986
Epoch 6/10
1339406/1339406 [==============================] - 28s 21us/step - loss:
0.0047 - acc: 0.9987
Epoch 7/10
1339406/1339406 [==============================] - 30s 22us/step - loss:
0.0041 - acc: 0.9988 0s - loss: 0.0041 - acc: 0.99 - ETA: 0s - loss: 0.0041
- acc: 0.998 - ETA: 0s - loss: 0.0041 - acc: 0
Epoch 8/10
1339406/1339406 [==============================] - 29s 22us/step - loss:
0.0039 - acc: 0.9989
Epoch 9/10
1339406/1339406 [==============================] - 29s 22us/step - loss:
0.0039 - acc: 0.9989
Epoch 10/10
1339406/1339406 [==============================] - 28s 21us/step - loss:
0.0036 - acc: 0.9990 0s - loss: 0.0036 - acc:
389185/389185 [==============================] - 3s 9us/step
...

Out[179]

0.8897876331307732
```

We got a small bump by increasing the hidden layers. Adding some more hidden layers to learn more, we get the following:

```
preprocessing = Pipeline([
    ("scale", StandardScaler()),
])

pipeline = Pipeline([
    ("preprocessing", preprocessing),
    ("classifier", KerasClassifier(build_fn=network_builder, epochs=10,
batch_size=128,
                                    verbose=1,
hidden_dimensions=(30,30,30,10), input_dim=74))
])

cross_val_score(pipeline, X, binarized_y)
```

The Epoch output is as shown here:

```
Epoch 1/10
892937/892937 [==============================] - 25s 28us/step - loss:
0.0671 - acc: 0.9709
Epoch 2/10
892937/892937 [==============================] - 21s 23us/step - loss:
0.0139 - acc: 0.9963
Epoch 3/10
892937/892937 [==============================] - 20s 22us/step - loss:
0.0100 - acc: 0.9973
Epoch 4/10
892937/892937 [==============================] - 25s 28us/step - loss:
0.0087 - acc: 0.9977
Epoch 5/10
892937/892937 [==============================] - 21s 24us/step - loss:
0.0078 - acc: 0.9979
Epoch 6/10
892937/892937 [==============================] - 21s 24us/step - loss:
0.0072 - acc: 0.9981
Epoch 7/10
892937/892937 [==============================] - 24s 27us/step - loss:
0.0069 - acc: 0.9982
Epoch 8/10
892937/892937 [==============================] - 24s 27us/step - loss:
0.0064 - acc: 0.9984
...
```

The output can be seen as follows:

```
array([0.97447527, 0.99417877, 0.74292446])
```

Execute the following command `pipeline.fit()`:

```
pipeline.fit(X, binarized_y)
get_network_test_accuracy_of(pipeline)

Epoch 1/10
1339406/1339406 [==============================] - 48s 36us/step - loss:
0.0666 - acc: 0.9548
Epoch 2/10
1339406/1339406 [==============================] - 108s 81us/step - loss:
0.0346 - acc: 0.9663
Epoch 3/10
1339406/1339406 [==============================] - 78s 59us/step - loss:
0.0261 - acc: 0.9732
Epoch 4/10
1339406/1339406 [==============================] - 102s 76us/step - loss:
0.0075 - acc: 0.9980
Epoch 5/10
1339406/1339406 [==============================] - 71s 53us/step - loss:
0.0066 - acc: 0.9983
Epoch 6/10
1339406/1339406 [==============================] - 111s 83us/step - loss:
0.0059 - acc: 0.9985
Epoch 7/10
1339406/1339406 [==============================] - 98s 73us/step - loss:
0.0055 - acc: 0.9986
Epoch 8/10
1339406/1339406 [==============================] - 93s 70us/step - loss:
0.0052 - acc: 0.9987
Epoch 9/10
1339406/1339406 [==============================] - 88s 66us/step - loss:
0.0051 - acc: 0.9988
Epoch 10/10
1339406/1339406 [==============================] - 87s 65us/step - loss:
0.0049 - acc: 0.9988
389185/389185 [==============================] - 16s 41us/step
```

By executing the preceding code we will get the following ouput:

```
0.8899315235684828
```

The best result so far comes from using deep learning. However, deep learning isn't the best choice for all datasets.

Summary

In this chapter, we had an introduction to TensorFlow, along with installing it and importing the MNIST dataset. We also learned about the various computation graphs, along with the tensor processing unit. This chapter also explained how to use TensorFlow for intrusion detection.

In the next chapter, we will study financial fraud and how deep learning can mitigate it.

10
Financial Fraud and How Deep Learning Can Mitigate It

Financial fraud is one of the major causes of monetary loss in banks and financial organizations. Rule-based fraud-detection systems are not capable of detecting advanced persistent threats. Such threats find ways to circumnavigate rule-based systems. Old signature-based methods establish in advance any fraudulent transactions such as loan default prediction, credit card fraud, cheque kiting or empty ATM envelope deposits.

In this chapter, we will see how machine learning can capture fraudulent transactions. We will cover the following major topics:

- Machine learning to detect fraud
- Imbalanced data
- Handling data imbalances
- Detecting credit card fraud
- Using logistic regression to detect fraud
- Analyzing the best approaches to detect fraud
- Hyperparameter tuning to get the best model results

Machine learning to detect financial fraud

Machine learning helps us flag or predict fraud based on historical data. The most common method for fraud-detection is classification. For a classification problem, a set of data is mapped to a subset based on the category it belongs to. The training set helps to determine to which subset a dataset belongs. These subsets are often known as **classes**:

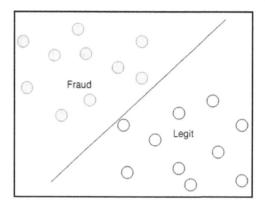

In cases of fraudulent transactions, the classification between legitimate and non-legitimate transactions is determined by the following parameters:

- The amount of the transaction
- The merchant where the transaction is made
- The location where the transaction is made
- The time of the transaction
- Whether this was an in-person or online transaction

Imbalanced data

Classification often deals with a major problem that occurs because there is a significant amount of data for one class, but a lack of data for the other. The financial fraud use case is where we face this problem; this happens because the number of fraudulent transactions that occur on a daily basis is much lower compared to the number of legitimate transaction. Such cases lead to scenerios where the dataset is biased due to the lack of accurate data.

Handling imbalanced datasets

There are several processes to deal with the issue of imbalanced datasets. The main goal of these processes is to either decrease the frequency of the majority class or increase the frequency of the minority class. Here, we'll list a few efforts that can help us get rid of the data imbalance:

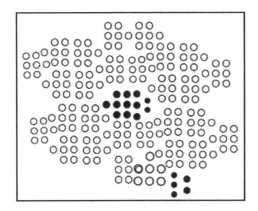

Random under-sampling

In this process, random selections are made from the class that has the majority of the data. This act is continued until both classes are balanced out. Though this method is good in terms of storage, but while random data reduction a lot of the important data points may get discarded. Another issue with this approach, is that it does not solve the problem of the dataset from which the random sample is picked being biased.

Random oversampling

This is the exactly opposite process of under-sampling; here, elements of the minority class are randomly added until the ratio between the majority and minority classes is close enough. The oversampling is a good method overall for addressing the issues that under-sampling faces. However, the major issue of oversampling is overfitting, where the results are too tailored to the input data.

Cluster-based oversampling

This approach to addressing imbalanced data uses K-mean clustering. The clustering algorithm is applied to both the majority class and the minority class in which each class is oversampled, such that each class has the same number of data elements. Though this is an efficient method, it suffers from the issue of overfitting.

Synthetic minority oversampling technique

Synthetic Minority Oversampling Technique (SMOTE) is a technique where synthetic data is generated by taking a subset of the data from the minority classes. However, none of the data is a replica of that in the minority class, thus overfitting is easily avoided. The synthetic data is added to the original dataset. This combined dataset is used to classify data. The good thing about this sampling is that there is no loss of information during the entire process.

Modified synthetic minority oversampling technique

This is a modified form of the SMOTE version of sampling. Here, the underlying distribution and noise in the data does not seep in the data.

Detecting credit card fraud

This chapter will test different methods on skewed data. The idea is to compare whether preprocessing techniques work better when there is an overwhelming majority class that can disrupt the efficiency of our predictive model. You will also be able to see how to apply cross-validation for hyperparameter tuning on different classification models. The intention here is to create models using the following methods.

Logistic regression

We start with importing all the required packages:

```
import pandas as pd
import matplotlib.pyplot as plt
from __future__ import division
import numpy as np

%matplotlib inline
```

Loading the dataset

We use a dataset from the 2017 Black Hat conference. We will be doing some basic statistical testing to better understand the data:

```
data =
pd.read_csv("https://s3-us-west-1.amazonaws.com/blackhat-us-2017/creditcard
.csv")
data.head()
```

The preceding code provides the data that has 31 columns in total.

We check for the target classes with a Histogram, where the *x* axis depicts the `Class` and the *y* axis depicts the `Frequency`, as shown in the following code:

```
count_classes = pd.value_counts(data['Class'], sort = True).sort_index()
count_classes.plot(kind = 'bar')
plt.title("Fraud class histogram")
plt.xlabel("Class")
plt.ylabel("Frequency")
```

Here is the output for the preceding code:

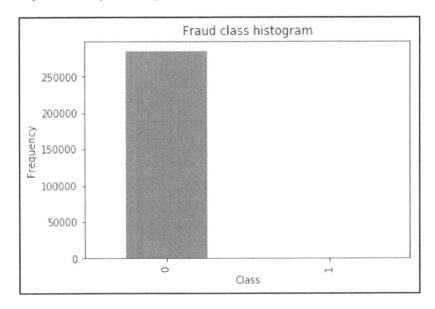

This histogram clearly shows that the data is totally unbalanced.

This is an example of using a typical accuracy score to evaluate our classification algorithm. For example, if we just use a majority class to assign values to all records, we will still have a high accuracy, but we would be classifying all one incorrectly.

There are several ways to approach this classification problem while taking into consideration this unbalance: Do we collect more data? It's a nice strategy but not applicable in this case:

- We approach the problem by changing the performance metric:
    - Use the confusion matrix to calculate precision, recall
    - F1 score (weighted average of precision-recall)
    - Use Kappa which is a classification accuracy normalized by the imbalance of the classes in the data
    - ROC curves calculates sensitivity/specificity ratio
- We can also resample the dataset
    - Essentially this is a method that will process the data to have an approximate 50:50 ratio.
    - One way to achieve this is by oversampling, which is adding copies of the under-represented class (better when you have little data).
    - Another is under-sampling, which deletes instances from the overrepresented class (better when we have lots of data).

Approach

1. We are not going to perform feature engineering in the first instance. The dataset has been downgraded in order to contain 30 features (28 anonymized + time + amount).
2. We compare what happens when using resampling and when not using it. We test this approach using a simple logistic regression classifier.
3. We evaluate the models by using some of the performance metrics mentioned previously.
4. We repeat the best resampling/not-resampling method by tuning the parameters in the logistic-regression classifier.
5. We perform a classifications model using other classification algorithms.

Setting our input and target variables + resampling:

1. Normalize the `Amount` column
2. The `Amount` column is not in line with the anonymized features:

```
from sklearn.preprocessing import StandardScaler
data['normAmount'] =
StandardScaler().fit_transform(data['Amount'].values.reshape(-1,
1))
data = data.drop(['Time','Amount'],axis=1)
data.head()
```

The preceding code provides the table that shows 5 rows × 30 columns.

As we mentioned earlier, there are several ways to resample skewed data. Apart from under-sampling and oversampling, there is a very popular approach called **SMOTE**, which is a combination of oversampling and under-sampling, but the oversampling approach is not done by replicating a minority class but by constructing a new minority class data instance via an algorithm.

In this notebook, we will use traditional under-sampling.

The way we will under-sample the dataset is by creating a 50:50 ratio. This will be done by randomly selecting x number of samples from the majority class, being x the total number of records with the minority class:

```
X = data.iloc[:, data.columns != 'Class']
y = data.iloc[:, data.columns == 'Class']
```

We count the number of data points in the minority class:

```
number_records_fraud = len(data[data.Class == 1])
fraud_indices = np.array(data[data.Class == 1].index)
```

We pick the indices of the normal classes:

```
normal_indices = data[data.Class == 0].index
```

Out of the indices we picked, we randomly select x number (`number_records_fraud`):

```
random_normal_indices = np.random.choice(normal_indices,
number_records_fraud, replace = False)
random_normal_indices = np.array(random_normal_indices)
```

We append the two indices:

```
under_sample_indices =
  np.concatenate([fraud_indices,random_normal_indices])
```

Appending the indices under sample dataset:

```
under_sample_data = data.iloc[under_sample_indices,:]
X_undersample = under_sample_data.iloc[:, under_sample_data.columns !=
'Class']
y_undersample = under_sample_data.iloc[:, under_sample_data.columns ==
'Class']
```

On displaying the ratio:

```
print("Percentage of normal transactions: ",
len(under_sample_data[under_sample_data.Class ==
0])/float(len(under_sample_data)))
print("Percentage of fraud transactions: ",
len(under_sample_data[under_sample_data.Class ==
1])/float(len(under_sample_data)))
print("Total number of transactions in resampled data: ",
len(under_sample_data))
```

The output of the preceding code is as follows:

```
('Percentage of normal transactions: ', 0.5)
 ('Percentage of fraud transactions: ', 0.5)
 ('Total number of transactions in resampled data: ', 984)
```

On splitting data into train and test sets, cross-validation will be used when calculating accuracies, as follows:

```
from sklearn.model_selection import train_test_split
# Whole dataset
X_train, X_test, y_train, y_test = train_test_split(X,y,test_size = 0.3,
random_state = 0)
print("Number transactions train dataset: ", len(X_train))
print("Number transactions test dataset: ", len(X_test))
print("Total number of transactions: ", len(X_train)+len(X_test))
# Undersampled dataset
X_train_undersample, X_test_undersample, y_train_undersample,
y_test_undersample = train_test_split(X_undersample,y_undersample,test_size
= 0.3,random_state = 0)
print("")
print("Number transactions train dataset: ", len(X_train_undersample))
print("Number transactions test dataset: ", len(X_test_undersample))
print("Total number of transactions: ",
len(X_train_undersample)+len(X_test_undersample))
```

The following output shows the distribution that we made from the preceding code:

```
('Number transactions train dataset: ', 199364)
('Number transactions test dataset: ', 85443)
('Total number of transactions: ', 284807)
('Number transactions train dataset: ', 688)
('Number transactions test dataset: ', 296)
('Total number of transactions: ', 984)
```

Logistic regression classifier – under-sampled data

We are interested in the recall score, because that is the metric that will help us try to capture the most fraudulent transactions. If you think how accuracy, precision, and recall work for a confusion matrix, recall would be the most interesting because we comprehend a lot more.

- *Accuracy = (TP+TN)/total*, where *TP* depicts true positive, *TN* depicts true negative
- *Precision = TP/(TP+FP)*, where *TP* depicts true positive, *FP* depicts false positive
- *Recall = TP/(TP+FN)*, where *TP* depicts true positive, *TP* depicts true positive, *FN* depicts false negative

The following diagram will help you understand the preceding definitions:

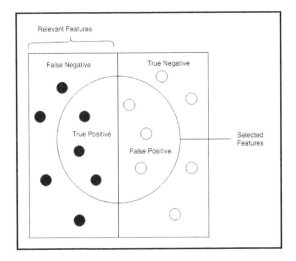

As we know, due to the imbalance of data, many observations could be predicted as False Negatives. However, in our case, that is not so; we do not predict a normal transaction. The transaction is in fact a fraudulent one. We can prove this with the Recall.

- Obviously, trying to increase recall tends to come with a decrease in precision. However, in our case, if we predict that a transaction is fraudulent and it turns out not to be, it is not a massive problem compared to the opposite.
- We could even apply a cost function when having *FN* and *FP* with different weights for each type of error, but let's leave that for now as that will be an overkill for this situation:

```
from sklearn.linear_model import LogisticRegression
from sklearn.model_selection import KFold, cross_val_score,
GridSearchCV
from sklearn.metrics import
confusion_matrix,precision_recall_curve,auc,roc_auc_score,roc_curve
,recall_score,classification_report
```

Ad-hoc function to print `K_fold_scores`:

```
c_param_range = [0.01,0.1,1,10,100]

print("# Tuning hyper-parameters for %s" % score)
print()

clf = GridSearchCV(LogisticRegression(), {"C": c_param_range}, cv=5,
scoring='recall')
clf.fit(X_train_undersample,y_train_undersample)

print "Best parameters set found on development set:"
print
print clf.bestparams

print "Grid scores on development set:"
means = clf.cv_results_['mean_test_score']
stds = clf.cv_results_['std_test_score']
for mean, std, params in zip(means, stds, clf.cv_results_['params']):
 print("%0.3f (+/-%0.03f) for %r"
 % (mean, std * 2, params))

print "Detailed classification report:"
print "The model is trained on the full development set."
print "The scores are computed on the full evaluation set."
y_true, y_pred = y_test, clf.predict(X_test)
print(classification_report(y_true, y_pred))
print()
```

The problem is too easy: the hyperparameter plateau is too flat and the output model is the same for precision and recall with ties in quality.

Tuning hyperparameters

We need to tune hyperparameters for better a recall. Parameter tuning refers to the better fitting of the parameters in a function such that the performance gets better.

The best parameters set found on development set:

```
{'C': 0.01}
```

Grid scores on development set:

```
0.916 (+/-0.056) for {'C': 0.01}
0.907 (+/-0.068) for {'C': 0.1}
0.916 (+/-0.089) for {'C': 1}
0.916 (+/-0.089) for {'C': 10}
0.913 (+/-0.095) for {'C': 100}
```

Detailed classification reports

The model is trained on the full development set. The scores are computed on the full evaluation set. Precision-recall f1-score support:

```
0 1.00 0.96 0.98 85296
 1 0.04 0.93 0.08 147
micro avg 0.96 0.96 0.96 85443
 macro avg 0.52 0.94 0.53 85443
 weighted avg 1.00 0.96 0.98 85443
```

We find the best hyperparameter optimizing for recall:

```
def print_gridsearch_scores(x_train_data,y_train_data):
 c_param_range = [0.01,0.1,1,10,100]

clf = GridSearchCV(LogisticRegression(), {"C": c_param_range}, cv=5,
scoring='recall')
 clf.fit(x_train_data,y_train_data)

print "Best parameters set found on development set:"
print
print clf.bestparams

print "Grid scores on development set:"
```

```
means = clf.cv_results_['mean_test_score']
stds = clf.cv_results_['std_test_score']
for mean, std, params in zip(means, stds, clf.cv_results_['params']):
print "%0.3f (+/-%0.03f) for %r" % (mean, std * 2, params)

return clf.best_params_["C"]
```

We find the best parameters set found on development, as shown here:

```
best_c = print_gridsearch_scores(X_train_undersample,y_train_undersample)
```

The output looks like this:

```
{'C': 0.01}
```

Grid scores on set:

```
0.916 (+/-0.056) for {'C': 0.01}
0.907 (+/-0.068) for {'C': 0.1}
0.916 (+/-0.089) for {'C': 1}
0.916 (+/-0.089) for {'C': 10}
0.913 (+/-0.095) for {'C': 100}
```

Create a function to plot a confusion matrix. This function prints and plots the confusion matrix. Normalization can be applied by setting normalize=True:

```
import itertools

def plot_confusion_matrix(cm, classes,
  normalize=False,
  title='Confusion matrix',
  cmap=plt.cm.Blues):

plt.imshow(cm, interpolation='nearest', cmap=cmap)
  plt.title(title)
  plt.colorbar()
  tick_marks = np.arange(len(classes))
  plt.xticks(tick_marks, classes, rotation=0)
  plt.yticks(tick_marks, classes)

if normalize:
  cm = cm.astype('float') / cm.sum(axis=1)[:, np.newaxis]
  #print("Normalized confusion matrix")
  else:
  1#print('Confusion matrix, without normalization')

thresh = cm.max() / 2.
  for i, j in itertools.product(range(cm.shape[0]), range(cm.shape[1])):
```

```
plt.text(j, i, cm[i, j],
horizontalalignment="center",
color="white" if cm[i, j] > thresh else "black")

plt.tight_layout()
plt.ylabel('True label')
plt.xlabel('Predicted label')
```

Predictions on test sets and plotting a confusion matrix

We have been talking about using the recall metric as our proxy for how effective our predictive model is. Even though recall is still the recall we want to calculate, bear mind in mind that the under-sampled data isn't skewed toward a certain class, which doesn't make the recall metric as critical.

We use this parameter to build the final model with the whole training dataset and predict the classes in the test data:

```
# dataset
lr = LogisticRegression(C = best_c, penalty = 'l1')
lr.fit(X_train_undersample,y_train_undersample.values.ravel())
y_pred_undersample = lr.predict(X_test_undersample.values)
```

Here is the compute confusion matrix:

```
cnf_matrix = confusion_matrix(y_test_undersample,y_pred_undersample)
np.set_printoptions(precision=2)

print("Recall metric in the testing dataset: ",
cnf_matrix[1,1]/(cnf_matrix[1,0]+cnf_matrix[1,1]))
```

We plot the non-normalized confusion matrix as follows:

```
class_names = [0,1]
plt.figure()
plot_confusion_matrix(cnf_matrix, classes=class_names, title='Confusion
matrix')
plt.show()
```

Here is the output for the preceding code:

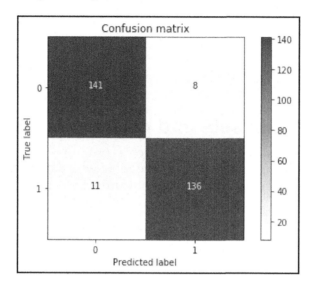

Hence, the model is offering a 92.5% recall accuracy on the generalized unseen data (test set), which is not a bad percentage on the first try. However, keep in mind that this is a 92.5% recall accuracy measure on the under-sampled test set. We will apply the model we fitted and test it on the whole data, as shown:

```
We Use this parameter to build the final model with the whole training
dataset and predict the classes in the test
# dataset
lr = LogisticRegression(C = best_c, penalty = 'l1')
lr.fit(X_train_undersample,y_train_undersample.values.ravel())
y_pred = lr.predict(X_test.values)

# Compute confusion matrix
cnf_matrix = confusion_matrix(y_test,y_pred)
np.set_printoptions(precision=2)

print("Recall metric in the testing dataset: ",
cnf_matrix[1,1]/(cnf_matrix[1,0]+cnf_matrix[1,1]))

# Plot non-normalized confusion matrix
class_names = [0,1]
plt.figure()
plot_confusion_matrix(cnf_matrix, classes=class_names, title='Confusion
matrix')
plt.show()
```

Here is the output from the preceding code:

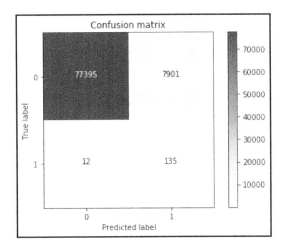

We still have a very decent recall accuracy when applying it to a much larger and skewed dataset. By plotting ROC curve and precision-recall curve, we find that the precision-recall curve is much more convenient as our problems relies on the positive class being more interesting than the negative class, but, as we have calculated the recall precision, we will not plot the precision-recall curves. AUC and ROC curves are also interesting to check whether the model is also predicting as a whole correctly and not making many errors:

```
# ROC CURVE
lr = LogisticRegression(C = best_c, penalty = 'l1')
y_pred_undersample_score =
lr.fit(X_train_undersample,y_train_undersample.values.ravel()).decision_fun
ction(X_test_undersample.values)
fpr, tpr, thresholds =
roc_curve(y_test_undersample.values.ravel(),y_pred_undersample_score)
roc_auc = auc(fpr,tpr)
# Plot ROC
plt.title('Receiver Operating Characteristic')
plt.plot(fpr, tpr, 'b',label='AUC = %0.2f'% roc_auc)
plt.legend(loc='lower right')
plt.plot([0,1],[0,1],'r--')
plt.xlim([-0.1,1.0])
plt.ylim([-0.1,1.01])
plt.ylabel('True Positive Rate')
plt.xlabel('False Positive Rate')
plt.show()
```

We get the following output:

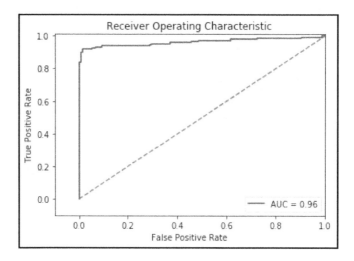

An additional process that would be interesting would be to initialize multiple under-sampled datasets and repeat the process in a loop. Remember: to create an under-sampled dataset, we randomly get records from the majority class. Even though this is a valid technique, it doesn't represent the real population, so it would be interesting to repeat the process with different under-sampled configurations and check whether the previous chosen parameters are still the most effective. In the end, the idea is to use a wider random representation of the whole dataset and rely on the averaged best parameters.

Logistic regression classifier – skewed data

Having tested our previous approach, it is interesting to test the same process on the skewed data. Our intuition is that skewness will introduce issues that are difficult to capture and therefore provide a less effective algorithm.

To be fair, taking into account the fact that the train and test datasets are substantially bigger than the under-sampled ones, it is necessary to have a K-fold cross-validation. We can split the data: 60% for the training set, 20% for cross validation, and 20% for the test data. But let's take the same approach as before (there's no harm in this; it's just that K-fold is computationally more expensive):

```
best_c = print_gridsearch_scores(X_train,y_train)
```

Best parameters set found on development set:

```
{'C': 10}
 Grid scores on development set:
 0.591 (+/-0.121) for {'C': 0.01}
 0.594 (+/-0.076) for {'C': 0.1}
 0.612 (+/-0.106) for {'C': 1}
 0.620 (+/-0.122) for {'C': 10}
 0.620 (+/-0.122) for {'C': 100}
```

Use the preceding parameter to build the final model with the whole training dataset and predict the classes in the test, as follows:

```
# dataset
lr = LogisticRegression(C = best_c, penalty = 'l1')
lr.fit(X_train,y_train.values.ravel())
y_pred_undersample = lr.predict(X_test.values)
# Compute confusion matrix
cnf_matrix = confusion_matrix(y_test,y_pred_undersample)
np.set_printoptions(precision=2)
print("Recall metric in the testing dataset: ",
cnf_matrix[1,1]/(cnf_matrix[1,0]+cnf_matrix[1,1]))
# Plot non-normalized confusion matrix
class_names = [0,1]
plt.figure()
plot_confusion_matrix(cnf_matrix, classes=class_names, title='Confusion
matrix')
plt.show()
```

Here is the output for the confusion matrix:

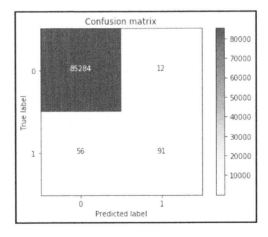

Before continuing, we need to change the classification threshold. We have seen that, by under-sampling the data, our algorithm does a much better job of detecting fraud. We can also tweak our final classification by changing the threshold. Initially, you build the classification model and then you predict unseen data using it. We previously used the predict() method to decide whether a record should belong to 1 or 0. There is another method, predict_proba(). This method returns the probabilities for each class. The idea is that by changing the threshold to assign a record to class 1, we can control precision and recall. Let's check this using the under-sampled data (C_param = 0.01):

```
lr = LogisticRegression(C = 0.01, penalty = 'l1')
lr.fit(X_train_undersample,y_train_undersample.values.ravel())
y_pred_undersample_proba = lr.predict_proba(X_test_undersample.values)
thresholds = [0.1,0.2,0.3,0.4,0.5,0.6,0.7,0.8,0.9]
plt.figure(figsize=(10,10))
j = 1
for i in thresholds:
 y_test_predictions_high_recall = y_pred_undersample_proba[:,1] > i

 plt.subplot(3,3,j)
 j += 1

 # Compute confusion matrix
 cnf_matrix =
confusion_matrix(y_test_undersample,y_test_predictions_high_recall)
 np.set_printoptions(precision=2)
print "Recall metric in the testing dataset for threshold {}: {}".format(i,
cnf_matrix[1,1]/(cnf_matrix[1,0]+cnf_matrix[1,1]))
 # Plot non-normalized confusion matrix
 class_names = [0,1]
 plot_confusion_matrix(cnf_matrix, classes=class_names, title='Threshold >=
%s'%i)
Recall metric in the testing dataset for threshold 0.1: 1.0
 Recall metric in the testing dataset for threshold 0.2: 1.0
 Recall metric in the testing dataset for threshold 0.3: 1.0
 Recall metric in the testing dataset for threshold 0.4: 0.979591836735
 Recall metric in the testing dataset for threshold 0.5: 0.925170068027
 Recall metric in the testing dataset for threshold 0.6: 0.857142857143
 Recall metric in the testing dataset for threshold 0.7: 0.829931972789
 Recall metric in the testing dataset for threshold 0.8: 0.741496598639
 Recall metric in the testing dataset for threshold 0.9: 0.585034013605
 ...
```

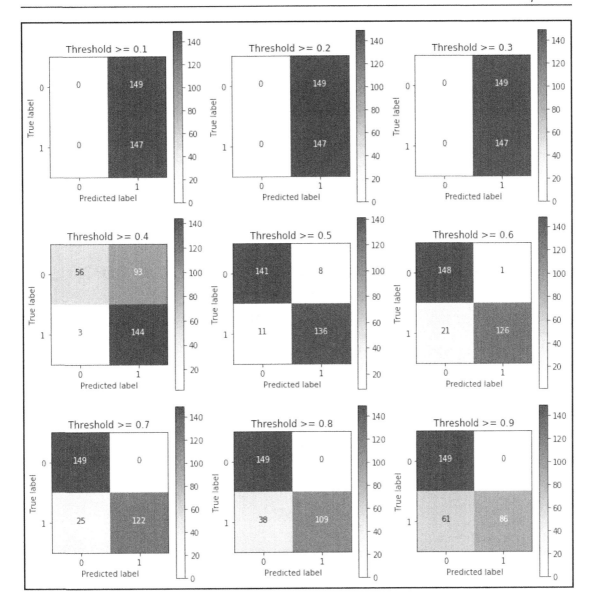

The pattern is very clear. The more you lower the required probability to put a certain in the class 1 category, the more records will be put in that bucket.

This implies an increase in recall (we want all the 1s), but at the same time, a decrease in precision (we misclassify many of the other classes).

Therefore, even though recall is our goal metric (do not miss a fraud transaction), we also want to keep the model being accurate as a whole:

- There is an option which is quite interesting to tackle this. We could assign cost to misclassifications, but being interested in classifying 1s correctly, the cost for misclassifying 1s should be bigger than misclassifying 0s. After that, the algorithm would select the threshold that minimizes the total cost. A drawback here is that we have to manually select the weight of each cost.
- Going back to changing the threshold, there is an option which is the precision-recall curve. By visually inspecting the performance of the model depending on the threshold we choose, we can investigate a sweet spot where recall is high enough while keeping a high precision value.

Investigating precision-recall curve and area

The following the code for investigating precision-recall curve:

```
from itertools import cycle

lr = LogisticRegression(C = 0.01, penalty = 'l1')
lr.fit(X_train_undersample,y_train_undersample.values.ravel())
y_pred_undersample_proba = lr.predict_proba(X_test_undersample.values)

thresholds = [0.1,0.2,0.3,0.4,0.5,0.6,0.7,0.8,0.9]
colors = cycle(['navy', 'turquoise', 'darkorange', 'cornflowerblue',
'teal', 'red', 'yellow', 'green', 'blue','black'])

plt.figure(figsize=(5,5))
j = 1
for i,color in zip(thresholds,colors):
 y_test_predictions_prob = y_pred_undersample_proba[:,1] > i

 precision, recall, thresholds =
precision_recall_curve(y_test_undersample,y_test_predictions_prob)

 # Plot Precision-Recall curve
 plt.plot(recall, precision, color=color,
 label='Threshold: %s'%i)
 plt.xlabel('Recall')
 plt.ylabel('Precision')
 plt.ylim([0.0, 1.05])
 plt.xlim([0.0, 1.0])
 plt.title('Precision-Recall example')
 plt.legend(loc="lower left")
```

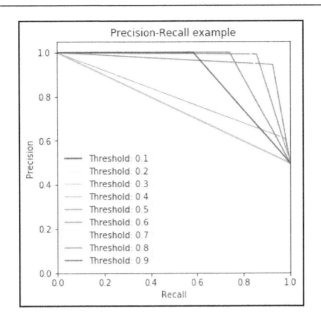

Deep learning time

Finally, we will use deep learning to solve the issue and look for the accuracy of the results. We will take advantage of the `keras` package to use the `Sequential` and `Dense` models, and the `KerasClassifier` packages, as shown in the following code:

```
from keras.models import Sequential
from keras.layers import Dense
from keras.wrappers.scikit_learn import KerasClassifier
```

We change our function to have multiple hidden layers in our network:

```
def network_builder(hidden_dimensions, input_dim):
    # create model
    model = Sequential()
    model.add(Dense(hidden_dimensions[0], input_dim=input_dim,
kernel_initializer='normal', activation='relu'))
    # add multiple hidden layers
    for dimension in hidden_dimensions[1:]:
        model.add(Dense(dimension, kernel_initializer='normal',
activation='relu'))
        model.add(Dense(1, kernel_initializer='normal',
activation='sigmoid'))
```

We will compile the model, use the logarithmic loss function, and the Adam gradient optimizer (which will be described in the next section).

Adam gradient optimizer

```
model.compile(loss='binary_crossentropy', optimizer='adam',
metrics=['accuracy'])
  return model
```

We find the best hyperparameter optimizing for recall:

```
def print_gridsearch_scores_deep_learning(x_train_data,y_train_data):
  c_param_range = [0.01,0.1,1,10,100]

clf = GridSearchCV(KerasClassifier(build_fn=network_builder, epochs=50,
batch_size=128,
  verbose=1, input_dim=29),
  {"hidden_dimensions": ([10], [10, 10, 10], [100, 10])}, cv=5,
scoring='recall')
  clf.fit(x_train_data,y_train_data)

print "Best parameters set found on development set:"
  print
  print clf.bestparams

print "Grid scores on development set:"
  means = clf.cv_results_['mean_test_score']
  stds = clf.cv_results_['std_test_score']
  for mean, std, params in zip(means, stds, clf.cv_results_['params']):
  print "%0.3f (+/-%0.03f) for %r" % (mean, std * 2, params)
```

Finally, as shown, we print the scores from the deep learning model:

```
print_gridsearch_scores_deep_learning(X_train_undersample,
y_train_undersample)

Epoch 1/50
 550/550 [==============================] - 2s 3ms/step - loss: 0.7176 -
acc: 0.2673
 Epoch 2/50
 550/550 [==============================] - 0s 25us/step - loss: 0.6955 -
acc: 0.4582
 Epoch 3/50
 550/550 [==============================] - 0s 41us/step - loss: 0.6734 -
acc: 0.6327
 Epoch 4/50
 550/550 [==============================] - 0s 36us/step - loss: 0.6497 -
```

```
acc: 0.6491
 Epoch 5/50
 550/550 [==============================] - 0s 43us/step - loss: 0.6244 -
acc: 0.6655
```

This produces the following output:

```
{'hidden_dimensions': [100, 10]}
Grid scores on development set:
0.903 (+/-0.066) for {'hidden_dimensions': [10]}
0.897 (+/-0.070) for {'hidden_dimensions': [10, 10, 10]}
0.912 (+/-0.079) for {'hidden_dimensions': [100, 10]}
```

We use this `hidden_dimensions` parameter to build the final model with the whole training dataset and predict the classes in the test dataset:

```
k = KerasClassifier(build_fn=network_builder, epochs=50, batch_size=128,
 hidden_dimensions=[100, 10], verbose=0, input_dim=29)
k.fit(X_train_undersample,y_train_undersample.values.ravel())
y_pred_undersample = k.predict(X_test_undersample.values)

# Compute confusion matrix
cnf_matrix = confusion_matrix(y_test_undersample,y_pred_undersample)
np.set_printoptions(precision=2)

print("Recall metric in the testing dataset: ",
cnf_matrix[1,1]/(cnf_matrix[1,0]+cnf_matrix[1,1]))

# Plot non-normalized confusion matrix
class_names = [0,1]
plt.figure()
plot_confusion_matrix(cnf_matrix, classes=class_names, title='Confusion
matrix')
plt.show()
```

We get the following output from the preceding code:

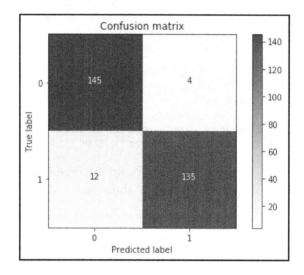

```
y_pred = k.predict(X_test.values)

# Compute confusion matrix
cnf_matrix = confusion_matrix(y_test,y_pred)
np.set_printoptions(precision=2)

print("Recall metric in the testing dataset: ",
cnf_matrix[1,1]/(cnf_matrix[1,0]+cnf_matrix[1,1]))

# Plot non-normalized confusion matrix
class_names = [0,1]
plt.figure()
plot_confusion_matrix(cnf_matrix, classes=class_names, title='Confusion
matrix')
plt.show()
```

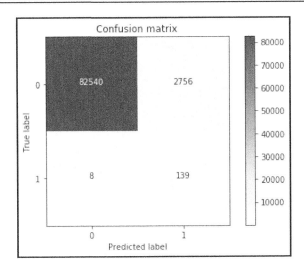

From the preceding graph, we know that this is the best recall so far that we've seen on the entire dataset, thanks to deep learning.

Summary

In this chapter, we used machine learning to detect financial fraud by handling imbalanced datasets. We also covered random under-sampling and oversampling. We looked at SMOTE as well as the modified version of SMOTE. Then we learned about detecting credit card fraud, which includes the logistic regression classifier and tuning hyperparameters.

This chapter also explained deep learning time as well as the Adam gradient optimizer. In the next chapter, we will explore a few different cybersecurity case studies.

11
Case Studies

In this day and age, password security is sometimes our first line of defence against malicious activity. SplashData recently released the worst passwords of 2018 by analyzing over 5,000,000 leaked passwords and looking at the most-used passwords. The top-10 list looks like this:

- 123456
- password
- 123456789
- 12345678
- 12345
- 111111
- 1234567
- sunshine
- qwerty
- iloveyou

SplashData had released this list annually in an effort to encourage people to use more secure passwords.

If you or someone you know uses a password on this list for any purpose, change it immediately!

In this chapter, we will follow in the footsteps of SplashData and perform our own password analysis on over 1,000,000 passwords that were leaked for one reason or another. We will study the following topics:

Introduction to our password dataset

Let's begin with the basics. We'll import our dataset and get a sense of the quantity of data that we are working with. We will do this by using pandas to import our data:

```
# pandas is a powerful Python-based data package that can handle large
quantities of row/column data
# we will use pandas many times during these videos. a 2D group of data in
pandas is called a 'DataFrame'

# import pandas
import pandas as pd

# use the read_csv method to read in a local file of leaked passwords
# here we specify `header=None` so that that there is no header in the file
(no titles of columns)
# we also specify that if any row gives us an error, skip over it (this is
done in error_bad_lines=False)
data = pd.read_csv('../data/passwords.txt', header=None,
error_bad_lines=False)
```

Now that we have our data imported, let's call on the shape method of the DataFrame to see how many rows and columns we have:

```
# shape attribute gives us tuple of (# rows, # cols)

# 1,048,489 passwords
print data.shape

(1048489, 1)
```

Since we only have one column to worry about (the actual text of the password), as a good practice, let's call on the dropna method of the DataFrame to remove any null values:

```
# the dropna method will remove any null values from our dataset. We have
to include the inplace in order for the
# change to take effect
data.dropna(inplace=True)

# still 1,048,485 passwords after dropping null values
print data.shape
(1048485, 1)
```

We only lost four passwords. Now let's take a look at what we are working with. Let's ensure proper nomenclature and change the name of our only column to text and call on the head method:

```
# let's change the name of our columns to make it make more sense
data.columns = ['text']

# the head method will return the first n rows (default 5)

data.head()
```

Running the head method reveals the first five passwords in our dataset:

	Text
0	7606374520
1	piontekendre
2	rambo144
3	primoz123
4	sal1387

Let's isolate our only column as a pandas 1-D Series object and call the variable as text. Once we have our series object in hand, we can use value_counts to see the most common passwords in our dataset:

```
# we will grab a single column from our DataFrame.
# A 1-Dimensional version of a DataFrame is called a Series
text = data['text']

# show the type of the variable text
print type(text)

# the value_counts method will count the unique elements of a Series or
DataFrame and show the most used passwords
# in this case, no password repeats itself more than 2 times
text.value_counts()[:10]
```

```
0          21
123        12
1          10
123456      8
8           8
5           7
2           7
1230        7
```

```
123456789        7
12345            6
```

This is interesting because we see some expected passwords (`12345`), but also odd because, usually, most sites would not allow one-character passwords. Therefore, in order to get a better picture, we will have to do some manual feature extraction.

Text feature extraction

In this section, we will start to manually create some features in order to quantify our textual passwords. Let's first create a new column in the data DataFrame called `length`, which will represent the length of the password:

```
# 1. the length of the password

# on the left of the equal sign, note we are defining a new column called
'length'. We want this column to hold the
# length of the password.

# on the right of the equal sign, we use the apply method of pandas
Series/DFs. We will apply a function (len in this case)
# to every element in the column 'text'

data['length'] = data['text'].apply(len)

# see our changes take effect
data.head()
```

Here is the output:

	Text	Length
0	7606374520	10
1	piontekendre	12
2	rambo144	8
3	primoz123	9
4	sal1387	7

Let's use this new column to see the most common passwords of five or more characters:

```
# top passwords of length 5 or more
data[data.length > 4]["text"].value_counts()[:10]

123456           8
123456789        7
12345            6
```

```
43162          5
7758521        5
11111          5
5201314        5
111111         4
123321         4
102030         4
```

These seem more like what we expected; we even see `111111`, which was on the list we saw at the beginning of this chapter. We continue now by adding another column, `num_caps`, that will count the number of capital letters in the password. This will eventually give us some insight into the strength of a password:

```
# store a new column
data['num_caps'] = data['text'].apply(caps)

# see our changes take effect
data.head(10)
```

We can now see our two new columns, both of which give us some quantifiable means of assessing password strength. Longer passwords with more capital letters *tend* to correlate to stronger passwords. But of course this is not the whole picture:

	Text	Length	num_caps
0	7606374520	10	0
1	piontekendre	12	0
2	rambo144	8	0
3	primoz123	9	0
4	sal1387	7	0
5	EVASLRDG	8	8
6	Detroit84	9	1
7	dlbd090505	10	0
8	snoesje12	9	0
9	56412197	8	0

We can visualize this data as a histogram of capital letters in passwords to see the distribution of the count of capital letters, which will give us a better sense of the overall usage of caps:

```
data['num_caps'].hist() # most passwords do not have any caps in them
```

Running this code will yield the following histogram, revealing a right skew of capital letters, meaning that most people stay on the lower end of capital letters:

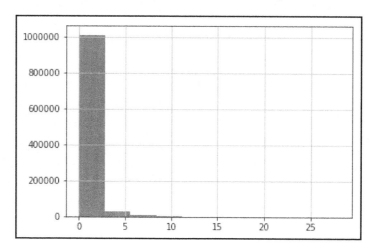

Calling the `describe` method of the DataFrame will reveal some high-level descriptive statistics about our data:

```
# grab some basic descriptive statistics
data.describe()
```

Here is the output:

	Length	num_caps
count	1.048485e+06	1.048485e+06
mean	8.390173e+00	2.575392e-01
std	2.269470e+01	1.205588e+00
min	1.000000e+00	0.000000e+00
25%	7.000000e+00	0.000000e+00
50%	8.000000e+00	0.000000e+00
75%	9.000000e+00	0.000000e+00
max	8.192000e+03	2.690000e+02

The `max` row of the length attribute is telling us that we have some massive passwords (over 8,000 characters). We will isolate the passwords that are over 100 characters:

```
# let's see our long passwords
data[data.length > 100]
```

The long passwords can be seen here:

	Text	Length	num_caps
38830	`><script>alert(1)</script>\r123Lenda#\rhallibu...`	8192	242
387398	`\r251885394\rmello2\rmaitre1123\rfk6Ehruu\rthi...`	8192	176
451793	`39<0Y~c.;A1Bj\r3ddd4t\r516ks516\rag0931266\rac...`	8192	223
517600	`12345\rhdjcb100\r060571\rkaalimaa\rrelaxmax\rd...`	8192	184
580134	`or1=1--\r13817676085\r594112\rmactools\r880148...`	8192	216
752693	`pass\rmbmb266888\r1988luolin\r15877487956\rcri...`	8192	180
841857	`==)!)(=\raviral\rrimmir33\rhutcheson\rrr801201...`	8192	269
1013991	`AAj6H\rweebeth\rmonitor222\rem1981\ralexs123\r...`	8192	269

We can clearly see that eight of the rows of our DataFrame became malformed. To make this a bit easier, let's use pandas to get rid of these eight problematic rows. We could do work to sanitize this data; however, this case study will focus on deeper insights:

```
print data[data.length > 100].shape # only 8 rows that became malformed
# to make this easy, let's just drop those problematic rows

# we will drop passwords that are way too long
data.drop(data[data.length > 100].index, axis=0, inplace=True)
(8, 3)


# 1,048,485 - 8 == 1,048,477 makes sense
print data.shape
(1048477, 3)


data.describe()
```

The following table is the output of the preceding code:

	Length	num_caps
count	1.048477e+06	1.048477e+06
mean	8.327732e+00	2.558635e-01
std	2.012173e+00	1.037190e+00

	Length	num_caps
min	1.000000e+00	0.000000e+00
25%	7.000000e+00	0.000000e+00
50%	8.000000e+00	0.000000e+00
75%	9.000000e+00	0.000000e+00
max	2.900000e+01	2.800000e+01

We will now turn to scikit-learn to add some automatic feature extraction.

Feature extraction with scikit-learn

We have seen the power of scikit-learn in this book, and this chapter will be no different. Let's import the `CountVectorizer` module to quickly count the occurrences of phrases in our text:

```
# The CountVectorizer is from sklearn's text feature extraction module
# the feature extraction module as a whole contains many tools built for
extracting features from data.
# Earlier, we manually extracted data by applying functions such as
num_caps, special_characters, and so on

# The CountVectorizer module specifically is built to quickly count
occurrences of phrases within pieces of text
from sklearn.feature_extraction.text import CountVectorizer
```

We will start by simply creating an instance of `CountVectorizer` with two specific parameters. We will set the analyzer to char so that we count phrases of characters rather than words. ngram_range will be set to (1, 1) to grab only single-character occurrences:

```
one_cv = CountVectorizer(ngram_range=(1, 1), analyzer='char')

# The fit_transform method to learn the vocabulary and then
# transform our text series into a matrix which we will call
one_char
# Previously we created a matrix of quantitative data by applying
our own functions, now we are creating numerical matrices using
sklearn


one_char = one_cv.fit_transform(text)
# Note it is a sparse matrix
# there are 70 unique chars (number of columns)
<1048485x70 sparse matrix of type '<type 'numpy.int64'>'
  with 6935190 stored elements in Compressed Sparse Row format>
```

Note the number of rows reflects the number of passwords we have been working with, and the 70 columns reflect the 70 different and unique characters found in the corpus:

```
# we can peak into the learned vocabulary of the CountVectorizer by calling
the vocabulary_ attribute of the CV

# the keys are the learned phrases while the values represent a unique
index used by the CV to keep track of the vocab
one_cv.vocabulary_

{u'\r': 0,
 u' ': 1,
 u'!': 2,
 u'"': 3,
 u'#': 4,
 u'$': 5,
 u'%': 6,
 u'&': 7,
 u"'": 8,
 u'(': 9,
 u')': 10,
 u'*': 11,
 u'+': 12,
 u',': 13,
 u'-': 14,
 u'.': 15,
 u'/': 16,
 u'0': 17,
 u'1': 18,
 u'2': 19,
 u'3': 20,
 u'4': 21,
 u'5': 22,
 u'6': 23,
 u'7': 24,
 u'8': 25,
 u'9': 26,
 u':': 27,
 u';': 28,
 u'<': 29,
 u'=': 30,
 ...
# Note that is auto lowercases!
```

We have all of these characters including letters, punctuation, and more. We should also note that there are no capital letters found anywhere in this vocabulary; this is due to the CountVectorizer auto-lowercase feature. Let's follow the same procedure, but this time, let's turn off the auto-lowercase feature that comes with CountVectorizer:

```
# now with lowercase=False, this way we will not force the lowercasing of
characters
one_cv = CountVectorizer(ngram_range=(1, 1), analyzer='char',
lowercase=False)


one_char = one_cv.fit_transform(text)

one_char

# there are now 96 unique chars (number of columns) ( 26 letters more :) )

<1048485x96 sparse matrix of type '<type 'numpy.int64'>'
   with 6955519 stored elements in Compressed Sparse Row format>
```

We get the following output:

```
one_cv.vocabulary_

{u'\r': 0,
 u' ': 1,
 u'!': 2,
 u'"': 3,
 u'#': 4,
 u'$': 5,
 u'%': 6,
 u'&': 7,
 u"'": 8,
 u'(': 9,
 u')': 10,
 u'*': 11,
 u'+': 12,
 u',': 13,
 u'-': 14,
 u'.': 15,
 u'/': 16,
 u'0': 17,
 u'1': 18,
 u'2': 19,
 u'3': 20,
 . . . . .
```

We have our capital letters now included in our attributes. This is evident when we count 26 more letters (70 to 96) in our vocabulary attribute. With our vectorizer, we can use it to transform new pieces of text, as shown:

```
# transforming a new password
pd.DataFrame(one_cv.transform(['qwerty123!!!']).toarray(),
columns=one_cv.get_feature_names())

# cannot learn new vocab. If we introduce a new character, wouldn't matter
```

The following shows the output:

		!	"	#	$	%	&	'	(	...	u	v	w	x	y	z	{	|	}	~
0	0	0	3	0	0	0	0	0	0	...	0	0	1	0	1	0	0	0	0	0

It is important to remember that once a vectorizer is fit, it cannot learn new vocabulary; for example:

```
print "~" in one_cv.vocabulary_
True

print "D" in one_cv.vocabulary_
True

print "\t" in one_cv.vocabulary_
False

# transforming a new password (adding \t [the tab character] into the mix)
pd.DataFrame(one_cv.transform(['qw\terty123!!!']).toarray(),
columns=one_cv.get_feature_names())
```

We get the following output:

!	"	#	$	%	'	(	...	u	v	w	x	y	z	{	|	}	~			
0	0	0	3	0	0	0	0	0	...	0	0	1	0	1	0	0	0	0	0	0

We end up with the same matrix even though the second password had a new character in it. Let's expand our universe by allowing for up to five-character phrases. This will count occurrences of unique one-, two-, three-, four-, and five-character phrases now. We should expect to see our vocabulary explode:

```
# now let's count all 1, 2, 3, 4, and 5 character phrases
five_cv = CountVectorizer(ngram_range=(1, 5), analyzer='char')

five_char = five_cv.fit_transform(text)
```

```
five_char
# there are 2,570,934 unique combo of up to 5-in-a-row-char phrases

<1048485x2570934 sparse matrix of type '<type 'numpy.int64'>'
  with 31053193 stored elements in Compressed Sparse Row format>
```

We went from 70 (we didn't turn off auto-lowercase) to 2,570,934 columns:

```
# much larger vocabulary!

five_cv.vocabulary_

{u'uer24': 2269299,
 u'uer23': 2269298,
 u'uer21': 2269297,
 u'uer20': 2269296,
 u'a4uz5': 640686,
 u'rotai': 2047903,
 u'hd20m': 1257873,
 u'i7n5': 1317982,
 u'fkhb8': 1146472,
 u'juy9f': 1460014,
 u'xodu': 2443742,
 u'xodt': 2443740,
```

We will turn off the lowercase to see how many unique phrases we can get:

```
# now let's count all 1, 2, 3, 4, and 5 character phrases
five_cv_lower = CountVectorizer(ngram_range=(1, 5), analyzer='char',
lowercase=False)

five_char_lower = five_cv_lower.fit_transform(text)

five_char_lower
# there are 2,922,297 unique combo of up to 5-in-a-row-char phrases

<1048485x2922297 sparse matrix of type '<type 'numpy.int64'>'
  with 31080917 stored elements in Compressed Sparse Row format>
```

With lowercase off, our vocabulary grows to 2,922,297 items. We will use this data to extract the most common phrases in our corpus that are up to five characters. Note that this is different from our `value_counts` before. Previously, we were counting the most common whole passwords whereas, now, we are counting the most common phrases that occur *within* the passwords:

```
# let's grab the most common five char "phrases"
# we will accomplish this by using numpy to do some quick math
import numpy as np
```

```
# first we will sum across the rows of our data to get the total count of
phrases
summed_features = np.sum(five_char, axis=0)

print summed_features.shape . # == (1, 2570934)

# we will then sort the summed_features variable and grab the 20 most
common phrases' indices in the CV's vocabulary
top_20 = np.argsort(summed_features)[:,-20:]

top_20 # == (1, 2570934)

matrix([[1619465, 2166552, 1530799, 1981845, 2073035, 297134, 457130,
406411, 1792848, 352276, 1696853, 562360, 508193, 236639, 1308517, 994777,
36326, 171634, 629003, 100177]])
```

This gives us the indices (from 0 to 2570933) of the most-commonly occurring phrases that are up to five characters. To see the actual phrases, let's plug them into the `get_feature_names` method of our `CountVectorizer`, as shown:

```
# plug these into the features of the CV.

# sorting is done in ascending order so '1' is the most common phrase,
followed by 'a'
np.array(five_cv.get_feature_names())[top_20]


array([[u'm', u't', u'l', u'r', u's', u'4', u'7', u'6', u'o', u'5', u'n',
       u'9', u'8', u'3', u'i', u'e', u'0', u'2', u'a', u'1']],
      dtype='<U5')
```

Unsurprisingly, the most common one- to five-character phrases are single characters (letters and numbers). Let's expand to see the most common 50 phrases:

```
# top 50 phrases
np.array(five_cv.get_feature_names())[np.argsort(summed_features)[:,-50:]]

array([[u'13', u'98', u'ng', u'21', u'01', u'er', u'in', u'20', u'10',
       u'x', u'11', u'v', u'23', u'00', u'19', u'z', u'an', u'j', u'w',
       u'f', u'12', u'p', u'y', u'b', u'k', u'g', u'h', u'c', u'd',
       u'u', u'm', u't', u'l', u'r', u's', u'4', u'7', u'6', u'o', u'5',
       u'n', u'9', u'8', u'3', u'i', u'e', u'0', u'2', u'a', u'1']],
      dtype='<U5')
```

Now we start to see two-character phrases. Let's expand even more to the top 100 phrases:

```
# top 100 phrases
np.array(five_cv.get_feature_names())[np.argsort(summed_features)[:,-100:]]
```

```
array([[u'61', u'33', u'50', u'07', u'18', u'41', u'198', u'09', u'el',
        u'80', u'lo', u'05', u're', u'ch', u'ia', u'03', u'90', u'89',
        u'91', u'08', u'32', u'56', u'81', u'16', u'25', u'la', u'le',
        u'51', u'as', u'34', u'al', u'45', u'ra', u'30', u'14', u'15',
        u'02', u'ha', u'99', u'52', u'li', u'88', u'31', u'22', u'on',
        u'123', u'ma', u'en', u'ar', u'q', u'13', u'98', u'ng', u'21',
        u'01', u'er', u'in', u'20', u'10', u'x', u'11', u'v', u'23',
        u'00', u'19', u'z', u'an', u'j', u'w', u'f', u'12', u'p', u'y',
        u'b', u'k', u'g', u'h', u'c', u'd', u'u', u'm', u't', u'l', u'r',
        u's', u'4', u'7', u'6', u'o', u'5', u'n', u'9', u'8', u'3', u'i',
        u'e', u'0', u'2', u'a', u'1']], dtype='<U5')
```

To get a more sensical phrases used in passwords, let's make a new vectorizer with lowercase set to `False`, and `ngram_range` set to (4, 7). This is done to avoid single-character phrases and we will try to get more context into what kinds of themes occur in the most common passwords:

```
seven_cv = CountVectorizer(ngram_range=(4, 7), analyzer='char',
lowercase=False)

seven_char = seven_cv.fit_transform(text)

seven_char

<1048485x7309977 sparse matrix of type '<type 'numpy.int64'>'
    with 16293052 stored elements in Compressed Sparse Row format>
```

With our vectorizer built and fit, let's use it to grab the 100 most common four- to seven-character phrases:

```
summed_features = np.sum(seven_char, axis=0)

# top 100 tokens of length 4-7
np.array(seven_cv.get_feature_names())[np.argsort(summed_features)[:,-100:]
]
```

```
array([[u'1011', u'star', u'56789', u'g123', u'ming', u'long', u'ang1',
        u'2002', u'3123', u'ing1', u'201314', u'2003', u'1992', u'2004',
        u'1122', u'ling', u'2001', u'20131', u'woai', u'lian', u'feng',
        u'2345678', u'1212', u'1101', u'01314', u'o123', u'345678',
        u'ever', u's123', u'uang', u'1010', u'1980', u'huan', u'i123',
        u'king', u'mari', u'2005', u'hong', u'6789', u'1981', u'00000',
```

```
u'45678', u'2013', u'11111', u'1991', u'1231', u'ilove',
u'admin', u'ilov', u'ange', u'2006', u'0131', u'admi', u'heng',
u'1234567', u'5201', u'e123', u'234567', u'dmin', u'pass',
u'8888', u'34567', u'zhang', u'jian', u'2007', u'5678', u'1982',
u'2000', u'zhan', u'yang', u'n123', u'1983', u'4567', u'1984',
u'1990', u'a123', u'2009', u'ster', u'1985', u'iang', u'2008',
u'2010', u'xiao', u'chen', u'hang', u'wang', u'1986', u'1111',
u'1989', u'0000', u'1988', u'1987', u'1314', u'love', u'123456',
u'23456', u'3456', u'12345', u'2345', u'1234']], dtype='<U7')
```

Words and numbers stick out immediately, such as the following:

- `pass`, `1234`, `56789` (easy phrases to remember)
- `1980`, `1991`, `1992`, `2003`, `2004`, and so on (likely years of birth)
- `ilove`, `love`
- `yang`, `zhan`, `hong` (names)

To get an even better sense of interesting phrases, let's use the TF-IDF vectorizer in scikit-learn to isolate rare phrases that are interesting and, therefore, likely better to use in passwords:

```
# Term Frequency-Inverse Document Frequency (TF-IDF)

# What: Computes "relative frequency" of a word that appears in a document
compared to its frequency across all documents

# Why: More useful than "term frequency" for identifying "important"
words/phrases in each document (high frequency in that document, low
frequency in other documents)

from sklearn.feature_extraction.text import TfidfVectorizer
```

 TF-IDF is commonly used for search-engine scoring, text summarization, and document clustering

We will begin by creating a vectorizer similar to the `CountVectorizer` we made earlier. `ngram_range` will be set to (1, 1) and the analyzer will be `char`:

```
one_tv = TfidfVectorizer(ngram_range=(1, 1), analyzer='char')

# once we instantiate the module, we will call upon the fit_transform
method to learn the vocabulary and then
# transform our text series into a brand new matrix called one_char
```

```
# Previously we created a matrix of quantitative data by applying our own
functions, now we are creating numerical
# matrices using sklearn
one_char_tf = one_tv.fit_transform(text)

# same shape as CountVectorizer
one_char_tf

<1048485x70 sparse matrix of type '<type 'numpy.float64'>'
   with 6935190 stored elements in Compressed Sparse Row format>
```

Let's use this new vectorizer to transform `qwerty123`:

```
# transforming a new password
pd.DataFrame(one_tv.transform(['qwerty123']).toarray(),
columns=one_tv.get_feature_names())
```

We get the following output:

!	"	#	$	%	&	'	(	...	u	v	w	x	y	z	{			}	~		
0	0.0	0.0	0.0	0.0	0.0	0.0	0.0	0.0	0.0	0.0	...		0.0	0.0	0.408704	0.0	0.369502	0.0	0.0	0.0	0.0	0.0

The values in the table are no longer counts anymore; they are calculations involving relative frequency. Higher values indicate that the phrase is either—or both—of the following:

- Used frequently in this password
- Used infrequently throughout the corpus of passwords

Let's build a more complex vectorizer with phrases learned up to five characters:

```
# make a five-char TfidfVectorizer
five_tv = TfidfVectorizer(ngram_range=(1, 5), analyzer='char')

five_char_tf = five_tv.fit_transform(text)

# same shape as CountVectorizer
five_char_tf

<1048485x2570934 sparse matrix of type '<type 'numpy.float64'>'
   with 31053193 stored elements in Compressed Sparse Row format>
```

Let's use this new vectorizer to transform the simple `abc123` password:

```
# Let's see some tfidf values of passwords

# store the feature names as a numpy array
features = np.array(five_tv.get_feature_names())
```

```
# transform a very simple password
abc_transformed = five_tv.transform(['abc123'])

# grab the non zero features that is, the ngrams that actually exist
features[abc_transformed.nonzero()[1]]
```

```
array([u'c123', u'c12', u'c1', u'c', u'bc123', u'bc12', u'bc1', u'bc',
       u'b', u'abc12', u'abc1', u'abc', u'ab', u'a', u'3', u'23', u'2',
       u'123', u'12', u'1'], dtype='<U5')
```

We will look at the non-zero `tfidf` scores, as shown:

```
# grab the non zero tfidf scores of the features
abc_transformed[abc_transformed.nonzero()]
```

```
matrix([[0.28865293, 0.27817216, 0.23180301, 0.10303378, 0.33609531,
         0.33285593, 0.31079987, 0.23023187, 0.11165455, 0.33695385,
         0.31813905, 0.25043863, 0.18481603, 0.07089031, 0.08285116,
         0.13324432, 0.07449711, 0.15211427, 0.12089443, 0.06747844]])
```

```
# put them together in a DataFrame
pd.DataFrame(abc_transformed[abc_transformed.nonzero()],
             columns=features[abc_transformed.nonzero()[1]])
```

Running the preceding code yields the table where you will find that the phrase 1 has a TF-IDF score of 0.067478 while bc123 has a score of 0.336095, implying that bc123 is more interesting than 1, which makes sense:

```
# Let's repeat the process with a slightly better password
password_transformed = five_tv.transform(['sdf%ERF'])

# grab the non zero features
features[password_transformed.nonzero()[1]]

# grab the non zero tfidf scores of the features
password_transformed[password_transformed.nonzero()]

# put them together in a DataFrame
pd.DataFrame(password_transformed[password_transformed.nonzero()],
columns=features[password_transformed.nonzero()[1]])
```

Running the preceding code yields a table in which the larger TF-IDF values is `%er` versus `123` that is, (0.453607 versus 0.152114). This implies that `%er` is more interesting and occurs less often across the entire corpus. Also note that the TF-IDF value of `%er` is larger than anything found in the `abc123` password, implying that this phrase alone is more interesting than anything found in `abc123`.

Let's take all of this a step further and introduce a mathematical function called the cosine similarity to judge the strength of new passwords that haven't been seen before.

Using the cosine similarity to quantify bad passwords

In this section, we will turn to some purely mathematical reasoning to judge password strength. We will use tools from scikit-learn to learn and understand password strength by comparing them to past passwords using vector similarities.

Cosine similarity is a quantitative measure *[-1,1]* of how similar two vectors are in a Vector Space. The closer they are to each other, the smaller the angle between them. The smaller the angle between them, the larger the cosine of that angle is; for example:

- If two vectors are opposites of each other, their angle is 180, and cos(0) = -1.
- If two vectors are the same, their angle is 0, and cos(0) = 1.
- If two vectors are perpendicular, their angle is 90, and cos(90) = 0. In the text world, we'd say that these documents are unrelated.

The following diagram shows the **Cosine Similarity**:

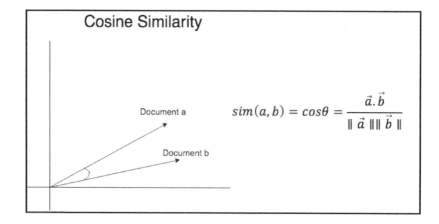

The goal now is to build a tool that takes in a password from a user and will spit back an assessment of how powerful that password is. This can be done many ways through various approaches. We will propose one now:

- Vectorize past passwords given to us in our dataset (through some scikit-learn vectorizer).
- Use the cosine similarity to judge the similarity between a given password and past passwords. The closer the given password is to past passwords, the worse we rank the password attempt.

Let's import an implementation of cosine similarity from scikit-learn:

```
from sklearn.metrics.pairwise import cosine_similarity
# number between -1 and 1 (-1 is dissimilar, 1 is very similar (the same))
```

We have already built a vectorizer, so let's bring it back. We can then use the `cosine_similarity` module to see the similarities between different passwords/strings:

```
five_cv

CountVectorizer(analyzer='char', binary=False, decode_error=u'strict',
        dtype=<type 'numpy.int64'>, encoding=u'utf-8', input=u'content',
        lowercase=True, max_df=1.0, max_features=None, min_df=1,
        ngram_range=(1, 5), preprocessor=None, stop_words=None,
        strip_accents=None, token_pattern=u'(?u)\\b\\w\\w+\\b',
        tokenizer=None, vocabulary=None)


# similar phrases
print cosine_similarity(five_cv.transform(["helo there"]),
five_cv.transform(["hello there"]))[[0.88873334]]

# not similar phrases
print cosine_similarity(five_cv.transform(["sddgnkjfnsdlkfjnwe4r"]),
five_cv.transform(["hello there"]))
[[0.08520286]]
```

Let's say we want to judge how good the `qwerty123` password is. We will first store it as a variable called `attempted_password`. We will then use our similarity metric on the **entire** password corpus:

```
# store a password that we may want to use in a variable
attempted_password="qwerty123"

cosine_similarity(five_cv.transform([attempted_password]), five_char).shape
# == (1, 1048485)
```

```
# this array holds the cosine similarity of attempted_password and every
other password in our corpus. We can use the max method to find the
password that is the closest in similarity

# use cosine similarity to find the closest password in our dataset to our
attempted password
# qwerty123 is a literal exact password :(
cosine_similarity(five_cv.transform([attempted_password]), five_char).max()
```

```
1.0000
```

It looks like `qwerty123` is a password that occurs as in the corpus. So it's probably not a great password to use. We can repeat the process on a slightly longer password, as shown in the following code:

```
# lets make it harder
attempted_password="qwertyqwerty123456234"

# still pretty similar to other passwords..
cosine_similarity(five_cv.transform([attempted_password]), five_char).max()
```

```
0.88648200215
```

How about using a password that is mostly a random assortment of characters, as shown here:

```
# fine lets make it even harder
attempted_password="asfkKwrvn#%^&@Gfgg"

# much better!
cosine_similarity(five_cv.transform([attempted_password]), five_char).max()
```

```
0.553302871668
```

Instead of finding the single closest password in our corpus, let's take the top 20 closest passwords and take the average similarity of them. This will give us a more holistic similarity metric.

We can think of this as a modified KNN in that we use a similarity metric to find the closest training observations. Instead of them using this information for classification or regression, we use it to inform our own judgements about password strength.

The following code shows the top 20 most-used similar password mean score:

```
# use the top 20 most similar password mean score
attempted_password="qwerty123"

raw_vectorization =
cosine_similarity(five_cv.transform([attempted_password]), five_char)
raw_vectorization[:,np.argsort(raw_vectorization)[0,-20:]].mean()


0.8968577221
```

The following code shows the top 20 most-used similar password mean score:

```
# use the top 20 most similar password mean score with another password
attempted_password="asfkKwrvn#%^&@Gfgg"

raw_vectorization =
cosine_similarity(five_cv.transform([attempted_password]), five_char)
raw_vectorization[:,np.argsort(raw_vectorization)[0,-20:]].mean()


0.4220207825
```

It is easy to see that smaller values imply better passwords, which are not similar to passwords in our training set, and are therefore more unique and harder to guess.

Putting it all together

To make all of our hard work easier to use, we need to pack it all up into a single, neat function, as shown:

```
# remake a simple two char CV
two_cv = CountVectorizer(ngram_range=(1, 2), analyzer='char',
lowercase=False)

two_char = two_cv.fit_transform(text)

two_char
# there are 7,528 unique 2-in-a-row-chars (number of columns)

<1048485x7528 sparse matrix of type '<type 'numpy.int64'>'
    with 14350326 stored elements in Compressed Sparse Row format>


# make a simple function using the two_char CV and matrix
def get_closest_word_similarity(password):
  raw_vectorization = cosine_similarity(two_cv.transform([password]),
```

```
two_char)
   return raw_vectorization[:,np.argsort(raw_vectorization)[0,-20:]].mean()
```

This function makes it easier to judge passwords quickly:

```
print get_closest_word_similarity("guest123") # very close to passwords in
the db

0.789113817

print get_closest_word_similarity("sdfFSKSJNDFKFSD3253245sadSDF@@$@#$") #
not very close to passwords in the db

0.47148393
```

We can take this one step further and create a custom password-tester class that will store in-memory vectorizations of passwords to make our algorithm easy to share:

```
# this is a complete data-driven automated password strength tester that
judges passwords without any human intuition.

class PasswordTester():
    def __init__(self, text):
        self.vectorizer = None
        self.password_matrix = None
        self.text = text

    def make_vectorizer(self, **kwargs):
        self.vectorizer = CountVectorizer(**kwargs)
        self.password_matrix = self.vectorizer.fit_transform(self.text)

    def get_closest_word_similarity(self, password):
        raw_vectorization =
cosine_similarity(self.vectorizer.transform([password]),
self.password_matrix)
        return
raw_vectorization[:,np.argsort(raw_vectorization)[0,-20:]].mean()

    def judge_password(self, attempted_password):
        badness_score =
self.get_closest_word_similarity(attempted_password)
        if badness_score > .9:
            return "very poor", badness_score
        elif badness_score > .8:
            return "poor", badness_score
        elif badness_score > .6:
            return "not bad", badness_score
        elif badness_score > .4:
```

```
            return "good", badness_score
        else:
            return "very good", badness_score
```

To use our custom class, we can instantiate it with custom vectorization parameters:

```
p = PasswordTester(text)
p.make_vectorizer(ngram_range=(1, 2), analyzer='char', lowercase=False)


p.judge_password("password123321")
('poor', 0.8624222257655552)

p.judge_password("Istanbul9999")
('not bad', 0.7928432151071905)

# generated from LastPass, a password management and creation service 10
digit
p.judge_password("D9GLRyG0*!")
('good', 0.41329460236856164)

# generated from LastPass, 100 digit
p.judge_password("ES%9G1UxtoBlwn^e&Bz3bAj2hMfk!2cfj8kF8yUc&J2B&khzNpBoe65Va
!*XGXH1&PF5fxbKGpBsvPNQdnmnWyzb@W$tcn^%fnKa")
('very good', 0.3628996523892102)
```

Summary

In this chapter, we got a holistic view of a single problem and got to use many of the lessons we've learned throughout this book. We were introduced to the password dataset, along with text-feature extraction and feature extraction using scikit-learn. Then we learned about using cosine similarity with scikit-learn.

Hopefully, this book has provided you with the tools you need to get started in data science and cyber security. Thanks for reading!

Other Books You May Enjoy

If you enjoyed this book, you may be interested in these other books by Packt:

Hands-On Cybersecurity with Blockchain
Rajneesh Gupta

ISBN: 9781788990189

- Understand the cyberthreat landscape
- Learn about Ethereum and Hyperledger Blockchain
- Program Blockchain solutions
- Build Blockchain-based apps for 2FA, and DDoS protection
- Develop Blockchain-based PKI solutions and apps for storing DNS entries
- Challenges and the future of cybersecurity and Blockchain

Mastering Machine Learning Algorithms
Giuseppe Bonaccorso

ISBN: 9781788621113

- Explore how a ML model can be trained, optimized, and evaluated
- Understand how to create and learn static and dynamic probabilistic models
- Successfully cluster high-dimensional data and evaluate model accuracy
- Discover how artificial neural networks work and how to train, optimize, and validate them
- Work with Autoencoders and Generative Adversarial Networks
- Apply label spreading and propagation to large datasets
- Explore the most important Reinforcement Learning techniques

Leave a review - let other readers know what you think

Please share your thoughts on this book with others by leaving a review on the site that you bought it from. If you purchased the book from Amazon, please leave us an honest review on this book's Amazon page. This is vital so that other potential readers can see and use your unbiased opinion to make purchasing decisions, we can understand what our customers think about our products, and our authors can see your feedback on the title that they have worked with Packt to create. It will only take a few minutes of your time, but is valuable to other potential customers, our authors, and Packt. Thank you!

Index

used, for detecting malicious URLs 87
used, for spam detection 128

M

machine learning algorithm
  classification problems 19
  clustering problems 20
  deep learning 22
  density estimation problems 22
  dimensionality reduction problems 21
  regression problems 20
  reinforcement learning 17
  supervised learning algorithms 15
  types 14
  unsupervised learning algorithms 16
machine learning algorithms
  ANNs 24
  Bayesian network (BN) 23
  decision trees 23
  genetic algorithms 24
  hierarchical clustering algorithm (HCA) 23
  random forests 23
  similarity algorithms 24
  support vector machines (SVM) 23
machine learning environment setup
  about 39
  data 39
  use case 39
machine learning
  about 8
  algorithms 22
  architecture 24
  categorization 18
  data 11
  for financial fraud detection 244
  implementing 31
  phases 12
  Python, using 32
  used, for detecting malicious URLs 87
  using, in cybersecurity 10
mail servers
  data, collecting 122
  IMAP email servers 122
  POP3 email servers 122
  SMTP email servers 122

malicious data injection
  within databases 166
malicious injections
  in wireless sensors 166
malicious pages
  detecting, with heuristics 79
malicious URL detection
  using, with decision trees 179, 182, 184
malicious URLs
  detecting, with heuristics 79
  detecting, with logistic regression 87
  detecting, with machine learning 87
mean absolute error (MAE) 29
mean squared error (MSE) 28
Microsoft
  reference 119
MNIST dataset
  importing 217
model 171
model engine
  data preparation 27
  feature generation 27
  testing 27
  training 27
model evaluation
  about 149
  sum of squared errors method, using 150
model, use case
  anomaly detection 175
  decision tree 171
  gini coefficient 172, 173
  random forest 174, 175
MongoDB
  PyMongo 38
  using, with Python 38
multiclass classification
  for URL classification 93
  one-versus-rest form 94

N

Naive Bayes classifier
  for multinomial models 197, 198
Naive Bayes theorem
  used, for detecting spam 124, 125
National University of Singapore SMS Corpus

Bayesian model combination (BMC) 71
Bayesian parameter averaging 70
boosting 70
Bucket of models approach 71

U

unlabelled data 12
unsupervised learning algorithms
  market basket analysis 17
  user behavior analysis 16
URL blacklisting
  about 77
  command URL 78
  control URL 78
  drive-by download URLs 77
  phishing URLs 78
URLs
  abnormalities, types 74, 76
  blacklisting 77
use case
  about 166
  data, features 168, 171
  dataset 166, 167
  model 171
  packages, importing 168
use cases, time series

reconnaissance detection 56
signal processing 54
stock market predictions 54
tackling 59
weather forecasting 55

V

validation dataset
  versus test dataset 195, 196
viruses 165

W

web-content-based feature 83, 84
whaling attacks 118
wide sense stationarity 46
Windows event logs
  account logon events 136
  account management events 138
  logon/Logoff events 135
  object access events 137
  used, for detecting network anomalies 134
Windows
  TensorFlow, installing 216
wireless sensors
  malicious injections 166
worms 165

Made in the USA
Monee, IL
18 March 2021

63142335R00175